Using the creative arts in therapy

This new edition of *Using the Creative Arts in Therapy* has been updated to include new developments in creative therapy and to reflect changing attitudes to the role of the arts in therapy. Its emphasis is on promoting health and encouraging healing, particularly self-healing. Designed for all those who are interested in using the arts in their professional practice, the book provides a general approach to the use of arts in special education, rehabilitation and health care.

The editor, Bernie Warren, has carried out pioneering work in this field for some twenty years. In three introductory chapters he gives a clear and concise account of the history and development of creative therapy, provides a basic framework for the use of creative activities with persons with a disability, and suggests many practical ideas and activities. The other writers, all creative specialists with extensive experience working in education, rehabilitation and health care, contribute chapters on folklore and ritual, visual arts, music, dance, drama, puppetry and storytelling.

Using the Creative Arts in Therapy is above all a *practical* book, giving insight into techniques, originating in the creative arts, that have proved beneficial in health care, rehabilitation and special education. It will be essential reading for students and professionals in a variety of fields – including education, nursing, social work and psychology – who wish to use the arts in their practice. It will also be of great help to creative artists interested in working in these fields.

Using the creative arts in therapy

A practical introduction
Second edition

Edited by Bernie Warren

London and New York

First edition published in 1984
by Croom Helm Ltd

Second edition published in 1993
by Routledge
11 New Fetter Lane, London EC4P 4EE

Simultaneously published in the USA and Canada
by Routledge
29 West 35th Street, New York, NY 10001

Reprinted 1996

Typeset in Times by
J&L Composition Ltd, Filey, North Yorkshire
Printed and bound in Great Britain by
Mackays of Chatham PLC, Chatham, Kent

British Library Cataloguing in Publication Data
A catalogue record for this book is available from the British
Library

Library of Congress Cataloguing in Publication Data
Using the creative arts in therapy: a practical introduction/
    edited by Bernie Warren.—2nd ed.
    p. cm.
    Includes bibliographical references and index.
    1. Arts—Therapeutic use. 2. Movement
therapy. 3. Creative ability. I. Warren, Bernie, 1953–
[DNLM: 1. Art Therapy. 2. Creativeness. 3. Dance
Therapy. 4. Music Therapy. WM 450 U85 1993]
RM931.A77U75 1993
616.89′1656—dc20
DNLM/DLC
for Library of Congress   92-48527

ISBN 0–415–08814–3

Contents

List of illustrations   vii
Notes on contributors   viii
Foreword   x
George C. Mager
Preface to the revised edition   xi
Bernie Warren
Acknowledgements   xiv

Part I   Why creative therapy?

1 Introduction   3
  Bernie Warren

2 Practical approaches to creative therapy   10
  Bernie Warren

3 Checklist of preparations and practical hints for leaders   15
  Bernie Warren

Part II   Practical activities

4 Folklore and ritual as a basis for creative therapy   25
  Rob Watling

5 Using the visual arts to expand personal creativity   35
  Roberta Nadeau

6 Dance: developing self-image and self-expression through
  movement   58
  Bernie Warren and Richard Coaten

7 Expanding human potential through music   84
  Keith Yon

8 Drama: using the imagination as a stepping-stone for personal
  growth   111
  Bernie Warren

9 Storymaking and storytelling: weaving the fabric that creates our
  lives   133
  Cheryl Neill

10 Creating community: ensemble performance using masks,
   puppets and theatre   161
   Wende Welch

   Name index   184
   Subject index   185

Illustrations

FIGURES

4.1 Schematic relationships between context, function and
    traditional material   27
10.1 Sock puppets   168
10.2 A neutral mask   169
10.3 Half-masks   177
10.4 Hand puppets   179
10.5 Rod puppets   181

TABLES

6.1 How you move   78
6.2 Basic descriptors   78

Contributors

Richard Coaten trained as a dancer and an actor. He has been involved in many innovative Arts for Health projects in Britain and has taught dance and movement to persons of all ages and abilities. Until recently, he was Arts Co-ordinator, The Arts Project, The Northern General Hospital, Sheffield. Currently, he works for Living Arts in Edinburgh.

George Mager initially trained as a pianist, dancer and actor. After a successful career on Broadway and in ballet, Dr Mager went to Harvard where he studied educational psychology. Currently he is a Professor of Educational Psychology at McGill University, Montreal, Canada, where he has taught for the last twenty years. In 1990 he was awarded the Order of Canada for his innovative work in the area of Arts and Integration.

Roberta Nadeau was born in the western United States and emigrated to Canada in 1973. She studied psychology and sociology as an undergraduate, graduating *cum laude*. She pursued graduate studies at Purdue University in the sociology of art, and is a painter, who has exhibited her works across Canada, a writer and an arts therapist. She has lectured in the United States, Canada, Europe and the Middle East. Currently she teaches part-time at the University of British Columbia and works as an art therapist in private practice in Vancouver, British Columbia where she also continues to paint.

Cheryl Neill is a storyteller and teacher. She has over twenty years experience teaching people of all ages and abilities. She has extensive experience in conducting professional development workshops in story-telling and drama and is the author of many original musicals. Currently, she teaches courses in both developmental drama and storytelling at Concordia University, Montreal, Canada.

Bernie Warren was born in England. He has worked as an actor, choreographer and musician. As a community worker, drama teacher and drama therapist he has worked with people of all ages and abilities. Bernie is currently Professor of Dramatic Art at the University of Windsor, Canada.

Rob Watling was born in England and received a first in English and folklife studies from Stirling University. Rob has worked as an actor, director, musician, drama teacher, community worker and drama therapist. His experience has been gained with a wide range of disadvantaged, disabled and disturbed individuals. Rob currently works as a media specialist and teaches Media Studies part time at Trent Polytechnic.

Wende Welch trained as a dancer, actress, puppeteer and mask-maker and has an MFA in Theatre Performance from York University, Canada. She has worked as a performer, designer and director with a number of professional companies in Canada and the United States most notably 50/50 Theatre Co. – a company dedicated to integration through the theatre arts. In addition to her professional work she currently teaches theatre performance at the University of Windsor, Canada.

Keith Yon was born on the island of St Helena and received his professional training in England at the Royal College of Music, the Guildhall School of Music and Drama and the Central School of Speech and Drama. His work bridges the boundaries between dance, drama and music and he has employed his innovative and eclectic style of working with a broad spectrum of people, covering a wide range of ages and abilities. Yon is currently a Senior Lecturer in acting-directing, voice-music at Dartington College of Arts, Totnes, Devon.

Foreword

No one needs to justify the value of the arts within a given society. That the arts, at times, hold up a mirror to a society that it may see itself reflected, or that the arts frequently lead the way that a society may enrich itself has been well documented over generations. The poet in the trenches and the painter in the studio have both brought beauty and meaning to our lives.

If there has been a demand for justification in recent years, it has been about the use of the arts in therapy. Art is art, some say. If there are therapeutic benefits to artistic expression, they are no different than the benefits to be had from committed involvement in just about anything – sports, academia, what you will. Others will argue that the high emotive aspects of art make it a perfect vehicle for introspection and possible growth. I shall not fight this battle here.

The value of this book is that it has been written by artists about their art forms. The contributors to this book have not relegated the arts to being mere tools for therapy, nor do they see therapy as the sole product of creative expression. What these authors have in common is the realisation of the value of creative expression as a means to empower oneself.

The radical therapists of the 1960s and 1970s taught us that therapy is a political activity and a means to bring about change, both personally and socially. Notions of adjustment to a status quo were strongly rejected. *Using the Creative Arts in Therapy* takes us a step forward and gives us suggestions to help us help others to change and grow.

The arts offer us so many possibilities that creative therapeutic activity can surely be one of them. Bernie Warren and his colleagues point the way to meaningful 'Arts for Health' activities.

Professor George C. Mager, C.M., Ed.D.
McGill University
August 1992

Preface to the revised edition

This book provides a *practical introduction* to 'Creative therapy': the uses of the arts (art, music, dance, drama, puppetry, storytelling and so on) and other creative processes to promote health and encourage healing. Implied in this working definition is that artistic and creative activities can help individuals accommodate to a specific disability; or recover from a specific medical or surgical procedure; or simply improve the quality of an individual's life. The definition of creative therapy in use throughout this book is different from the first edition. It reflects the move away from *curing* (something done to someone else) *to promoting healing* (which 'involves some notion of self-help'[1]) and/or *maintaining health*. The current move towards 'Arts for Health' suggests there are benefits to simply participating in creative activity. This is clearly distinct from art(s) therapy connoting the treatment of a condition that produces 'ill-health' and is (at least in the mind of the writer) a healthy and honest development. The revised edition of this book attempts to reflect this development.

Like the first edition, this book is divided in two parts. The first part (which is predominantly unchanged from the previous edition) presents a general approach to the use of the arts and other creative processes in special education, rehabilitation and health care settings. Chapter 1 serves as a brief introduction to the history and development of creative therapy. Chapter 2 presents the reader with a basic framework for the use of creative activities with persons with a disability and Chapter 3 presents a simple annotated checklist for leaders.

Part II contains chapters from contributing authors, who each address themselves to their specific creative specialisation. Many of the chapters in this section are the same as in the first edition; however, there are two new chapters and some notable additions to other material. Regrettably the addition of the new material meant that David Stebbing's chapter on the physical roots of movement had to be left out of this edition.

Virtually unchanged from the previous edition are Rob Watling's chapter on the significance of folklore and other traditional material (Chapter 4) and Roberta Nadeau's chapter on visual art (Chapter 5). Both

Yon's chapter on music (Chapter 7) and my own on drama (Chapter 8) have been revised. The chapter on dance (Chapter 6) has been thoroughly overhauled by Richard Coaten and myself.

Finally there are two new chapters in this edition. Storytelling, although mentioned by several contributors, was a notable omission from the previous edition. Cheryl Neill's chapter (Chapter 9) rectifies this omission. Wende Welch's chapter on masks and puppets in ensemble performance (Chapter 10) serves to unite various aspects of the performing and the visual arts and acts as a fitting closure to the practical section of the book.

Each of the authors contributing to the book is primarily a practitioner. Throughout this volume we have tried to provide the reader with access to material which requires a minimum of training to understand and apply. The intention is to provide ideas and activities that allow professionals from a variety of fields[2] to expand their present knowledge and skills concerning the use of creative therapy. In so doing, we hope that professionals will increasingly make use of processes and activities drawn from the creative arts within their professional practice as they strive to help improve the quality of their clients', patients' or students' lives.

It is important to record that although this book is primarily concerned with creative therapy, the authors strongly believe that the ideas, games and activities cited in this volume are valuable to all people irrespective of age or ability. This belief is borne out by the working practices of the contributing authors, all of whom have worked in the fields of recreation, special education and health care and as practising artists. What is more important, we see the links between these different areas of application as being essential to the development of our work, complementary rather than mutually exclusive: an important concept in this age of increased specialisation and empire-building.

It is important to realise that this book does not provide a panacea for all problems, nor will it make the reader an instant creative specialist. However, it will give an insight into *some* of the techniques, originating in the creative arts, that have proved beneficial in health care, rehabilitation and special education settings in aiding individuals to gain better understanding and control of their bodies and emotions. One outcome of this is that they are better able to explore their own 'unique creative thumbprints'[3] within the fabric of their daily lives.

This, then, is primarily a practical book. However, above all else it is a book about helping to develop human creative expression and enabling all people to be themselves, and to express that self to others in a creative and socially acceptable manner. It is this primary goal that the authors work towards in all their work believing that if we succeed in providing everybody access to meaningful avenues for creative expression, the improvement in the quality of human life will make creative therapy, and books like this, redundant.

Bernie Warren
Windsor, Ontario
July, 1992

NOTES

1 L. Moss (1987) *Art for Health's Sake*, Carnegie Trust, Dunfermline, UK.
2 Including but not confined to education, nursing, social work, psychology and the visual and performing arts.
3 All human beings, irrespective of their abilities or limitations, are capable of making their own 'thumbprint', that is a 'mark' made in sound, line, colour, form, shape or movement that no one else could ever make in exactly the same way. It is this mark which states 'I exist. I have meaning' and it is a reflection on an individual as a unique human being. Most importantly this unique creative thumbprint can be thought of as the essential building block of all creative expression.

Acknowledgements

This book is the result of many years of hard work carried out, often unsung, by dedicated professionals working in various parts of the world. Many of these unsung heroes and heroines (without whom this book would never have seen the light of day) are mentioned by contributors throughout this work. There are still many other people who invariably remain unacknowledged, yet their contribution to this young and fast-growing body of knowledge is considerable. I would like to take this space to express my sincerest gratitude to all those people with whom I have worked as facilitator, teacher, therapist and friend. The amount I have learnt from you, about the strength of the human spirit struggling against adversity, is truly immeasurable.

I wish to thank all the contributors to both editions of this book; especially Roberta Nadeau who was instrumental in the development of the first edition. In addition, I wish to mention Peter Senior, whose work in the field of Arts for Health has been an inspiration over the years.

I must also thank Donna Harling who so excellently helped in all stages of the original manuscript and Kerrin Patterson for her excellent work on the revised edition of this book. In addition I must thank Julie Ortynsky for her invaluable assistance in re-editing the chapter on music. Above all, I want to thank Edna P. for her editorial suggestions and for her sense of humour.

To all these people (friends, colleagues and 'clients' alike) I dedicate this book.

Part 1

Why creative therapy?

Chapter 1

Introduction

Bernie Warren

The growth of interest in creative therapy[1] has occurred over a relatively short time. This interest has developed as a result of the successes achieved by arts specialists working in health care, rehabilitation and special education settings. Many of these successes have been unexpected, certainly not planned and, in some cases, inexplicable. Over the last ten to fifteen years, an understanding of the benefits gained from the use of the arts in healing and for health has been growing. This has occurred as more and more specialists work in this area, as more administrators are willing to experiment using the arts in their institutions and as methodological research is interwoven with anecdotal reports of the effects of this work. As a result, this mixture of experiment, research and anecdote has built a body of ideas, skills and knowledge that has at its core the essence of human existence; a need for each of us, no matter what our age or ability, to reaffirm ourselves and to communicate with others.

The concept of creative therapy (as a discipline or group of methodologies) is relatively new. However, its roots can be found in the continual but ever-changing relationship between culture, artistic activity and social development. Some writers have gone so far as to suggest that the arts and society are inextricably linked and that the health of a society is reflected in the pool of artistic activity the society creates – and vice versa. Similarly, it has been suggested that individuals exercising their right to make their own creative mark may be considered as a sign of a healthy individual. However, unlike many societies that preceded us, our technologically advanced industrial society has clearly separated art from life. We have words that allow us to categorise and subdivide art forms. Our society has successfully isolated individuals from artistic creation. As a result art is defined in terms of artifacts, products that can be discussed and criticised – often because of their economic rather than their aesthetic or spiritual contributions to society as a whole.

Over the centuries we have created the concept that artistic creation is the responsibility of a few gifted individuals. In so doing, we have denied the majority of individuals within our urban and technologically advanced society their birthrights: that, as a human being, everyone has the right to make his or her own 'unique creative thumbprint' – one that no one else could make. We all have a need to make this 'mark', not because we necessarily wish to be the reminders to a future generation of a long-lost culture but because each creative mark reaffirms the self. It says 'I am here', 'I have something to express'.

As the workplace has become increasingly dehumanising and sterile (with fewer and fewer outlets for creative expression) it is not surprising that the arts have come to be seen as therapy. However, *Therapy* (which implies a prescribed course of treatment with predetermined expected results for a specific diagnosed condition) and *the Art(s)* (which at least in part suggests an exploration, one that usually finds the notion of predetermined expectation anathema) are strange bedfellows. Art is not a medicine that must be taken three times a day after meals. However, it can feed the soul, motivate an individual to want to recover and, in certain circumstances, cause physiological changes in the body.[2]

Happily, more and more people are becoming aware that being involved in the process of artistic creation is every bit as important and in many cases more important than the end product. The definition of Creative Therapy in use throughout this book reflects this move away from curing (an end product – and usually something that is done to someone else), to promoting healing and/or maintaining health, which as Moss (1987) points out are processes that involve 'some notion of self-help'. The recent move towards 'Arts for Health' (which suggests the benefits of participation in creative activity) as distinct from art(s) therapy (which implies the treatment of a condition that produces 'ill-health') is a healthy and honest extension of these developments.

Slowly people are becoming aware of their creative potential, their need to make their mark. As a result more and more individuals who, because of birth, crisis or accident had previously been denied their rights as 'full members' of their society, are finally gaining access to the arts. The results, in some cases, are quite staggering. Individuals, previously seen as useless, incapacitated or catatonic have begun to speak, move more freely and in some cases, over a time, take a full and active part in society.

However, it is important to remember that the arts do not stand in isolation and are most definitely not in themselves a cure for all ills. Nevertheless, in each individual's act of creation, the arts engage the emotions and free the spirit. This can encourage individuals to do something because they want to and *not* just because someone else decides it is good for them. The arts can motivate in a way possibly no other force can. It is only through making a mark that no one else could make, that we express the individual spark of our own humanity.

So, why creative therapy? In essence because reintegration of artistic processes within a social context can help promote the growth of a healthy individual and a healthy society. This is essential not only to an individual's but also to a society's well-being. Unfortunately modern industrialised societies have excluded many people from their right to indulge in these artistic processes. In using the creative arts in health care, rehabilitation and special education settings, and seeing the resulting growth in self-image, self-esteem and healthy social interactions, society as a whole is being handed a mirror concerning what is possible for all its members if only they are given the opportunity.

EMPLOYING CREATIVE THERAPY

The settings in which creative therapy is used vary tremendously. This diversity reflects the wide application and power of simply participating in a creative activity. However, it also reflects the diversity of theoretical frameworks and approaches that arts specialists hold, and the wide range of professional conditions within which they must practically implement their skills. However, it is beyond the scope of this book to deal in detail with the many and varying philosophical and theoretical frameworks that creative specialists make use of, implicitly or explicitly, in their working lives.[3]

For individuals beginning to explore this area, part of the problem is in the 'literature'. Writers and speakers on the creative therapies[4] have stumbled over definitions for more than thirty years. Much of the problem has been caused by attempting to define what individual creative therapies are, rather than looking at what they do. As a result a great deal of time has been spent attempting to answer the question '*what* is Art Therapy, Music Therapy, etc.?' Moreover, rather than establishing the benefits to health and well-being of artistic activity itself, the 'therapeutic legitimacy' of artistic activity has been established, defined and calibrated in terms of other bodies of knowledge, most notably psychotherapy, medicine and psychology.

For at least the last fifteen years creative specialists have been struggling to answer the 'wrong' question. For the question is perhaps better phrased as *when* are the arts 'therapy', or, better still, what artistic activity – poetry, music, etc., would be beneficial to this individual at this particular moment? In addition, many creative specialists have tried to demonstrate just how much they are like psychotherapists and psychoanalysts. However, few creative specialists accentuate their greatest strength, the thing that makes them different, their expertise in their art form. It is little wonder that despite many protestations to the contrary, creative therapy remains firmly under the grip of the medical community!

Throughout this book a switch of focus is suggested from the arts as therapy to the arts for health: a switch from assessing the product to indulging in the process. I am certainly not alone in the conviction that (irrespective of the leader's style of working) initially it is the act of making a mark, not its effect on an outside professional, that is of greatest value in reintegrating mind, body and soul.[5] These marks may allow the professional an insight into the individual's way of encountering and deciphering the world, but this is really no more than a beacon, a guide to possibilities for the next stage in the process.

I am a great believer in working towards demystification. As already mentioned, the act of creation (of expressing self through a creative activity) is part of both our heritage and our birthright. There is nothing mystical about it. Each of us can create something unique and meaningful to ourselves. However, so that we may make use of creative experience, we each need to understand the techniques and ideas that allow us to be creative.

Professional artists always look towards expanding their knowledge and understanding of the skills, techniques and processes that allow them to be creative in their own medium.[6] There is nothing mystical about being creative: all that is necessary is access (to materials, teachers, books, etc.), understanding (of the techniques and ideas related to a particular medium such as painting or storytelling) and application of this understanding in a medium that best allows individuals to express themselves: a medium that allows them to be creative.

The problem is that creativity cannot be switched on like a light bulb. You have to have the right power circuit, the right environment in which to create. In creative therapy the starting point for the development of a supportive and creative environment is always the leader. The leader is usually the most important factor in the direction and development of each individual involved in any session. For the leader sets the tone, provides direction and chooses the material in which individuals will participate. This is true of any leader and is particularly true of the leader employing the creative process in health care, rehabilitation and special education settings.

In employing creative activities in special settings, leaders have to know and understand three basic factors. They should know themselves, their creative medium and the members of their group both as individuals and as members of their group. All the concepts, ideas and techniques at an individual's disposal will be wasted if a leader cannot make them accessible to others. Knowledge and understanding of these three basic factors greatly facilitate a group's access to the creative process.

The first factor is probably the most difficult. Very few people know themselves totally. The external stimuli to which we are all exposed change constantly. We are always having to cope with new pieces of information, some that threaten our beliefs and some that reinforce them. Not everyone can be centred or achieve perfect harmony; however, most leaders can become aware of their strengths and weaknesses, and I believe that this awareness is crucial to being a successful leader. It is particularly important to be aware of our own vulnerability – the areas that are 'taboo', ways of working that each of us finds difficult, and even groups of people with whom we feel uncomfortable working. If we don't acknowledge these 'vulnerable' areas, it is certain that at some point an individual or group of individuals will discover our Achilles' heel. It is unlikely that any of us will ever be perfect. However, becoming aware of the many facets of our character and working towards increasing the quality and quantity of our positive characteristics and reducing our negative points help to build an awareness of ourselves.

Knowledge of self and security in that knowledge can go a long way to facilitating the controlled release of a group's creative energies.[7] Only when leaders create a positive and self-confident atmosphere can the members of a group start to feel secure enough to express themselves. In simple terms, the group have to trust the leader before they can trust themselves. It is only when they have confidence that the leader will not subject their creative work to unnecessary and negative criticism and that all of their work will be treated confidentially that they will feel fully secure in investing part of themselves in their creative work. When individuals are able to do this they start to grow in confidence and self-esteem. Ultimately being content with who we are at any given moment in our lives, feeling secure in our self goes a long way towards being a successful leader for our focus remains on individuals in our group rather than on ourselves.

In working with any group of individuals,[8] an understanding of our own working style and favourite medium is particularly important. In addition, knowing different techniques within that medium is essential to the choosing of activities that are suitable to a group's individual and specific needs and abilities. The creative process actively engages the senses and the emotions and must be experienced – it cannot simply be reproduced. We each have to have experienced the challenge of being faced with a blank piece of paper, or an empty stage, or the request to improvise around a theme to understand the problems it can present for others. The root of creation is in experience: not only experiencing the act of creation, but also allowing that act to recreate previously experienced emotions, events, feelings – channelling them through that creative expression.

Individuals have differing needs. This is as true for creative expression as it is in any other area. These may change from time to time. At one point a visual medium may be the most conducive to an individual's need to express him or herself, whereas at another time, for the same individual, singing may be the essential outlet. I work primarily in the performing arts. However, I am also very visual and many colleagues have commented that as a theatre director I 'sculpt' the space, nevertheless when I try to paint or draw often I experience breakdown in communication between my mind and body. Whenever I attempt to work with paint or charcoal or even clay my hands are unable to create what my mind is asking them to produce. As a result, I become frustrated very quickly. Yet the more I work with each visual medium, the easier it becomes for me. This is true for many other people.

A slow and patient approach is often necessary. In many cases, individuals need to express themselves in a particular medium, for example sound, but do not possess the technical skills to 'say' exactly what they want to. This may be the result of physical restrictions, or simply, as in my case in the visual arts, a limited experience in that medium. Part of the job of a leader is to provide members of a group with the skills, the vocabulary if you like, with which to express themselves in that medium.

Over the past few years I have come to believe that it is necessary for leaders of creative therapy sessions to help individuals learn the language of the creative medium. Each creative art has a different set of grammars (its technical rules and structure) and vocabulary (forms of expression) that we need to acquire if we are not to be frustrated when we try to express inner thoughts or feelings. It is important that leaders take the time to become familiar with the inner forms of their discipline and create an environment where each individual can learn the language of the creative medium. This learning of the language is crucial to long-term success in creative therapy; or to put it another way pre-packaged fast foods can sustain an individual for a short while but there is really no substitute for good home-cooked meals.

Knowing ourselves and our art forms are essentials, but these need to be linked to the needs of the individuals within the group. We need to structure our sessions so that everyone, individually and collectively, feels secure, that they feel we can and do provide them with the vocabulary, inner structures and the materials by which they can express themselves. In the next chapter I will address myself to the fundamental question of how these basic ideas can be transformed by the inexperienced leader into practical realities.

NOTES

1 'Creative therapy': the use of the arts (art, music, dance, drama, puppetry, storytelling and so on) and other creative processes to promote health and encourage healing. Implied in this working definition is the use of artistic and creative activities to help individuals accommodate to a specific disability; or recover from a specific medical or surgical procedure; or simply improve the quality of an individual's life.
2 One example of this is the effect of humour and laughter in the process of healing. So clear is the value of laughter that some Canadian and American hospitals have humour rooms to promote self-healing particularly in stress and auto-immune related illnesses, for example cancer, heart disease and stroke.

3 For the reader interested in this area, I suggest they look first at Feder and Feder (1984).
4 This term is used in this context as a catch-all for the multitude of other sub-disciplines within this area of study and activity, for example, art therapy, music therapy, drama therapy, poetry therapy, dance therapy, play therapy, bibliotherapy, etc.
5 When an individual is immersed in creative activity (as an observer but more particularly as a participant) they are lost in the 'creative moment' – a liminal state that brings together different aspects of our being (physical, intellectual, emotional and spiritual) in a way that offers unique opportunities for healing to take place.
6 This is equally important for leaders of creative therapy sessions; particularly in terms of the needs for members of their group to learn the language of an art form. See discussion later in this chapter.
7 I have long been fascinated by my observations of professional colleagues whom I admire. They seem to have the capacity, irrespective of their medium, to extend a circle of energy around the group that acts as a support – as a comforter and friend. It is something I refer to as the leader's 'parental circle' because of its relationship to the support we generally come to expect from our parents. This is something for which I strive constantly.
8 Most of the discussion of group work applies just as well to working with an individual.

SUGGESTED READING

Feder, E. and Feder, B. (1984) *The Expressive Arts Therapies*, Feder Publications, Sarasota, FL.
Moss, L. (1987) *Art for Health's Sake*, Carnegie Trust, Dunfermline, UK.

Chapter 2

Practical approaches to creative therapy

Bernie Warren

PREPARATION AND PLANNING[1]

Very few creative specialists organise and fund their own programmes. Most are employed by public health authorities, hospitals, schools, social work departments, rehabilitation centres or other similar public or private institutions, to work within very specific limits with a particular group. It is very important that you clarify the conditions of your contract before starting work with your group. In particular, the who, why and what of the agreement are essential. These questions are:

Who   will I be working with?
Why   am I being employed? and
What   am I expected to achieve?

Subsidiary but nevertheless crucial questions are:

When   are we expected to meet?
Where   do these meetings take place?

The answers to the first three questions will enable you to form some ideas concerning *how* the goals set for you and the group might be achieved. The answer to the last two questions will provide a thousand organisational problems, which will make the *why*, the *what* and the *how* more difficult.

The starting point for any creative session is to find out who is in your group. In the initial stages your employer or supervisor will probably present you with a very sketchy outline of the people with whom you are expected to work. In many cases this will provide you with little or no useful information. This is often unintentional and occurs because of an unfamiliarity with the sort of information that will prove useful in running the session. It is important that you find out the information you feel is important.

The kinds of basic questions one needs to ask are:

How many people will be in the group?
Does anyone use a wheelchair or other ambulatory aids?

Is everyone able to communicate? Do any individuals have difficulties with speaking, hearing, seeing?
Does anyone have epilepsy? A heart condition?
Will I have any professional or voluntary assistance in my sessions?

Wherever possible, try to get specific information. To be told someone has a 'mental handicap' or is 'disabled', is far too general. Try to find out if the members of the group have similar abilities and ages. The age of the participants is particularly important, as this will be a factor to be considered when choosing your material. If someone uses vague terms to describe an individual's behaviour, such as 'she exhibits schizophrenic tendencies', try to get them to explain what they mean. Also, try to find out under what circumstances these specific behaviours occur. Having said all of this, try to leave yourself room to make your own judgments. It is surprising how happy, co-operative and creative some individuals, whom others see as aggressive, withdrawn or disturbed, can be when given a warm and friendly environment in which they have a chance to express themselves.

Usually, the composition of a group (the number, ages and abilities of the individuals within it) is resolved over the first two or three sessions. Often I read the information given to me about the group only very briefly before the first session and try to 'forget' it, or at least not refer to it consciously, during the running of that session. After the session is over, I compare my perceptions of the group members, based on my observations during the session, with those given to me before I started. I always keep my first session simple and fairly undemanding. In it I use activities that are relatively non-threatening and which act, for me, as a gauge of the abilities of the members of that group. These I refer to as diagnostic tools, and in the sections on dance and drama I give examples of some of these activities.

It is also important to be aware that an individual's talents or abilities may lie dormant for a long period, surfacing only when a particular activity engages them. It is for this reason that the contributing authors lay great store on the activities in a session being, above all, enjoyable. There are times when this rule may be broken as some of the material that may surface might be anything but pleasant. However, there is little benefit to be gained from applying the creative therapies if they are viewed in the same light as having to take medication! Enjoyment is an essential motivating factor in enabling individuals to overcome their limitations. So often when working with the creative process, individuals will do something that is not only unexpected but also is beyond their previously exhibited capabilities. The arts have that extraordinary power to engage the emotions and so motivate individuals to strive beyond their limits because they are enjoying themselves.

In asking yourself 'Who am I working with?' you are slowly able to answer some of the questions relating to the *how* of the contract. However, it is important to know *why* you are working with the group and *what* your supervisor or employer is expecting from you and the group. These may be $64,000 questions, for your perceptions of what you are doing may differ, sometimes drastically, from those of an outside observer. It is here that creative specialists are often trapped by a belief that it is necessary to label their work as therapy so that it can be seen to be valuable and therefore defensible in monetary terms. However, this extension of the now rather dated debate about the arts as recreation, education or therapy has in large part been blunted by the move towards Arts for Health. Nevertheless, it will be important for you to clarify your position to your employer within the context of your contract.

There are many creative specialists working with people with special needs in the fields of rehabilitation, education and health care. Only a small percentage of such specialists have been trained in psychology, psychotherapy or medicine; yet many are employed as specialists. At the other extreme, individuals with professional training in psychology or psycho-therapy or occasionally medicine *and* one or more art forms are employed to introduce the arts as recreation within institutions. It is always important to recognise and state clearly, both to yourself and to your employer, the limits to your training, experience and expertise. It is also helpful to explain your philosophical and theoretical orientation as all of these help clarify 'What is expected of me?' which in large part modifies the more significant question of 'Why am I being employed?'

In this era of accountability and malpractice suits it is essential that you identify what your expertise and orientation are early on, to avoid misunderstandings. For example, an employer may ask you to work as an 'art therapist' and when you stop using craft kits and move towards personal creative expression he or she will 'slap your wrists' for creating waves; or you may be asked to work as a 'drama games co-ordinator' when what is being asked of you is that you function as a drama therapist. Make sure, in establishing the *why* and *what* of your contract, that you are willing and able to do what is asked of you. There is no point pursuing a contract where you are doing something beyond your experience and training or where it is just not your way of working. In both cases you, your group and your employer are unlikely to benefit from or be satisfied with the situation. The result is that your contract is likely to be a short and unhappy one.

The *where* and *when* of the contract are possibly the biggest problems facing any leader of creative therapy. All too often we meet with our groups too infrequently and in surroundings that do not satisfy our needs. It is important that you attempt to secure the most suitable room in the building. It is quite likely that fourteen other people will be wanting to use that room at exactly the same time. I strongly suggest you do not attempt to share it with them. If you are unable to secure the most suitable room, at least attempt to get one that meets some of your needs. If you are working in the visual arts, you will need a sink – having one 'just down the hall' can be extremely frustrating for you and the group. If you are running a dance/movement session, a carpeted room restricts the possibilities for rolling on the floor. Each of us will have specific needs, but whatever else happens, *try* to get a room that is not a thoroughfare or shared by another group. This is very important in generating a sense of security for your group.

Another factor in establishing the security of a room is to check on its other uses. Try, where possible, to avoid rooms that group members associate with less pleasant activities. Again, this may be impossible; however, it is worth the effort.

A major factor in establishing trust is the continuity and scheduling of your sessions. Avoid requests to change the timing of the sessions in midstream. Also, try to avoid time slots that occur just after group members have had a meal. The frequency of your group sessions is often out of your hands, but you should decide what the optimum number of sessions is each week – two or three sessions is probably a good number to aim for. The length of the session will depend on the activities you plan to engage in and the age and ability of your group. As a rough rule of thumb, the visual arts need longer sessions than drama or music, with dance/movement probably requiring shorter but more frequent sessions.

The reality is that you will have very little say in the *where* or *when* of your contract. The room and the time slot for your sessions were probably decided before you were hired. It is important that when you do find yourself in an environment or a timetable that is all but unworkable, you strive towards changing these to satisfy your needs more adequately. In the meantime, you simply have to make the best of a bad job. Sometimes the knowledge gained from working in unsuitable conditions can be a valuable learning experience. At others it will be a nightmare, which will stay with you all your working life.

The *how* of the contract is a dynamic experience. It occurs in relationship to the why, where, when, what and who of the contract. There is no single or simple answer to it and consequently it is the most difficult aspect of the contract to discuss. While there are a few excellent books[2] that make suggestions about how to cope with this volatile area, ultimately each individual has to find their own way of negotiating the moment by moment problems that are faced by creative specialists working in this field. It is almost impossible to use a plan that has been created before the session, for this is too static and cannot make allowances for dynamic changes within the group. Leaders have to rely a great deal on their training, past experience and intuition to help guide and plan sessions. Often this is done by 'thinking on your feet'. The *how* of the contract is essentially the sum of knowing who you are, knowing your art form and knowing your group. It is about making use of *your* material to meet the needs of *your* group. This will not only mean different things to different people, but will also mean different things to the same person at different times or with different groups.

I strongly recommend that you attempt to gain role-flexibility as a leader. Even if you only work with one group, at different times the needs of the members will be different. For example, sometimes they will want you to be a parent figure telling them what to do, at others they will want you to be an impartial observer, and at still others they will want you simply to be part of the group. It is important that you do not get stuck in an inflexible style, which does not allow room to move. On occasion, what the group wants from you is not what you see as their needs at that time, or the role they cast you in may not be suited to you or you may feel unable to carry it off. It is important that you work within your limits but try to meet the needs you identify in the group.

Working on role-flexibility can be difficult. One way of learning role-flexibility is to try to get experience of working with other groups. Try to work with other group leaders, observe their style but always remember who you are. It is important not to move simply from one extreme to the other. Make changes one small step at a time, for any sudden changes can be very threatening to the group.

The problem is that leadership style and role-flexibility are particularly personal. They are learned and not taught. They become an integral part of a leader's way of working, but they are also dictated by the medium you work in and by specific activities within that medium. Personal creativity can be stifled if you constantly tell individuals exactly what to do. Yet some groups need clear, concise and constraining instructions in the early stages of their development. Remember, the more directions you give, the less room you allow for personal creativity.

This chapter dealt with the basic problems of contract that a leader faces. The contract represents the framework in which you have to operate. A great deal of the contract is initially beyond your control. The content of your session and your style of leadership are uniquely your own. In Chapter 3 I will outline some hints for the smooth running of a session – a checklist of ideas that may prove useful.

NOTES

1 What follows may seem obvious to many readers nevertheless it is alarming just how many people do begin sessions without considering basic planning.

2 For example two books written for drama teachers, J. Neelands (1984) *Making Sense of Drama*, Heinemann, Oxford, and N. Morgan and J. Saxton (1987) *Teaching Drama*, Hutchinson, London, may be helpful in this area and I strongly recommend anyone working in a clinical setting read M. Cox (1978) *Structuring the Therapeutic Process*, Jessica Kingsley Publishers, London.

Chapter 3

Checklist of preparations and practical hints for leaders

Bernie Warren

Below I have outlined some observations and questions that I feel are important to the running of a successful session of creative therapy. I feel the questions are relevant to anyone leading a creative session, irrespective of their background, experience, style(s) of leadership or the groups with which they are working; however, these factors will obviously affect the answers that each of us gives to these questions. The checklist below reflects my personal concerns, namely: being clear on my responsibilities as leader; treating the people I work with, irrespective of age or ability, as unique human beings;[1] and providing a structure in which people can enjoy themselves, be creative and work towards overcoming the mental, physical or emotional conditions that they face in their daily lives.

The checklist, which is annotated, covers the three basic phases of running a practical session of creative therapy, that is before, during and after each session. Many of the points may be obvious to you, some you may think about only occasionally and others you may not have thought about before. After a while, most of the suggestions and questions that follow become so much an integral part of a leader's way of working that you can strike them from your checklist, as you will be doing them automatically.

QUESTIONS TO BE ANSWERED BEFORE STARTING THE SESSION

(1) Who am I working with?

(a) How many people will be in the group? Will this number be constant? *Often this number will fluctuate. Someone may be ill, need to go to surgery, X-ray, dentist, hairdresser or a million and one other places. Be patient and be prepared for these changing numbers.*

(b) What are the ages of the group members? Are they approximately the same age?

(c) What are the *abilities* of the group members? Can they all walk? Is there a common link between members of the group? For example, are all the individuals in the group recovering from a stroke?

It is always important to plan specifically for your group. No two groups are ever exactly the same, but obviously experience gained with similar groups is very valuable. The key is in choosing activities that allow group members to succeed.

(d) Do I know everything I need to know about the members of this group? For example, are any members of the group on medication that will limit their creative potential (e.g. heavy sedation)?

It is highly unlikely that you will know everything you would like to know before the start of the first session. You will almost certainly gain valuable information from your own work.

(2) What are my responsibilities as leader?

(a) In what capacity am I being employed? Teacher? Facilitator? Leader? Therapist?

(b) What am I expected to do with the group? Is my job to engage the group directly in creative activities, or am I employed to seek actively to change specific behaviours?

(c) If my job is to change specific behaviours, what is the time-frame in which I am expected to do this? Is this realistic?

(d) Am I capable of carrying out what has been asked of me?

(e) Do I need to renegotiate my 'contract'? That is, what I am expected to achieve with the group through my creative medium (see also 'Questions to be Answered after the Session is Over').

If your job description and your duties clash, there is a need to clarify exactly what is expected of you. There is also a need for you to make clear to your employer/supervisor what skills you possess. There is a vast difference between accepting a challenge and misrepresenting your abilities. Often you may need to re-educate your employer or supervisor about why you work creatively and what skills you possess in relation to the perceived needs of your group.

(3) Pre-session planning

(a) When is the session scheduled? How often do I see the group and for how long each session?

(b) Do the group members know where and when we meet? Do the other professional staff who work with them also know this information?

Often you will have no say in the frequency or timing of your sessions. If your sessions are too long, allow time for simply talking and being with the members of the group. If the session is too short, allow yourself time before and/or after the session to be with the group. This unstructured 'talk time' is often essential to allow an individual to develop a trust in you. It also provides a time to share what has been happening in the group's lives.

(c) What space do I need to work in? Does the space I have been allocated meet these needs? For example, does it have running water and enough chairs? Is it comfortable? If not, how can I make do with the space allocated?

It is essential that you make clear to the person dealing with scheduling and administration exactly what your needs are. Demand the impossible – go for what you would want ideally and barter from there!

(d) Will I have any assistants? Will they be volunteers or professionals? Do they know the group members? Do they know my way of working? Do they know what my goals are?

It is not unusual for your assistants to know the group better than you. This can be an extremely valuable asset. Make use of these people. Wherever possible, run workshops for them before working with your group. Take them into your confidence; share ideas and information with them. One word of caution – always remember that, no matter what happens, you are responsible for the running of the creative sessions, consequently when push comes to shove you must have the final word.

(4) Planning the session

(a) Given all the information I now have, how can I best achieve my goals? These may be different from those suggested by your employer or supervisor.

(b) What activities will best match my strengths with the perceived needs of the group and their abilities?

(c) How much structure do I need to provide for the group so they can actively engage in these activities?

Much of this may have to be left open until after your first session. Try to provide, in the first few sessions, activities, structures and language systems that allow you room to change direction without breaking the trust and security you are developing.

(d) What equipment will I need? Is this to be provided for me? Am I expected to take my own art supplies? Tape recorder? Musical instruments?

Many creative specialists always carry their own materials around with them. It is perhaps the one way of ensuring you have exactly the materials you need. Try to be reimbursed, or given an equipment budget to cover these costs.

(e) Is the room with which I have been provided still going to function well for me? Do I need to negotiate another space?

This may be difficult, but always try to get the room that suits you. If you need a sink for art work, or a piano, or a clean space to roll on, keep on pressing for your needs. It may be difficult explaining to someone unfamiliar with your creative medium why you need these facilities but keep on trying.

POINTS TO LOOK FOR AND QUESTIONS TO ASK YOURSELF DURING THE SESSION

(1) Immediately prior to the session

(a) Is all the equipment I need for this session here?
(b) Are all the group members here? What is the general mood of the group? Is it in keeping with my plans for this session?
In some cases you may want to keep that mood. In others, you may wish to dispel it. Either way, you may feel the need to change your plans. Flexibility of approach is one of the keys to successful and creative leadership.

(2) Running the session

(a) Did I introduce myself? Does the group know why I am here and what we will be doing together? How do they react to this?
(b) Do I know the individuals in this group?
Every group is different. Every individual in every group is unique. Each makes their mark differently. The medium in which they are most creative differs. Name games, sharing information and allowing group members to feel they are part of the group's decision-making process is essential. All too often, leaders do not even consider asking a group what they would like to do.
(c) Am I warming up the group for the activities to come?
The warm-up sets the tone for the rest of the session. If the session is to be 'physically strenuous', it is important to warm up the joints and the muscles. If imagination is to be the focus of the session, exercises to warm up the imagination will be needed. If there is lethargy at the beginning of an active session, it's very unlikely that your group will be prepared to expend any energy without being coaxed.
(d) How are group members responding? Who is outgoing? Who is shy?
(e) Am I introducing the activities in a way that people can understand? Am I working at their pace?
(f) Am I providing the right amount of structure to allow the group to be creative?
(g) Am I meeting the individual needs of the group? Am I aware of changes occurring in these needs throughout the session?

Throughout the session, no matter how actively involved you are, you must be sensitive to the needs of all the group. This requires tremendous amounts of concentration and, in particular, paying close attention to all the observed behaviours of your group. Make sure you are using language that the group understands. You may need to vary your language level, that is the complexity of words, your language system – the way you put sentences together, and try to reinforce your requests with gestural clues to communicate with all the group's members. Always remember to work at your group's pace, but also always start each activity at the beginning and not just where you finished last time with this or some other group. As to the structure, you will have to sense if you need to let go of the reins or pull them in even more. This is something one learns with experience and unfortunately experience can not be gained from any book.

(h) Am I simply filling the session up with 'busy time'?

(i) Am I enjoying myself?

If you are not enjoying yourself, it is almost certain that no one else will be. However, be careful that you are not the only person enjoying yourself. Remember who the session is for; it is often important to remind your assistants about this too. If you do get caught in a 'playing to the crowd' mentality, the session may degenerate into 'busy time': a lot happening, but nothing being done.

(j) How can I end this session on a positive but relaxing note?

Lying on the floor, listening to tranquil music, gentle rocking in pairs, telling the group a story, while they lie on the floor with their eyes closed, working with a parachute – are all examples of examples of ends to a session that are both relaxing and positive.

(3) Immediately after the session

(a) Does everyone know when the next session will be? Do I need to send notes back with certain individuals?

(b) Does everyone have all the possessions they arrived with?

(c) Do I have everything I came with?

(d) Have I checked all the lights are out? Water turned off? Is the room in reasonably the same state I found it?

This is particularly necessary as janitors and cleaners are possibly the most important professionals we encounter.

QUESTIONS TO BE ANSWERED AFTER THE SESSION IS OVER

(1) Evaluating the session

(a) How did the group respond? To me? To my material? To other members of the group? Was this as I expected?

(b) How did I feel about the session – good, uneasy, bad? Can I pinpoint a reason for this? The room? My presentation? My contract? My material?

(c) Did I meet any of my goals this session? Did I identify new goals during the session?

(d) Have I made a written note of my observations and feelings about the session yet?

I feel it is extremely important to keep written records. These should not just be a clinical account of what happened. They should include observations of what went on, how the group members participated and how you felt the session went. I have kept a journal of every session I have ever run and these have proved invaluable, not only during but also after the sessions have finished.

(2) Planning for the next session

(a) Am I on the right track? Do I need to change my approach? My material? My medium? Do I need to renegotiate my contract?

(b) Who are the individuals in the group who need special attention? How can I best meet these needs without disturbing other members of the group?

(c) What shall I do next time? How can I link it to what we have already done so that it builds on these experiences?

The answers to these questions will be extremely specific. The only observation I will make is that it is essential that you link your material to your own personality and to the personalities in your group!

(d) Have I scheduled time for a break between sessions?

In the long run it is essential that you timetable 'space' for yourself to replenish the energy you have expended. You cannot pour from an empty cup.

The most important thing to remember is that everyone in the room is a human being. You, your assistants and the members of your group all have good and bad days. All of you will experience frustration and elation, failure and success. If you can bear that in mind, you will be a long way down the road to allowing the people you work with the opportunity to expand their own horizons through creative activity.

The rest of this book is devoted to practical activities that will allow you to share the power of the arts with others.

NOTE

1 It is important to remember that individuals in any group, irrespective of their ability or disability, should be encouraged to take responsibility for their own

lives. This requires that the leader treat each individual with respect. More importantly, leaders need to be careful not to make decisions for members of the group, for the arts are best seen as an expression of each individual's uniqueness; they cannot be done to or for people. It is this quality that enables creative activity to provide the opportunity to empower individuals.

One book that has been very useful to me in this context is H. Exley (ed.) (1981) *What It's Like To Be Me*, Exley Publications, Watford.

Part II

Practical activities

Chapter 4

Folklore and ritual as a basis for creative therapy

Rob Watling

Folklore is that part of any culture that is transmitted by word of mouth or by custom and practice. It includes folk literature (folktales, poems, songs, dramas), folksay (proverbs, riddles, rhymes, dialect), customs and beliefs, music, dance and ethnography (the study of arts, crafts and the manufacture and use of artifacts). It is important to realise that modern industrialised societies have folklore in the same way as American Indians or Australian aborigines. Nor should we think of folklore as 'the things our grandparents used to do' for it is a vital part of the way all societies operate. There is as much folklore in the city as in the jungle.

This traditional material, wherever it is found, belongs to the people who use it. They have devised it when they have wanted it, transmitted it from generation to generation, adapted it when necessary, and discarded it when they have no further need for it. It is constantly changing, and almost infinitely variable. It is functional (as we shall see later) and it has stood the test of time. Traditional societies do not have creative therapists, but neither do they seem to be snowed under with the sorts of problems that we, as leaders, are helping our clients to tackle. Without making a romantic appeal for some sort of return to a simpler, more ethnocentric way of life, I believe that we do have important lessons to learn from tradition and have found my working knowledge of folklore invaluable to me in many of my sessions. It has served both as a source of material and as part of a theoretical model of what happens in creative therapy sessions. However, before we look at some of the applications of folklore we need to know a little more about the subject.

Many of the early folklorists, working in the nineteenth century, concentrated purely on collecting large quantities of material. They wanted to list the things people did – the songs they sang, the rituals they performed, the tales they told or the tools they used. Collections of this information were compiled but it was some years before people began to realise that the material was not enough by itself. It was not sufficient to know that 'Waly Waly' was a Scottish ballad. They began to ask who sings it, to whom, where and when? Where was it learned, how is it remembered and why does it exist at all? Is it just a sad song? Is it a cautionary tale? Is it a record of an important event in a society unable to perpetuate its history with pen and ink? This new generation of students wanted to know about the *context and the function of the living material*. It is context and function that interest us, too.

Folklore can serve an enormous range of functions. A simple folktale can, in certain contexts: relate the history and wisdom of a society; reinforce custom and taboo; teach skills by example; explain the mysteries of the universe and our place within it; amuse and entertain; offer solutions to personal and practical problems . . . the list is very long and other types of material can have as many varied functions. Here are four particular examples:

The Anang in Nigeria, like many other African tribes, use proverbs as a central part of their judicial system. Plaintiff and defendant quote proverbs (widely used as the embodiment of tribal wisdom) to support their cases.[1]
In China, while the tyrannical Chin Shih Whang was having the Great Wall built, folksongs emerged as an expression of the people's feelings: their grief at the death of so many labourers, their fury at the enforced break-up of so many families as men were sent away to build the wall, their opposition to the capital punishment of those who refused to go. Popular protest songs, passed on by word of mouth, are still around today.
The Inuit of North America will sometimes have a singing duel to settle a dispute in a non-violent way (violence is not welcome in the close confines of a winter settlement). The combatants sing songs at each other with the intention of ridiculing their opponent into submission. They channel their antagonism into a functional, conclusive ritual (Burket-Smith 1971: 59, 164, 173).
In Norse mythology, on the other hand, combatants will indulge in an insult-flinging competition as a precursor to a battle. Here the idea seems to be to goad your partner into action and to prepare yourself for victory.

This notion that folklore can and should be studied in terms of its context and function is central to us if we wish to apply traditional material to creative therapy. We could sit in a circle and sing war chants. We could perform traditional Swiss dances, tell each other Russian folktales or play Welsh street games; however, as leaders we need to understand what it is we are doing and with whom. We, too, need a firm notion of the context and function of our material and the way in which these elements relate to each other. This relationship can be described by a simple diagram (Figure 4.1), in which the shading denotes areas of change and mutual influence. When any one of the variables in the figure alters, it may affect one or both or neither of the others.

Take, for example, the game of 'London' described later in this chapter. Traditionally when played by a group of children, it is 'just a game'. Its

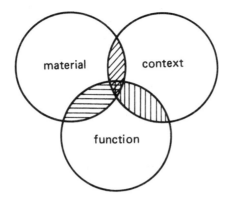

Figure 4.1 Schematic relationships between context, function and traditional material

context might be described as a backstreet game, played by friends in their leisure time. The function of the game appears to be fun; something to pass the time; perhaps a chance to consolidate friendship or to practise competitiveness. If we change the context by playing this game in a creative therapy session, what else do we change? Perhaps we change nothing, as we can play this game for its own sake. However, we could decide to use this game with a group who need to develop gross motor control. Now we could add the function of teaching people to stop quickly and to control their balance to our list. It is still the same material but now with new context and function. We can go further (as in the 'collective' version of the game that I describe) and change the rules of the game. It is no longer everyone for themselves but an exercise in co-operation. Context, function and material are variables for us and the group to alter as we wish.

Folklore is a powerful, accessible, adaptable source of material, which offers us insights into the way people act and interact with each other and the environment. Once we understand some basic principles of the way in which it operates, we are able to apply some of this material in a therapeutic way. The rest of this chapter outlines some practical ways this can be done, with particular reference to traditional games, folk narratives and simple rituals.

TRADITIONAL GAMES[2]

I have tried to suggest games of different types in this section, varying from the energetic to the slow and contemplative. All of them, I hope, contain the essential element of fun referred to in other parts of this book. By way of explanation, I have used the term 'It' to describe the player who is working against the rest of the group, usually in an effort to catch them. 'It' is often called 'He', 'Her', 'On' or 'On it' in Britain.[3]

Stick in the Mud

This is an excellent game with which to start a session and one that is always a great favourite. It is often called 'Sticky Glue', 'Release', 'Ticky Underlegs' or 'Underground Tag'.

One player is 'It' and chases the others. Anyone 'It' touches must stand with their arms outstretched and their legs apart – they are 'stuck in the mud'. They must stand still until another player frees them by crawling between their legs. They may then run off again. Sometimes players are required to call 'SOS' or 'Release' while they are stuck in the mud. 'Its' job is to get everyone stuck in the mud, which is not easy. I quite often have two 'Its' to make the game less frustrating. The first and/or the last people to be caught are 'It' next time round.

This is a fast, energetic game involving a variety of movement and body shapes, basic teamwork and usually quite a lot of noise. It can be useful as an exercise for those needing to develop simple spatial awareness and can easily be adapted for different ability groups. Slowing the game down to a walking pace can be useful, so can changing the 'freeing' act for a simpler manoeuvre. Some people find it easier to stand near a wall when they have been tagged and to hold up an arm or a stick to form an archway. They are released when someone goes through the arch (this is sometimes called 'Tunnel Touch'). Alternatively, the game can be made more demanding: players must move around the room in a particular way; you must crawl backwards through a captive's legs to free them; play the game linked to a partner so that pairs of people have to crawl through two sets of legs. As ever, the possibilities are endless and can be matched to the abilities of your group or used to lead them into new areas of movement and activity.

Sun and Frost

This is a version of Stick in the Mud played in Stornoway in the Isle of Lewis and was collected by the Opies from an 11-year-old girl who said,

> 'You all stand in a row and one person picks the nicest face for the sun, and the rest that's left they all put on ugly faces and pick the ugliest [for the frost]. The people that's left all go out and the frost goes after them and if they're caught they have to stand still till the sun tips them and they will get free. That's how you play the Sun and Frost.'
>
> (Opie and Opie 1969: 111)

The obvious symbolism in this game can be of use to many groups over and above the physical benefits of movement. I have sometimes extended the idea and asked the Frost to 'really freeze' the players and the Sun to thaw them out with a warm hug and a nice sigh. There are many other traditional games where quite intimate body contact is perfectly acceptable, and they can be used, among other things, for the recognition of body parts.

London

A game with incredibly wide circulation, this is known in various parts of the world as 'Red Light, Green Light', 'Ochs am Berg', 'Eins zwei drei – sauer Hering!', 'Uno, due, tre, stella', 'Grandmother's Footsteps' or simply 'Freeze'.

Originally played across a street or a yard, 'It' stands facing a wall with all the other players on the opposite side of the road. The object is for them to creep up and tap 'It' on the shoulder, but at any moment 'It' may suddenly turn round. Anyone 'It' sees moving (even a hand) is sent back to the start. 'It' may look round any number of times but is often required to count silently to ten between each go or to say a short phrase in his or her head to give the others a chance. The first player to get right across is the next 'It'.

This game is immensely popular and is nearly always played with complete equanimity. This has much to do with the quality of the 'It' role, for 'It' has considerably more control over the proceedings than in chasing and tagging games. This is one of those rare games where 'It' is the coveted role, but has the additional advantage that everyone else can feel that they are succeeding – even the ones who are sent to the back to the start, for they are now hidden by the people in front of them and can move forward more quickly. A headstrong dash for the finish is rarely successful and the quiet individual can often win by stealth. I have seen many players delight in the attention they receive in being sent back over and over again. It is rare for players to accuse one another of cheating or to refuse to accept 'Its' verdict.

In creative therapy sessions the game is useful in a number of ways. It is fun, of course, and can relax a group very quickly, helping to create a good working atmosphere. It improves concentration and alertness and can be used to develop body awareness, balance and gross motor control. Faced with a group of adolescent boys who were having difficulty making group decisions and acting co-operatively, I developed a variation we called 'Group London'. There was still one 'It' but the rest of the group had secretly to select one of their number as the one they wanted to 'make it' to the other side. Their job was to help him get across by shielding him from view, or by 'sacrificing' themselves and drawing 'Its' attention away from him. The dynamic of the game changed dramatically and I have used it on a number of occasions as a link between more self-centred games and exercises to develop group cohesion.

As a widely known game, London also serves as a good example of another benefit of traditional material. Many people playing these games will remember their own variant and can make a positive contribution to the session (something they might otherwise find difficult). I have run whole sessions with all the activities suggested by group members from their own repertoire of traditional material.

Muk

This game is part of the traditional winter activity of the Inuit (Eskimo). The players sit talking and joking in a circle with 'It' in the centre. Suddenly 'It' will say 'Muk' (the Inuit word for silence) whereupon no one must make a sound however, 'It' is allowed to tell jokes, fool around, pull faces or whatever until someone breaks the Muk. Then the group gives that person a comic name (traditionally the name of an animal). This person then either replaces the 'It' or joins them as part of a growing team of animals who will eventually descend on the last silent member of the group.

Ostensibly a game about the breaking down of barriers between individuals (one of the social functions for the Inuit), in our society this game can easily become an exercise in reinforcing these barriers. This is particularly likely in a group where people have problems with communication and self-presentation and 'It' can quite quickly feel threatened and ostracised. The leader is at liberty to make capital out of this (perhaps moving on to more intensive work) or to defuse the situation by having more than one person in the middle. You may wish to stop the game when there are still three or four people in the outer circle to avoid the group applying all its coercion on one individual, but this last breakdown can have a unifying effect on the group and restore the element of fun.

IRISH WAKE GAMES[4]

The traditional Irish funeral was a fascinating mixture of solemnity and joviality. In common with the funeral rites of many cultures, it served as an opportunity not only to pay respect to the dead but also to celebrate life and the living. Most, if not all, of the amusements have now been separated from the modern Irish wake, largely in response to the disapproval of the church, but we still know enough about them and the way they were played to understand at least some of their functions in this context.

The wake itself, where relatives and neighbours would watch over the coffin until the funeral, was partly a chance for people to express their respect and to show their mourning. It also served to guard the coffin overnight from evil influences – which could mean spirits, the devil, body-snatchers or all three. There would be much drinking and eating at a wake and there was as much singing and dancing as at any other Irish gathering. However, there were also these games to help people stay awake and relatively sober at their task. There were riddles, trials of strength and dexterity, tricks of all sorts and forfeits galore, all acting as a confirmation, a celebration of the living at a time of deep respect for the dead.

Pig in the Sty

One person (traditionally a woman) stands in the middle of a ring of players who link arms as securely as possible. Outside the ring is another player (usually a man). His job is to kiss or tag the girl in the middle either by reaching over the ring of linked players or by forcing his way through. (At this stage the ring may decide to let the girl escape and to keep the man prisoner.) All the other players try to frustrate the man's attempts until he is successful or resigns.

This game can be used in a number of ways: to act as a warm-up, to channel physical aggression, to develop co-operative energy, to break down barriers to physical contact (which can here be intimate but safe), to illustrate rejection and corporate disapproval or to promote a discussion of traditional sex roles. The game can easily be adapted by encouraging different techniques: use no hands; everyone has eyes closed; tickling is allowed; use persuasion to gain entry into the circle; cheat; etc.

Do the Opposite

This was a common amusement at the wakes and one that I have found popular with all sorts of groups, the object being to trick people into making simple mistakes. Two players, for example, hold a scarf between them and are told to do the opposite of any instruction you give them. You tell them to hold it tight and they should let go, you tell them to pick it up and they should leave it alone, you tell them to keep it away from other people and they should give it to a new couple. Any mistake (and there are many) is punished with a forfeit – I use a hit on the head with a balloon. The game is, once again, infinitely variable and can easily be adapted to the abilities and concentrative powers of most groups. It is great fun to watch, for humour is a great leveller. Once everyone has been fooled (including you, for the leader should join in whenever possible in these games) the whole group has greater access to each other as individuals.

Cumulative games

Another adaptable concentration exercise is the cumulative memory game. The first player in a circle, for example, says 'I went to market yesterday

and bought a cow.' The second player says, 'I went to market yesterday and bought a cow and a sheep.' The third says, 'I went to market
yesterday and bought a cow, a sheep and a sack of corn.' This continues
with each player adding something new to the list. Again it must be used
at an appropriate level for the group. Some groups will be able to go round
the circle several times without making a mistake; for others it will be a
considerable achievement if they can repeat what their neighbour has
just said. Be prepared to use memory aids (pictures, mime, sound-clues)
and look for ways to develop additional skills in the same game (recognising the idea of 'sets of things', counting, non-verbal communication,
etc.).

TRADITIONAL NARRATIVES[5]

Storytelling can be a fulfilling experience in its own right. Traditional tales,
poems, ballads and dramas (as well as some modern literary ones) embody
all sorts of wisdom: teachings, history, parables and advice; for folk
narratives are often the living encyclopaedia and life-manual of the non-
literate society. Even the simple act of being a member of an audience can
be calming and nearly everyone loves to be told a story. We need not limit
ourselves to straightforward tale-telling sessions, however useful they may
be, but can reinforce their meanings and messages in a number of ways.
It can often be valuable to ask groups to externalise their reactions to a
narrative in discussions, in paintings and sculptures, in a dance perhaps,
or by acting out some of the scenes. Ask your group to project their ideas
of what happened before the start of the story and what happens
afterwards. Use the narrative and its accessibility as a platform for all sorts
of expression and discovery.

Since it is often the hero or protagonist with whom we are meant to
identify, who encounters our own predicament and symbolises ourselves,
it can often be valuable to use a traditional narrative as the basis of a
guided fantasy. In this exercise each member of the group listens to the
story and acts out the part of the central character as the adventure
unfolds: doing what the protagonist does; 'seeing' what he sees; 'feeling'
what he feels; and learning (often intuitively) what the hero learns. A
whole wealth of human experiences can be fed into each group member,
who need not be self-conscious about the quality of their performance as
it is directed inwards rather than out at an audience.

RITUAL AND CREATIVE THERAPY

Rituals have always formed an important part of the collective and
individual actions of people throughout the world. From the Indian dance

to the swinging of Catholic incense, from the blood sacrifice on a new boat to the 'wetting of a baby's head' in an English pub, from the rain dance to the children trying not to step on the cracks of the sidewalk, rituals are anchors of certainty in a precarious sea. At the moment of ritual we know exactly where we stand.

There are many times when an individual or a group need, in exactly the same way, to know where they stand: at the start of a session; when a new member joins the group; when a group member faces a crisis or shares a moving experience; at the close of the session. At moments like these it can sometimes be helpful for a group to use some sort of ritual as a collective expression of a shared experience. The predictability of ritual can help to take the slightly frightening edge off a session. There is one regular weekly group I attend whose members are comforted not just by our occasional use of simple ritual but by our predictable, almost ritualistic use of traditional games as a mainstay of our work together. They know what to expect from the sessions and can learn to understand their place within them.

But a word of warning. I have been a member of several workshops and sessions where a ritual has been artificially imposed on a group. 'We are now going to show our unity for each other's feelings and experiences by joining with everyone in the room and silently communing with each other', said the therapist. Unfortunately it was obvious that the group wanted, on this occasion, to reflect individually on their own experiences. They were a square peg being tapped remorselessly into a round hole. Any worthwhile ritual expression must have its roots in the nature of the therapeutic experience. It is material that must be appropriate to the context and suited to its intended function. It is not hard to develop rituals with and for a group, but we must insist that our modern-day material takes a lesson from its traditional counterpart. All creative activity must work as an expression, not as an imposition, and folklore (the carrier of wisdom, faith, joy and learning for thousands of years) has never successfully been imposed on anyone.

NOTES

1 J. C. Messenger, Jr. 'The Role of Proverbs in a Nigerian Judicial System', in Dundes (1965) pp. 299–307.
2 Still the definitive work on the traditional children's games from England and Wales is the Opies' (1969) *Children's Games in Street and Playground*. There is an enormous wealth of material in the Opies' work, including versions of the first three games in this section.
3 P. V. Gump and B. Sutton-Smith, 'The It Role in Children's Games', in Dundes (1965) pp. 329–36. This article contains a fascinating preliminary discussion of some of the possible functional applications of selected 'It' games.
4 For a fuller study of this material in context, see S. O'Suillebahn (1969).
5 For a more elaborate discussion see Cheryl Neill, Chapter 9 in this volume.

SUGGESTED READING

Bettelheim, B. (1979) *The Uses of Enchantment*, Penguin, Harmondsworth.

Brewster, P. G. (1952) 'Children's Games and Rhymes', *The Frank C. Brown Collection of North Carolina Folklore*, vol. 1, pp. 29–219, Durham University Press, Durham, North Carolina.

Briggs, K. (1977) *A Sampler of British Folk Tales*, Routledge, London and Boston.

Brown, W. K. (1974) 'Cultural Learning through Game Structures: A Study of Pennsylvania German Children's Games', *Pennsylvania Folklife*, 22: 2–11.

Brunvand, J. H. (1978) *The Study of American Folklore*, 2nd edn, Norton, New York.

Buchan, D. (1973) *A Scottish Ballad Book*, Routledge, London and Boston.

Burket-Smith, K. (1971) *Eskimos*, Crown Publishers, New York.

Child, F. J. (1965) *The English and Scottish Popular Ballads*, 5 vols, Dover, New York.

Clark, E. E. (1960) *Indian Legends of Canada*, McLelland and Stewart, Toronto.

Dorson, R. M. (ed.) (1972) *Folklore and Folklife: An Introduction*, University of Chicago Press, Chicago.

Dundes, A. (ed.) (1965) *The Study of Folklore*, Prentice-Hall, NJ.

Eckhardt, R. (1975) 'From Handclap to Line Play', in *Black Girls at Play: Perspectives on Childhood Development*, pp. 57–101, Southwest Educational Development Laboratory, Austin.

Ferretti, F. (1975) *The Great American Book of Sidewalk, Stoop, Dirt, Curb and Alley Games*, Workman Press, New York.

Frazer, J. G. (1936) *The Golden Bough*, Macmillan, London.

Friedman, A. B. (1977) *The Penguin Book of Folk Ballads of the English-speaking World*, Penguin, Harmondsworth.

Gluckman, M. (1962) *Essays on the Ritual of Social Relations*, Manchester University Press, Manchester.

Grimes, R. (1982) *Beginnings in Ritual Studies*, University Press of America, Lanham, MD.

Luthi, M. (1976) *Once upon a Time: On the Nature of Fairy Tales*, Indiana University Press, Bloomington and London.

McNeill, F. (1957) *The Silver Bough*, Routledge, Glasgow.

Newell, W. W. (1963) *Games and Songs of American Children*, Dover, New York.

Opie, I. and Opie, P. (1959) *The Lore and Language of Schoolchildren*, Oxford University Press, Oxford.

Opie, I. and Opie, P. (1969) *Children's Games in Street and Playground*, Oxford University Press, Oxford.

Orlick, T. (1978) *The Cooperative Sports and Games Book*, Readers and Writers, London.

O'Suillebahn, S. (1969) *Irish Wake Amusements*, Mercier, Cork.

Van Gennep, A. (1960) *The Rites of Passage*, Routledge, Boston and London.

Chapter 5

Using the visual arts to expand personal creativity

Roberta Nadeau

Because of the quiet contemplative, personal approach needed to produce in the visual arts, there are large expansive areas of inner exploration that go hand in hand. These inner experiences are of particular value to those who are using the arts with persons with a disability. Most other art forms require another person to have a full encounter with what that particular art form can give. In the visual arts we can provide tools, knowledge of materials and experience with drawing and painting, which can allow individuals to take with them, wherever they go, the potential for further work. We have the wonderful opportunity to enrich their lives and creative potential.

Even in a crowd, the visual arts encourage a capacity to work in solitude. The artist's eye is always seeing, sensing and feeling the atmosphere around at that moment. If the inner peace for such exploration is not present in the person or persons we are working with in our initial contacts, we can at least see such peace of mind as part of our goal in introducing visual arts sessions. In this hectic, fast-paced world, all people can gain from knowing greater inner peace. Such peace comes from self-knowledge and an appreciation of each person's unique, individual, creative mark which may in turn provide opportunities for increasing self-confidence and self-esteem.

The wonderful beauty of the arts, in all forms, is that human emotion is involved in a raw and uncensored manner. Feelings flowing are essential for artistic experience. Freud, Jung, Plato and Aristotle are but four of the thinkers who have clearly defined the value of the arts in human growth and development. Freud helped us to be more aware of the unconscious and the necessity of the human being to have a full conscious as well as unconscious life. Dreams are essential to a healthy person. The professional artist and the inexperienced participant have in common the fact of being at their best as creators of visual imagery by their capacity to tap the unconscious and, as a result, to present in line, colour and form a mark that is individually their own, unable to be produced by any other individual in exactly the same way, ever.

The artist has always been a barometer of the health of a society. In addition, it is from the work of the artist that anthropologists, historians, archaeologists, etc. make the deductions so important to our present understanding of humanity's time on earth. Little of the written word has survived the centuries of human existence; actors die within their respected lifetimes; music survives and yet changes with each new person who sings the note or plays the score. Yes, art changes too. However, sculpture, ceramics, and work in gold, silver and other metals have survived earthquake, fire, erosion and time. They have given to us from other centuries the visual information to conclude that certain instruments were used to make music, that certain types of theatre were important to the people of specific times, and that governments were organised in certain configurations. In essence, what we know of human history is a result of the work of the artist and artisans of particular times and cultures.

Despite often impossible barriers to creativity, the artist has been, through all time, a person of unquenchable thirst to know, see, feel and express through their work what they are experiencing. The art of any period of history is generally several decades ahead of actual social change: pre-Russian Revolution art and pre-French Revolution art being only two examples. This response is the result of a phenomenon quite like having an extra sense. To the practising artist it can be a blessing as well as a burden, in that the capacity to respond to, record and assess the world around cannot be turned off. The artist does not work a 9-to-5 day nor does an artist take a holiday. Art is a way of life, not a way to make a living. The creative mind is at work full time, even in communication with the muses of artistic inspiration while sleeping.

All artists will testify to the fact that in producing one drawing or painting, ideas are therein born for another ten or more works. The finished product may at times be a great success or a great failure. It does not matter. What does matter is the continuation of discovery. This process is what we have to share with the people with whom we work. As Fred Gettings (1966) has said, 'Art is of value for the way it improves the mind and sensibilities more than for its end products.' Because of this exciting process and all-inclusive *seeing and feeling,* which are essential, it becomes easier to understand the enormous value of encouraging experience in the visual arts for those persons with a disability . Through teaching individuals to see what is around them, to express their feelings and constantly affirm the fact that they, and only they, can make those particular marks on paper or canvas, you increase opportunities for those people to know more about themselves and their unique rights for respect and self-love.

The uses of line, form and colour are emotional encounters. There is even greater emotion involved once colour is introduced. It is important to know and to feel sure about the fact that art deals with human emotion, as quite often the act of putting line or colour on paper can produce cathartic emotional responses for the individual producing the work. Their excitement, tears and frustrations are to be dealt with sensitively – not in any way dismissed. For they are an integral part of the art process, and the arts play a vital role allowing for increased quality of life-experience for those with whom we are working.

Creativity is still a mysterious element of the human brain. Over centuries there have been attempts to understand, to clarify, and still scholars admit that we know little about what creativity is. However, readings and research suggest that the creative activity provides opportunities for self-discovery and personal development. For persons who have some form of disability, though, there are too often few if any opportunities to realise their potential. So simple is the procedure that it at times seems to me amazing that, for far too long, art materials have been seen by some as foreign, dirty (much cleaning up required), frightening ('we have no control') and misunderstood. Thus arts experience is denied to people who can gain so very much from it.

PREFACE TO PRACTICAL ACTIVITIES

Art materials

The art materials of concern to me in this writing are those that allow for two-dimensional expression: graphite, charcoal, conte, ink, pastels, paint, paper, pens, brushes, canvas and board. For a person who already has a limitation in physical or mental skills, it is essential not to create more barriers by improper selection of materials. The materials should be of the best amateur artist's *quality* available to you. Papers, canvas or boards must be of good size and quality. How destructive to say that you care to share the visual arts experience with a person with a disability and then to see only frustration because of easily torn paper, limp or lifeless colours, or 'self-destruct' creations, which are a pain to produce and a sorrow to the individual as their work is deposited in a waste can.

Pencils (graphite)

Art pencils range from very hard leads to soft and very soft leads. For the purposes we are talking of here, purchase and use only HB, 2B, 4B or 6B pencils. Art pencils can be purchased from the HB end of the range to 10B; however, too soft a lead will defeat your purposes as the work created too easily smears. The importance of the soft leads is that it takes less physical pressure to produce a mark and even the most inhibited person will not find it difficult to deal with having once begun. We all are guilty of concluding that we cannot do something and of being terrified to try. A simple, well chosen pencil and a piece of large drawing paper can provide hours of exploration and accomplishment.

Charcoal

Like graphite pencils, charcoal comes in varying weights or degrees of hard to soft. Again, buy large sticks, which are easy to grasp, soft and, as a result, quick to make distinctive marks and absolutely excellent for the intense black areas that can be created. Charcoal does get messy and for some people that alone can be a healthy and constructive experience because 'institutional' preference is for 'clean at all times'. For a person to be told, 'You have done nothing wrong, all will wash off when we are finished', is to be allowed to feel good, and is an affirmation of your belief in the individual's right to experience the joys of all levels of the tactile beauty and pleasure the creating of visual art allows.

Charcoal can also add new dimensions when an art gum eraser is employed to lift areas of black away. The 'positive space' imagery or design can be created through the efforts of working into a large black space. Positive space is the actual design area. Negative space is the artistic term used for the space around the initial or essential design. For some people this can be particularly gratifying, for they are creating an element of magic. I try to employ as much fantasy and magic-related conversation as is fitting to inspire and excite exploration.

Conte

Conte is a stick resembling a unique blending of oil-pastel and charcoal. It, also, is available in a variety of soft to hard selections and in raw sienna and burnt umber (beautiful earth tones), black and white. Here, as before, buy the softer, easier-to-use materials. The beauty of conte is the feel of silk in your fingers and the tremendous variation of marks, designs, lines and forms that can be made. The sticks, as with charcoal, have great versatility. A stick worked on its side gives wide sweeping flows of colour. The conte is easily smoothed or varied in intensity with the fingers or a tissue rubbing the paper. Persons with limited muscle control can achieve delightful results because of the fluid capacities of the medium itself, and you will be happy to know that there is not as much washing up needed as happens with charcoal.

Pastels

These come in the form of chalk pastels or oil pastels. I use both in my work and recommend that both be a part of your art supplies. Poor quality in choice will lead to two unfortunate problems: (a) the colours will be pale and bland, and (b) there will be great difficulty for some people to experience the goals you wish to achieve, in that the pigment simply will not move easily over the paper. One of the great beauties of pastel is that you are working with pure pigment, which has been rolled with a limited amount of oil to create a medium of pure colour. There are many varieties of good pastels for student or amateur work. Before buying, however, make certain that the colours are bright and the pigment is easily transferred to whatever surface would be worked upon. Even the most frightened or restrained individual can be moved to do preliminary explorations, purely by the excitement of the brilliant colours. The chalk pastels are soft and chalk-like in their feel in your hand. The oil pastels are more similar to crayon in feel, and yet are pastels, with all their wonderful qualities of colour intensity and capacity to be manipulated or mixed using fingers or tissues.

Paint

Painting is a joyous experience that, as you will read later, must be introduced at the correct time to people to avoid frustrations and thus limitations to the gains that can come from the process. Again, your purchases must be made with concern for intensity of true colour and the manufacturer's quality of pigment transfer. I choose to buy tube water-colours, as so often the cake watercolours are difficult for many of those with whom I work to be able to know the fun of flowing colour as it explodes before them. I repeat: in working with people who already have imposed physical, mental or emotional difficulties, it is essential that we as facilitators for the arts do not put more barriers in their way by poor choices of materials. I never work with oil paints with groups. If a certain person wants to paint in oils, that becomes an individual decision between myself and the person involved. The turpentine needed as medium for moving the pigment in oil paints is very poisonous, and if an individual has allergic reactions to the turpentine, you have great problems on your hands. Acrylic paints are water-based, and water is used as the painting medium to vary thickness of paint and to clean brushes or hands. For many people interested in moving to thicker paints, I advise the purchase of acrylics.

Watercolours, particularly from the tube, are most adaptable. You can teach a person or group how to obtain gradations in washes or to paint in wild, bright colours. To produce a gradient of washes, you take a brush fully loaded with pigment. Strokes are made on the paper, and then, adding only water to the brush, a progressively lighter wash can be obtained. This provides, in work with persons with a developmental disability or seniors who are senile, opportunities to spark imagination with suggestions of a certain element of magic, which has become theirs with the use of the paints, the brush and water.

Brushes

As mentioned before, buy good quality brushes. If cared for well, they will provide years of service to the artist's hand. I am not suggesting the purchase of sable brushes, but I hope to make it clear that a cheap 'bargain' will soon leave parts of the brush on a person's work. Efforts to remove a bristle can lead the way to the famous 'self-destruction' activity, which frustrates and can be heartbreaking. Also, brushes must be large – at least size 10 or larger – with adequate handles. There are some brushes produced by art supply companies that have a plain, unpainted and unvarnished handle. If you are able to buy a variety of these brushes, you will see how their less slippery finish is a true blessing for certain individuals. The brush is an extension of the hand or foot of the person painting, and should be introduced as a tool. I will speak later of the importance of this understanding. As a tool, the brush can add variety to the experience with paint. It can provide unlimited variety in stroke, and in dabbing, pulling and swirling of colour. If you are unfamiliar with all a brush can do in your hands, I advise many lovely hours of exploration and fun before you introduce paint brushes to a person with a disability. As with any element of knowledge or experience, we can only teach what we know.

Inks

These come in many colours and can be applied with pen or brush. The uses of inks as a medium of expression should be judged according to the people you are working with and their particular interests, capabilities and desires to express themselves in various media. Inks, rather like oil paints, take closer supervision or, at times, a one-to-one working relationship. Inks can produce great delight when used in mixed media works, and again, for certain individuals, much excitement when waterproof inks are used and then watercolour or pastel is painted 'magically' over the original line. For individuals with limited imagination, you as the facilitator may at times need to suggest media and approaches that can unlock some of the imagination that is simply lying dormant, since no one before has given it much of a chance. This is true for everyone, not simply those with a disability. The opportunities provided to people all through life to explore their creative potential are so very limited that they seem proof enough to me that we are tapping a powerful source. If it was not so powerful, why should true creative experiences be denied to so many?

General beginnings

Introduce one art medium at a time, allow for full exploration and understanding of all the things one can do with a pencil, charcoal, pastel, etc.

Encourage an end to timidity by only providing large pieces of paper – paper at least 18 by 24 in (45 by 60 cm). Even the person with extreme limitations in movement will be able to feel the desire to extend their reach. In my experience (as facilitator of such extension of motor skills) I have quite often seen attempts to reach the top and sides of the paper that have surprised the care professionals in charge of the particular individuals on a daily basis. Such extension was seen as unlikely if not impossible.

Some people can be assisted if you keep Velcro as part of your supplies, to wrap around the hand of someone who has little muscle extension to assist in holding a drawing medium or a paint brush. Also, putting mixed watercolours or tempera paint in empty liquid soap bottles (any plastic bottle that can easily be squeezed) may enable those with little fine motor control to enjoy all the glorious feelings of the painting experience.

Remain continually observant of persons in need of help or encouragement, but please constantly remind yourself that the beauty of the visual arts is the essential nature of *quiet inner discovery*. Constant interruptions or comment can break the inner peace of another person. We have been given a birthright to produce. We have not been given the right to disturb another's creative space. In my experience I have found that, presented with a quiet, mutually respectful atmosphere, the individual or group with whom you are working will wish to create an atmosphere respectful of all in the room. For some people, just to feel such mutual regard for their own thoughts, work and capacity to think can be as beneficial to them as the entire creative process or their finished products.

Classical music, well chosen and played softly, can be a tremendous aid in producing an atmosphere conducive to creative activity. Here, however, I warn: know the music you choose and why it will work. If you are unsure or uncomfortable with the music, you can do harm rather than good. Bach's music for classical guitar and lute have been standbys for me, in that they produce steady, quiet, soothing conditions of great musical beauty.

Provide a means of storage or transport to protect the creations of the people with whom you are working. Very few individuals have financial opportunities to buy proper portfolios. However, these can be made by you and the persons in the group by saving all cardboard, sheets from packing cases, backs from drawing pads, etc. These simple materials and a little masking tape and time provide the person creating with a means of safe transport, and in some cases the only storage they personally can know, as this packaging protects their work while it is stored under their beds or in a closet in one particular type of institution or another. If you have an arts or crafts room to work in, it is essential to provide storage for works finished or in progress. Some 'special populations' require that you find a way to lock their work away safely. Destruction or misuse of their completed works by another person, no matter how innocent or accidental the initial cause of such damage, may mean months of effort to re-establish the same quality of freedom in their artistic expression.

Have plenty of supplies and a large amount of paper. There is at times nothing so inhibiting to artistic creativity than to see limited supplies and thus, for example, to fear using the last remnant of a stick of red pastel. Having adequate supplies available has also, in my experience, produced a mutual regard and patience within a group. They know that even if they must wait a few minutes for the use of a certain material, it will not be gone.

Erasers should be viewed as tools and not as means of instant correction. Far more exciting results can be obtained by looking at other options of correction, such as darkening negative space or creating variations in shape and form that may not have been thought of if there were not a desire to change a form.

There is a great need for volunteer help if you are working with a group larger than three or four in number. Also I have had occasions where sisters, mothers, fathers, etc. have come along to a session to observe, as they also provide transport. After numerous occasions on which comments were made, such as 'No, that isn't the way a tree looks', or 'No one has hair that colour', I decided that all volunteers or visitors would be given paper and encouraged to work. Suddenly, they too were having the same explorations and discoveries; soon negative and sometimes destructive comments stopped. Do remember that your volunteers are there to help you. Give them clear directions and encourage them to learn by doing what the artistic process involves. Otherwise they are more of a hindrance than a help.

Keep written records for yourself of your interactions with the various people with whom you work. These records are essential to your personal effectiveness as a leader and to your preparation in creating the proper time-and-space elements for each individual. The goal of one aiding others through the visual arts is to see positive change in self-esteem and self-expression, and an increase in motor skills and the quality of physical and emotional health of the persons with whom we work.

Be patient, very patient, if you have an individual who sits back only watching for a number of sessions. There have often been so many terrifying experiences piled one upon another to cause true and justified alarm when introduced to a new situation. Having created an atmosphere respectful of creative work, we then must learn to accept the flow of individual personalities. The rewards for such patience are great. An elected mute surprised all when she began to speak to me during an art session. She had sat watching for four sessions before participating. A severely handicapped young man made the first efforts ever to do things by himself and was so convinced that he had found his special way of successful expression that he asked if I could arrange a proper exhibition for his works. His family took him on holidays and he took all his completed creations in the makeshift portfolio I provided to show everyone. He had sat watching for five weeks before becoming involved. These are but two examples of the success that comes with patience and understanding. As certain people sit around the room watching, for sometimes even three to five sessions, when they, of their own will, approach you there is a rush of excitement and creative expression. For as they have watched, they have come to terms with the situation and have answered for themselves all the ever-so-important questions regarding how far to trust you as a person. Once the gift of trust has been exchanged, there is no end to the opportunities for creative self-expression.

Help yourself and others to get to know one another's names by starting each group art session with introductions. These exchanges of names can vary as the weeks of sessions move on. For example, members can give their name and then state their favourite colour or name of their favourite medium or image to draw or paint, etc. As will have been said by all the contributors to this book in one way or another, the recognition of a person's name and the time spent in helping others to know names can be very important. All that some individuals may have that they can truly call their own is their name. By recognising the importance of their name, you are recognising the value you place on their existence.

As many people in the populations we work with have been isolated from society, the sharing and showing of art history books can be time well spent. There is a whole other world within the realm of the visual reproductions of other artists. Too many people are exposed to nothing other than calendar art, television and a few, poorly done, entertainment-geared publications. Select the best and share the names of artists and the time in history in which they lived. Talk about what kind of painting you are looking at, or what the sculpture was carved from, etc. One or two pieces of work to share each session can be an amazing catalyst. If you are still working in pencil, charcoal and conte, show black and white drawings. Once working in colour, move into sharing reproductions of paintings. I had one young woman in a group of people with developmental disabilities ask me very honestly one session, 'Roberta, could you help me make a Mona Lisa?' I responded with the gentle remark that it would help us both if one of us were a Leonardo da Vinci. That exchange led to many small discussions: never present too much to absorb at any time about Leonardo da Vinci. The purity of her keen interest was a true joy. Many an art history professor should be as lucky as I have been with students so enthusiastic and thirsty for knowledge.

It is essential, in helping others create art, that you have respect for the independent and unique mark they, and only they, can make. Even in a clinical setting, it is essential not to intrude, ask unneeded questions or interrupt unethically the process of which we are privileged to be a part. If a person wishes to tell you about their work, you have received a double gift. You were initiator of the process and are included in the individual's enthusiasm and emotions about what they are producing or have produced.

One such exchange I shall cherish always. There was a severely multi-handicapped young man of 24 years who was in a group art session. He always arrived ready and eager to start. At this time the Falklands war was in full turmoil and he seemed to produce nothing but images of what he felt was going on. These images began to flow once we had worked together for a couple of months and he had all the media, except the paints, to choose from. One painting in pastel had a dark stormy sea, a dark troubled land, and a number of buildings. One of those buildings was a brilliant mix of pink, orange and yellow. The structure absolutely glowed from the paper. He asked 'Do you know why that building is there?' I had no idea. 'That building is where *the peace talks are going on.*' This exchange opened a door for us to discuss all his many weeks of battleships, tanks, etc. He had hoped that by drawing all these images he could get the war to stop. His words were, 'War is such a horrible waste of life.' Interference in his process of emotional release regarding the war, which was getting so much press and TV coverage, would have been unethical. Possibly such interruption might even have stopped his process of slowly creating adequate visual armies displayed on sheet after sheet of paper until he was ready to create the peace talks within his gloriously coloured building. Then there was, in the news media, only discussion of future peace talks. This young man was ahead of the politicians and more capable of producing honest images than some professional artists I know about.

Lastly, an important element regarding the value of the creative process upon which I could easily write an entire chapter: do encourage honest expression. Even if a person has ugly, angry feelings, which are finding their way to the work, you are succeeding, for these expressions are real. Work towards integrity and quality in the work of all people, and encourage truth of experience and sight. There is great damage done through allowing overly sentimental and stereotypical art to be produced by any individual. The value of involving anyone, particularly those defined within 'special populations', is lost if you passively allow the 'pretty' images. Because of lack of or limited exposure – and then at times only to the 'kit' art experiences, some people can easily arrive in your session knowing no other imagery than the sickly sweetness of stereotyped art forms. By encouraging the re-awakening of inner self and presenting activities that remove one immediately from such production, you can begin to encourage expressions of truth and personal satisfaction.

PRACTICAL ACTIVITIES

My focus in this section will be on the use of the visual arts with a variety of people, with suggested activities which readers can adapt to their own particular theoretical frameworks or job descriptions. Personally, my professional approach is to offer actual experience within the visual arts and to know that the individuals involved will need to be attended to differently and responded to differently, and that the use of the arts in their lives must be individually defined.

I believe in the arts for all the various and glorious reasons described by myself and other contributors to this book. My intense personal conviction regarding the healthiness of the arts experience for all people relates to the essential nature of the arts to provide for every person – man, woman, child, disabled or able-bodied – an avenue of personal expression. Only you can make that particular sound or line or movement. The other art forms dealt with in this volume sit more secure and removed from the tragic results of the trap I am presently concerned with. The visual arts have a hand-in-hand friendship with craft or, as I prefer to call it, the applied arts. The trap is that too many people administrating, giving economic support for arts programming, have in mind something very different from our purpose here.

Kits serve a merchandising purpose, not an artistic experience. Yet for so very many, 'arts programmes' kits are seen as the root of creative action. The final products are sold as commodities in gift shops. Often they are interesting to display, for, if the individual with a disability has been able to move all threads as demanded, or paint pre-programmed proper colour in the proper space, you have a presentable but unstimulating and impersonal piece of work. These kits, green ware, paint-by-number sets, etc. do not allow an individual to express his or her feelings, to expand his or her capacity as a human being to feel, see or respond. As a result, such kits *must* be avoided at all times. The human mind is capable of tremendous creative ventures, which are all too frequently ignored or wasted because there are not enough people wishing to take the necessary time. Such kits also lead to the stereotypical reproduction of emotion. Our aim is to allow the people with whom we are working every opportunity to discover how wonderfully unique and special is the fact that they have known life and can share their feelings with us. To that aim, all our work should be directed.

Initial experience

People are often concerned and reluctant to participate fully when presented with a new experience. We must judge carefully what we introduce to an individual as a first visual arts experience. There are very few people who have not known, experienced, the use of the pencil. Even people I have known lacking arms have used a pencil from very early in their lives. A good graphite pencil, as I have described, should be used on large sheets of paper. Have everyone begin with drawing circles all over the paper, and, depending upon their individual abilities, encourage them to try to make the circles as similar in size as possible. The same should be done with ovals, lines and scribbles, the effort being to make the person comfortable with producing a line another person is seeing, and to break down all barriers to the famous saying 'I cannot do art.' These elemental forms are basic to most motor efforts used in writing. The fact that such simple efforts can bring true feelings of accomplishment are worth every minute spent. Every experience from there forward will reduce further and further an individual's inner fear. My own years of work with others has shown that there are people who will repeat, over and over again, the same imagery because they received such true pleasure from the first encounter. The circles or ovals will recur in works in pastel and paint enhanced or matured through other experiences, yet a reminder of how important the first good feelings were.

Pencil

Pencil circles, rectangles and scribbling all over the page. Tell the group: 'You can do nothing wrong. Art gives you freedom to express yourself as you wish.'

If I see a person being particularly withdrawn and afraid to begin, I ask them to hold the pencil or other drawing or painting medium. Then I slowly begin to move that person's hand (or foot). There will come a point where you can feel the person begin to take over the action. At that point I slowly release guidance and simply let my hand go for a ride. It will be obvious when you can lift your hand away and not have to give such assistance. For an individual with a limited range of muscle movement or motor control, this can be most important in assisting their efforts.

Charcoal and conte

After a session or two with a pencil, I then introduce charcoal, a messy, breaking-free experience which renders on paper intense blacks and assorted variations thereof. Charcoal should be demonstrated as used in a direct drawing form; then with the stick on its side with the wonderful swirling effects that can be produced; smudging of the charcoal once laid upon paper; erasing – 'lifting' of charcoal with an art gum or charcoal eraser; encouraging people to feel the exciting fun of rubbing the charcoal on their fingers and then using their fingers as tools to create design elements. Hours of much pleasure to all can be spent. Simply make certain you have taken soap and towels.

Conte, although a different medium, can be used in much the same manner. The stick on its side can produce wonderful areas of variation. Into that area of pigment a person can again utilise the art gum eraser, or a tissue, to produce a variety of special effects. Actually, conte is more easily manipulated than charcoal.

Pastels

The chalk pastel is my personal choice as the medium through which I introduce people to colour. I have very specific reasons for this. When we as artists are working with a person with a disability, there is great advantage in keeping, for as long as necessary, the pigment in contact with the fingers or toes. Not only are we, as people, more aware of the feeling of the medium against our skin, but we are also closer to the transfer of colour to paper, canvas or board. The intimacy of this process can be cathartic for some people experiencing the arts for the first time.

Colours can be layered, mixed, smudged or wiped away, leaving hints of pigment. All varieties of creative activity with colour teach fundamental understanding about colour and about mixing. The rich pigment of the chalk pastel allows for easy demonstrations and explorations of the *primary* colours: red, yellow and blue, and the *secondary* colours: violet, green and orange, which are derived from the mixing of the primary ones.

Each person responds differently on an emotional level to colour. The emotions and feelings evoked by certain colours are good to discuss. Small dramatic activities can be introduced where a person shows how a colour makes them feel – by the use of facial expression or body movement.

Oil pastels

Oil pastels are easily over-layered, smudged, rubbed, etc. However, their particular qualities create unique results and experiences. For the individual clearly desiring to rub a drawing medium clear through the paper this can be of great benefit, in that layer upon layer of colour can be added and the product will only become richer – that is, as long as you have provided paper outside the 'self-destruct range'.

For a group of people working together over a number of sessions and who have been introduced to oil pastel, I have a 'trust game' (such jargon is a matter of personal definition, in that in the visual arts we are not dealing as directly with group activities as are those of our contemporaries working in music, the dramatic arts or in guided fantasy through the avenues of folklore). This activity is to present to the group a large and sturdy piece of paper. The paper is passed one to the other as they individually work on their own creations. Each person should be given an adequate amount of time with the paper so as to make the contribution they wish. Their name should be signed on the bottom, with your help if necessary. Once everyone has added to the image of colour and form, the paper should be clipped to a drawing board. Then, gathering everyone around you, put turpentine on a rag and begin to rub the work. Turpentine acts upon oil pastel as upon oil paints; it is the medium for moving the pigment. Under a turpentine rag and with a little directed guidance on your part, a fascinating and beautiful group project can result. This is particularly pleasing to those persons with severe limitations to their muscle movements. Even the energy expended in one small corner of the paper by a person with a severe disability has added equally to the overall beauty of the finished product. Such group projects I try to hang where they can serve as a reminder of group cohesion and of the elements of 'magic' that we, as leaders, can put to our service. This activity usually leads to people wishing to experiment on their own drawings. I agree, as long as they will allow me to move the rag with their direction. 'Poison' is a word even the most severely limited individual understands. It is simple. You care enough for them to help them, but not to see anyone be ill or injured.

Oil pastel can also serve as a 'resist' for other media and greatly increases the opportunities for some people to experience the joys of the unexpected in the visual arts. When the person, or group, is ready to move on to experiences with paints, I first add oil pastels in mixed media work. I will speak more about this shortly. Once the individuals you are working with have experienced both chalk and oil pastels, it is advantageous to present both for exploration. As each medium responds differently to smudging, rubbing and intermixing, the results of beauty and fun can be delightful. Also you will soon be able to see how quickly certain people choose certain ways of working that provide them the most successful route to the goal they desire to reach, even if it appears to be not far removed from play to the observer. Picasso once said, 'To draw you must close your eyes and sing.' Working with certain persons within the range of our interests gives us increased insight into how much truth is in Picasso's understanding of the uniquely tactile, sensual and direct process of drawing.

Many works in pastel are known to us, through art history books, as paintings. Such a definition is largely the result of the paint-like quality of many pastel works. It is also related to the fact that pastels are such pure pigment. As I have said before, allowing the relationship between mind and hand to be as close as possible to the drawing or painting medium has many advantages for all who have a desire to experience colour. The emotions are more easily tapped because the paint-like flow of pigment on paper is so immediate.

Painting

I have already pointed out my particular desire for the use of tube watercolours. Egg cartons (of the plastic variety) or small cake tins can allow hours of unending enjoyment and exploration. Always begin by giving each person only the primary colours. By this time there has been an introduction to colour mixing during our time spent with pastels. However, a new experience results the moment you put a brush into the hand or toes of someone you are working with. The paint brush is a tool and it must be remembered that it can, for some, be a new barrier to creative activity. The brush allows new sensations but reduces the sensations of tactile immediacy with the medium. Assistance and patient, steady, guarded care must be taken, depending on the needs of the individuals with whom you are working.

I begin painting experiences by putting a bit of yellow, red and blue into spaced areas of the egg carton. We look at what happens when yellow is mixed with a bit of blue. The element of magic, or capacity to feel a power of control over a painting medium, can be, for some, the first experience with feelings of accomplishment and self-destination ever known. As I write I smile with delightful memories of the expressions on the faces of some people with whom I have worked and their incredible pride: 'I made *purple!* Look, it is purple.'

I help them see how the brush, loaded with pigment, gives a very intense colour, and how adding water alone to the brush will produce lighter and lighter washes. A bright red can become the faintest pink hue so simply, so pleasantly. One spring as the lilacs were in bloom and a group with which I had been working had begun explorations in paints, the demonstration of washes led a young woman with a developmental disability to produce the loveliest, softly whispered interpretation of spring blooms I think I have ever seen. She was not a master artist, with all the knowledge and understanding of the medium she was working with, yet the emotion that flowed on to the paper made some of my professional colleagues' work look quite weak by comparison. She expressed the wonder of light, colour, fresh new smells of the earth and the blossoms on the trees in a way I would be proud to approach in my own work.

There are many ways to use a brush: as a wash – the brush on its side, utilising the point to draw clear distinct lines, or by using the tip of the brush dotted straight down on the paper to produce spots, leaves, parts of a flower, a person's curly hair, etc. The brush, as a result, begins to offer extensions to creative process.

Slowly I add more colours from the tube watercolours to the palette of the people I am working with. Patience is truly a virtue in working in the visual arts, for if your excitement for a person to know more media or colours exceeds good judgment, you can end up with frustrated and sometimes frightened people – some who never return to the visual arts experience.

Also, depending upon the individual or the group, you may have to limit experiences with colour totally to pastel or coloured pencils. This may, for example, be necessary, as I have found, when the group you are working with is very large and your support staff is small or non-existent. Painting in such situations could lead to utter frustration for all, especially as there is a probability of water jars being knocked over or paints being confused. Spilt water is spilt water, granted, yet such spills can destroy the work of many and are not worth the risk. The objective of the arts facilitator/leader is to provide creative experiences in self-exploration and it is of the greatest importance that we understand that we must consciously be aware of preventing situations which, by their nature, produce feelings of guilt or failure. If a person is angry with him- or herself or his or her own work, and purposely destroys what he or she has produced, we must accept that as their right. Group annihilation of all work within range of the running water of an overturned jar is avoidable.

In working with people with emotional disabilities, we may often see outward destruction of the work produced. The anger is directed at their product and releases or responds to the emotions expressed in the process of creating the work. Conversation, one to one, about the work and your response can often provide insights important to the success of further creative activity with that particular person. Your own analysis of such behaviour depends entirely upon your training and your 'contract'.

Mixed media

After all media have been introduced and dealt with individually, then and only then do I introduce mixed media investigations. After this point all arts media will be presented for a person's choice. The desire to experiment and to have fun is basic to human nature. There need be little direction given, simply your constant availability if there are problems, and your capacity to help and to encourage excitement in the people around you to try something new.

Collage

Collage work can be very rewarding for certain people, depending upon the restrictions they personally bring to an arts session. I save magazine photos for their beautiful array of colours and other assorted papers for their textures. Tear them up before presenting them if you are aware that people will only see the imagery and not the colours. Give a sturdy piece of paper or illustration board as a back surface and, with rubber cement from the jars, allow for imagery creation from torn shapes and areas of colour. To individuals with cerebral palsy, or those paralysed in other ways with limited use of their arms, this can be a most beneficial experience.

The frustration of struggling to have colour stay where one wants can be overcome with the assistance of yourself or a volunteer to wipe on the rubber cement for the people you are working with. Then as many variations of form or imagery as they desire can be explored. The fumes from rubber cement can be a problem for some people. Thus here, as in all cases, do know well the group or individual with whom you are working.

Rubber cement is pleasant to use for, once dry, the clear extra glue can simply be rubbed from the surface of the work. Some of the white non-toxic classroom glues can be used as well. However, they have one severe problem: many cause great wrinkling and here again a beautiful work becomes a sad completed work as it turns into a relief map. I imagine we have all tried the ubiquitous flour and water and we know of the discouraging crinkling and wrinkling of which I speak. Again I say, there have been many art and craft programmes offered to those 'less fortunate than we' and tragically all too often without a desire to see quality products result from the great rewards of a quality arts process. You simply cannot have one without the other. Because an individual may have a disability does not allow us, in programme planning, to offer second-class experiences: the arts are too powerful, too important to human experience.

Working with music

Some people are truly frightened to begin making marks on a piece of paper. They are afraid of judgment, of ridicule and exposure. I find that the introduction of music to the atmosphere of the session is most helpful. If you are going to use music, please know what music you are choosing and exactly what you expect to be the positive results of such a choice – as some music can be an unforgivable interruption to the creative process. Certain classical music, folk music and guitar can provide an avenue of personal transformation from a state of fear to one of actually flowing with the elements of the music itself. One young woman with a developmental disability I worked with asked, as a piece of Allan Stivell's Celtic harp music finished, who it was and how the name was spelt. I wrote the name on the blackboard for all to see, and she actually signed her particular finished pastel work 'Allan Stivell'.

Specialised activities with music

Certain music can be an excellent stimulus to creative activity, especially music well chosen by you to have certain rhythms, tempos and beats, which make automatic response to the music difficult, if not almost impossible. Even if the individual has extensive limitations to their personal move-ments, their minds can and do still respond. I generally put the music on after everyone has the particular art materials for that session. Then I ask for all to listen to the music for a little while and then to choose a particular medium that they wish to use, and to respond on paper as they would like to have what they see in their mind be understood by others. Slowly the efforts of all can be freed to a new level of experimentation and joy – especially if you take the time to choose music with variations which provide a creative stimulus, giving direction but allowing room for personal expression.

Partner 'trust' exercise

If you have persons who are finding it difficult to get along, who possibly live in the same group home, work in the same sheltered workshop, or are in the same permanent care unit, then possibly via an arts experience exchange some of their feelings towards one another can be dissipated. In addition, it can help those concerned to understand better, or even to appreciate more their own capacity for patience. I must, however, add a warning: please know your group well and the two particular persons whom you involve in the activity, and expect no miracles. If you are unsure, change your own 'mind frame' to make sure you see this activity as a *game* and nothing more – a game to be experienced for the fun and artistic exploration.

We all feel rather possessive about our own work. It is natural and healthy. In fact, it is what I have spent the last number of pages writing about. If you have any questions about the following activity, work through it with a fellow artist or interested party before using it with a specialised group.

The specific activity consists of pairs of people who will work together. One piece of paper is given, and conte, pencils, chalk and oil pastels are provided. The instructions are as follows. First, you, Billy, will begin. John is asked to watch and feel what might be the thoughts, colour desires and mood (these descriptive terms must be adjusted according to the group with which you are working). John watches silently and observantly. Then, at your discretion, you ask Billy to give the paper to John and for Billy to observe in the same concerned way. The paper goes back and forth several times, John and Billy making their own reinterpretation of their response to the imagery already on paper. The finished product should be hung in the arts session space or the exercise repeated at another time so that the participants can each have an agreed product as a possession.

I ask the reader to remember that some distances between individuals are there for reasons. At times unknown to us, cruelties have occurred that are too inhuman for us to deal with in creative arts sessions. We *must* be perceptive and never ask more of an individual than he or she can give at the particular moment. Also, we must understand and show compassion towards those in our sessions who have been hurt so deeply as to be unable to respond to another individual at all. Sometimes we only know who these people are from behavioural signals, for which we must constantly have our antennae out. We are not to be judges, only to recognise that, even among 'normal' people, cruelties may be imposed by a person which make respect for that individual impossible, in fact unethical. If we can understand this fact of life, why, then, do so many arts specialists, social workers and psychologists feel that such problems do not affect those people who are described by some as handicapped, retarded, deaf, blind and so on? Human emotion is our common denominator. If one cannot hold total respect for individuals who do not want to work with those who have hurt them, then we had better go into another field where we are not dealing with the arts and with human beings and their emotional 'backpacks', which have collected survival equipment we shall never have the privilege to know.

Group 'trust' exercise

In this activity, I always use music and involve the entire group. The activity begins with each person being given a large piece of paper. Then they choose the media they want to work with. Once everyone is set and ready to produce, I explain the rules of the game:

1 Names are put on the back of the paper and the paper is turned over. The drawing will now be placed on the surface facing you.
2 Then each person is to work along with the music I put on the tape recorder *until* the music stops. Once the music is stopped, then each person passes the paper on which they are working to the person on their right. Each person again begins when the music starts. Music is stopped and the papers are passed again.

This continues until all the pieces of work have moved in a full circle. Simply, choose one member of the group and watch carefully for when their paper returns to them. At this point all members will again have their original work. It is important to select lively music. 'Stage show' music seems to work the best in creating an atmosphere of gaiety and fun. There will be some individuals who always watch their drawing as it moves around. I have even had people who are less than friendly say to another, 'Don't ruin my picture.' Even though there may be a few interpersonal problems, you should keep your eyes on the exercise as it is so very valuable as a shared activity, as an exercise in sharing. The success of the game will depend on your ability to allow people to know the great pleasure in all participants sharing and in being able to take home or back to their room a piece of work that has been produced by everyone in the arts session. I have done this many times with a wide variety of people with a disability and have seen nothing but pleasure and goodwill increase among members of the group.

Music and drawing game

In this game people are again placed in pairs. Each has his or her own piece of paper upon which they are working. If the person sitting facing another decides to add a form, colour or design to the other's work, they simply reach across and work on the other drawing. Again, lively, spirited music should be used, which creates a feeling of fun. There are very few times in which any negative behaviour has been exhibited. If you handle the game's explanation well, it will be understood to be a game and as an experience most beneficial for all. However, some people need to be individually encouraged to touch the other's paper. We learn as human beings through such exchanges that new ideas often follow as a result of the inspiration given by another person's interpretation. Also, the opposite paper is always upside down to yours and the perspective is automatically changed as a result. The goal is to encourage trust and understanding through the exercise, which is structured in such a way as to encourage patience with another person reaching over and putting their mark upon your work. This effort to reach can be a physical extension activity as well.

One only has to be involved for a few minutes in any work to have a personal identification that says, 'This is my drawing.' To relax with another person's intrusion upon our space has implications that go far beyond the art session itself. Goals such as these are a large part of the beauty of the arts as human exchange. We learn much about ourselves and other people, and the knowledge that we gain is essential for producing good art as well as for healthy relationships.

Creating pictorial images through suggested fantasy

For some individuals, if not a large majority of all people, there has been limited use of the imagination. We need, as arts facilitators, to have tricks up our sleeves to unlock creative thinking, or to remove blocks so long in place that it becomes a major part of our professional intention with certain persons.

One way I have found successful as well as most pleasurable for everyone is to select a fairy-tale or other story that is rich in visual imagery. Then, giving everyone paper and a selection of media, I begin reading the story with interest and excitement. As they listen to my reading they are to produce a work that expresses the way they pictured the story or the way they felt. Images, colours and emotions, all are interpreted through each person's own perceptions. A well chosen story can unlock many of the blocks to creative thinking. The elderly person quite often finds great imagery provoked by stories that are historical-traditional in their nature. The great richness that can be shared from having lived through so much of human history can be a beginning for awakening the creative spirit of a folk artist.

If the people with whom you are working have had little exposure to some of the great beauty of imagery-provoking stories, you should not panic as they sit engrossed in the story and unable to work. The images will flow later, with such an obvious receptiveness for storytelling that you will have an indication of the likelihood of success, should the exercise be repeated.

SUMMARY

In this chapter it has been my desire to provide an introduction to art materials and their use. I have included only a few of the many games and exploratory exchanges that can be employed.

I purposely left out any of the psychologically oriented games or personal activities. My decision is related to my firm belief in the visual arts experience as a first-quality emotional experience for all people. I also have a concern for the specific intent of many such activities and the necessary psychological training that should accompany such work.

Also, I have not spent much time in dealing with the art-related activities that are known so well by everyone, for example the gluing of macaroni in all shapes and forms to create designs, or of cracked eggshells on a surface to be painted. I know the reader can think of many more. Simply look in any elementary teacher's art directives and you have loads of such ideas. I am concerned with allowing emotional release and personal growth through the visual arts.

Your job is to provide good supplies, enthusiasm and creative inspiration. You will be needed as a keen and conscientious observer. Most difficulties can be overcome with a little help from you.

If you are fortunate enough to be working with a group of people in a situation where an exhibition of their works can be organised, that each selected as their own choice to represent them, you have the opportunity for a grand ending to what can be anything from weeks, months and sometimes years of working together. Such exhibitions should have a good accessible space and an 'opening' where others are invited and refreshments are served. This is a wonderful way to show people your appreciation for their efforts and to encourage further work and self-development through the visual arts experience. When such opportunities are not available, because of the conditions of the working situation, I have found that a finale can be accomplished through enjoying refreshments together. I give a present of pastels, paper, paints, or whatever would mean the most and be most needed. Then the highly emotional experience of having created art together does not end on a low note with simple goodbyes exchanged. You have been able to continue the inspiration.

I close with a reminder. We are working with other human beings through an emotional and highly expressive medium. We must always remain extremely humble in our interactions with others during working sessions. Openness to new experience is what we are encouraging and we too must remain open. So very much of what I have learned has been in response to what I have been taught by those whom I teach.

It is often thought that art is a form of recreation, indulged in by those who shun hardship. True artists are never at rest; like Rodin they labour at their work with passionate devotion, from early morning until dark; indeed, after daylight fades, the dreaming muse begins to torment the mind until it can plunge again into manual expression.

> The principles on which art is built are fundamentally the same as those of life itself. Sincerity of soul, accuracy of the outward and inward eye, constancy and patience are indispensable to any real accomplishment, be it art or merely living – perhaps the greatest art of all.[1]

ACKNOWLEDGEMENTS

For wisdom gained from working with other people I am forever grateful to Dr Dolores Armstrong and Dr Walter Hirsch. I thank them and all who, by their example, have given me such wonderful insights into the human spirit.

I thank Robert Whyte, Donna and John Harling, Sara Widness and Robert McInnis for always believing in me and my work and all the artists, writers and poets of all time, for their unending inspiration.

Lastly I thank my children, Joe, Pat, Anthony and Noelle, for enriching my life and understanding of human existence, for always keeping my viewpoints fresh and clear and for returning to me so much love.

NOTE

1 Malvina Hoffman (1965) *Yesterday is Tomorrow*, Crown, New York.

SUGGESTED READING

Arnheim, R. (1969) *Visual Thinking*, University of California Press, Berkeley and Los Angeles.

Atack, S. (1980) *Art Activities for the Handicapped*, Souvenir Press, London.

Edwards, B. (1979) *Drawing on the Right Side of the Brain*, J. P. Tarcher, Los Angeles.

Feder, E. and Feder, B. (1981) *The Expressive Arts Therapies*, Prentice-Hall, Englewood Cliffs, NJ.

Gettings, F. (1966) *You are an Artist: A Practical Approach to Art*, Hamlyn, New York.

Kramer, E. (1971) *Art as Therapy with Children*, Schocken Books, New York.

Langer, S. (1942) *Philosophy in a New Key*, Harvard University Press, Cambridge, MA.

Langer, S. (1967) *Mind: An Essay on Human Feeling*, Johns Hopkins Press, Baltimore.

Liebmann, M. (1986) *Art Therapy for Groups*, Brookline Books, Cambridge, MA.

Liebmann, M. (ed.) (1990) *Art Therapy in Practice*, Jessica Kingsley Publishers, London.

Ludins-Katz, F. and Katz, E. (1989) *Arts and Disabilities: Establishing the Creative Art Centre for People with Disabilities*, Brookline Books, Cambridge, MA.

May, R. (1979) *The Courage to Create*, Bantam, London.

Pavey, D. (1979) *Art-based Games*, Methuen, London.

Ulman, E. and Dachinger, P. (1975) *Art Therapy in Theory and Practice*, Schocken Books, New York.

Chapter 6

Dance

Developing self-image and self-expression through movement

Bernie Warren and Richard Coaten

All living organisms, at least once in their lives, exhibit behaviours that could be referred to as dancing. Human beings are no exception. We are constantly pursuing movements that have repetition and rhythm and can be subdivided, by an outside observer, into movement themes or phrases. Many modern choreographers often build on these natural movement sequences to create dances that audiences pay money to watch.

Within all of us there is a dancer. Washing our faces, digging the garden or baking bread can all be viewed as our own personal pieces of choreography, our own special dances. These movement sequences have special meaning for us and yet it is unlikely that most of us will ever 'perform' for another in hopes of reward, money or applause. However, they do reaffirm our being.

The movements we make as human beings are so intricately linked with dance that many learned authorities spend hours debating when an action, or series of actions, ceases to be movement and starts to enter the realms of dance. This pedantic academic argument concerning the physiology, mechanics and aesthetics of movement – is mainly irrelevant to the individual wishing to employ dance/movement in special education, rehabilitation or health care. It is important, however, to realise that dance/movement serves many, very important functions for all human beings.

For all of us the body is an instrument of expression and in childhood it is through the movement of our bodies that we start to build a picture of our world. As we develop we explore our capabilities and start to learn what our bodies can do. This exploration and movement of our body parts leads to a growing awareness of our body's structure and to the growth of body image. Not only is this early corporeal exploration important to the developing self-concept of young children, but also throughout life this testing and usage of our bodies would appear to be linked to cognitive development, particularly in the areas of assimilation and recall of new information.

More important still is the link between dance/movement and emotion.

The movements we initiate, the body shapes we form and the responses we present to external stimuli usually reflect our inner emotional state. The way we move, the way we stand, our gestures – all express (sometimes more accurately than the words we speak) what we feel at any given moment; in essence they express the 'sub-text' below our verbal communications. The belief in sub-textual communication through movement has created the concept of dance as a mirror of the soul. This in turn has led to many referring to dance as the mother of all tongues because movement cuts across all language barriers and speaks to individuals at a primal, emotional level. For some people, particularly those born into highly technological and industrialised societies, which increasingly shun the expression of emotions, this can be *very* threatening. As a result emotional energy, instead of being naturally expressed, becomes pent up and is often dissipated through destructive or anti-social behaviour.

At its simplest level, a dance is a statement of emotion expressed through movement. To control the statement, to make it more specific, to produce colour and texture within the emotional statement, so that an observer (audience) responds, empathises or understands, requires a great deal of training, technique and 'emotional integrity'.[1] This is the arduous route undertaken by the professional dancer. However, as already mentioned, at any one time we all have at least one dance within us. Often people with a disability have a great need to allow their dance to see the light of day, for both physiological and emotional reasons. Yet all too often it is these individuals who are denied the chance to explore this emotional release through dance and movement.

For people with a disability, the dance experience can be particularly valuable. For the person with a cerebral palsy, dance/movement can offer an opportunity to gain control over muscle spasms creatively. For the person who is withdrawn, a dance may allow them the opportunity to make a creative statement about themselves. For those of us making use of dance/movement in special education, rehabilitation or health care it is important to be aware of the positive benefits of dance/movement for gross and fine motor control, neurological functioning, circulatory stimulation and so on. However, it is equally important to remember that the movements that form part of an individual's unique dance are an emotional response. It is this emotion that lifts the sequence of actions beyond the purely mechanical level of physical exercise, such as can be gained through racquetball or swimming. Dance allows an individual the chance to make a personal creative statement about their feelings through the movements they carry out. This will often have other benefits in more physiological areas, particularly for those people who have a physical disability.

The implicit benefits that can be gained through dance/movement sessions are not easily achieved. For these benefits to be gained by individuals, it is important to engender a sense of fun and personal achievement throughout the sessions. If a sense of enjoyment and personal satisfaction is lost, the mechanical, physiological and neurological benefits that can ultimately occur as a result of dance/movement sessions will also be lost: as interest, motivation and self-satisfaction will give way to boredom, repetition and alienation from being just another trained dog jumping through the same old hoops.

What follows is a selection of exercises, games and ideas that many professionals have employed in our work with special client groups. The activities do *not* have some mystical power that can transform the neophyte into a dance/movement specialist. However the material is enjoyable, easy to use and normally 'successful', even in the hands of individuals with little formal training in dance or movement. Always remember that each group, and each individual within a group, has specific needs; sensitively choosing material suited to those needs will go a long way to making your sessions both enjoyable and successful.

PRACTICAL ACTIVITIES

The material presented here is a cross-section of activities employed by professional dance/movement specialists. Some of the material is 'universal' and is also used by drama and music specialists in their work. However, the roots of all the activities are in movement. The examples cover four of the basic goals a dance/movement specialist may be seeking to achieve with a particular client or group, namely: gaining greater control of isolated body parts; improving body image; achieving controlled emotional release; and becoming more socially adept. In many cases these goals are interlinked, for with greater control of individual body parts in turn comes a better appreciation of the body schema and therefore, an improved body image. This knowledge, and control of the body and its extremities, in turn facilitates the channelling and releasing of emotion through movement expression.

All the activities outlined require little in the way of practical equipment. For most, a selection of percussion instruments, or a tape recorder or record player to provide the suitable musical stimulus are all that is required. In addition we suggest that you always carry with you a variety of styles and tempos that can encourage a wide range of movement possibilities. Initially it is advisable that you use music that you like and that you know creates the desired response in you. Certain activities may require specialised equipment and in these instances mention is made of this in the text. In addition, our own particular musical preferences for particular activities are also noted in the text.

As a final basic practical hint, we suggest that participants attending dance/movement sessions should wear loose comfortable clothing, wherever and whenever possible. However, for some people, particularly in the first few sessions, wearing 'special' clothes can be very threatening and often counterproductive. Nevertheless, so that participants can achieve the greatest range of personal movement, it is important to work towards this simple goal.

The dance/movement activities are presented here under four sub-headings: Warm-up, Body Awareness, Group Awareness and Dances. It will become obvious to even the most inexperienced person that this way of categorising activities is purely a matter of convenience, as many of the activities outlined here could just as easily have been put under at least two of the other headings!

Finally, try not to become so entrenched in the goals you are seeking to achieve for your group, and the individuals within it, that you stop being sensitive to a particular individual's immediate needs, or lose sight of the importance for all your group to become actively and enthusiastically involved in the session. Enabling individuals to enjoy each session, to have fun with you, goes a long way towards the transformation of these sessions from simply being labelled as therapy to being truly beneficial for participants.

There are many ways to warm up a group.

WARM-UP

As with all other performing arts, a 'warm-up' period is an essential part of each session. The 'warm-up' is particularly important for people who rarely use their bodies, and well chosen warm-up activities will greatly reduce the chances of physical injury. Ideally, the warm-up should meet the needs both of the group and of the activities that comprise the session. If the activities to follow are to be physically demanding, then a thorough body warm-up is necessary to avoid sprains, strains or muscle tears. If the activities are to be more contemplative, emphasising sensitivity rather than activity, then a suitable warm-up is necessary. The warm-up also provides a time for the group to become accustomed to the leader's style and this helps with building trust, a sense of adventure and a shared energy. At a physical level, warm-ups also help to improve circulation and neuro-muscular stimulation. Themes, ideas and movement motifs begun in this early part can readily be developed later on, helped by the leader's own creative alertness[2] to these new possibilities.

Here are three simple warm-up activities. Unless otherwise stated, all activities are described from the point of view of the group leader.

Rob's Little Finger Game

This is an excellent preparation for tag games or a physically demanding session; although the title itself is perhaps a little misleading. You can use this activity not only as a physical warm-up but also as a means of getting people to smile through the use of a dose of 'humour of the unexpected'.[3] Tell the group we are to do a very strenuous activity and ask if they think they are ready to do this. Then ask the group to stretch out their right hands. After a brief pause to allow people to wonder what will happen next, tell them to wiggle their thumbs. Always ask the group to be careful, not to strain themselves. After a short wiggle tell the group to drop their right arms. As soon as they have their right arms by their sides, ask them to stretch out their left hand and wiggle that thumb. Inform them of the importance of working both sides to balance out the body energy – 'You might look lopsided if you only exercise one thumb.' Slowly increase, without stopping, the parts of the body that are being moved, adding to the thumb: fingers, wrist, elbow, shoulder on one side, and then the other thumb, fingers, wrist, elbow, shoulder on the other side, finally adding the head, neck and hips until people are moving all their body parts at the same time and hopping from one leg to the other around the room singing 'God Save the Queen' (or the appropriate national anthem). The effect is a chaotic mass of arms, legs, fingers and hips, counterpointing a rather august and nationalistic tune and almost invariably creates a light and humorous atmosphere.

This game is a good work-out for all the body. It can also become quite physically demanding. Most importantly, it can be a very valuable diagnostic tool. It enables the leader to elicit information about the basic capabilities of the group early on. For example, does everyone in the group know where their knees are? Can everyone isolate a single movement such as moving their thumb? Can they carry out more than one task at any one time? Does everyone understand 'control' words such as stop, wait, listen, etc? Do they laugh at your jokes? If an individual fails to carry out a command, there may be a number of reasons. For example, he or she may not understand the request. He or she may not associate the word 'thumb' with the relevant body part, or may be bored with the activity or deliberately disobeying – the possibilities are almost limitless.

It is important to remember that the warm-up gives the leader an insight into the likely capabilities of the group. This information may prove useful during the rest of the session. As a final note on this game, many years ago while attending a conference where this game was played, the leader of the group was a pianist who had no right hand. As a result he presented a very interesting adaptation of this game. Readers might wish to reflect on the simple changes they would have to make to adapt this game for people with limb loss or similar physical disabilities.

I Am Me – a name game

This game can be played in two stages. In the first stage, the group stands in a large circle. In turns, each member of the group jumps in the air and as they land they say their name, for example 'Bernie'. This can slowly build until as soon as one person has landed the next person starts to jump, creating a 'jumping jack wall of sound'. This leads on to the next stage, where the group moves as individuals around the room observing the following ritual. The ritual consists of a linked pattern of movements and words, for example, to make a personal statement about themselves.

Movement	Stomp	Stomp	Jump
Statements	I	AM	SUSAN
	I	FEEL	HAPPY
	I	WANT	ICE CREAM

This sequence is repeated until you feel the group has had enough. The first part of the triad is always 'I am', but the second and third parts can be varied; for example I NEED, I HATE, I LOVE, I FEAR or whatever are the needs of your particular group. In each case the statements are linked to the movement, for example:

Movement	Stomp	Stomp	Jump
Statements	I	AM	JOHN
	I	LOVE	SLEEPING
	I	HATE	WORK

In each case the statements are always individual personal statements.

This game can be particularly valuable in enabling people to express their emotions vehemently without becoming 'spotlighted'[4] or having the group focus on their problems, because their statements will be part of the group's 'wall of sound'.

Should you wish to bring the statements 'into the open', to be shared with the group you can get the group back into a large circle and then ask each member of the group to cross the circle in the prescribed ritualised manner. As leader you can choose which emotions you wish each person to describe or this can be left up to members of the group. This can lead to group discussion or simply increase your store of information concerning the group.

Follow My Dance I

This is an adaptation of follow the leader using music and is a very enjoyable activity to follow on from an unstructured or loosely shaped beginning. Bring the group into a circle either sitting or standing so that each person has a good view of everyone else in the group. It might be valuable to play a name game immediately before starting 'Follow my Dance' just to jog a few memories. In the dance there is a 'dance leader' who responds to the music playing. The rest of the group then tries to copy the leader's actions. This leadership role is then rotated among all the members of the group. The role is passed on by making eye contact with someone in the group for example Sheila and saying 'Let's all follow Sheila.' Another way is to pass a scarf round the circle. Here, the leader walks round the inside of the circle holding out the scarf for the new leader to take. This encourages choice on the part of the participants. The whole group then watches and simultaneously tries to copy Sheila's actions. In certain cases it is helpful to take control and suggest it is time to pass the leadership role on, or that an individual should continue for a little longer.

This is an extremely valuable and enjoyable dance and can be used as a diagnostic tool.[5] Through careful movement observation[6] it is possible to gain an insight into the abilities and attitudes of participants in a relatively short space of time with little need to resort to clinical files or other sources of second-hand information.

An extremely important part of this dance is that it enables each member of the group to be 'spotlighted'. For a time everyone is the centre of attention and has power over the group. There is the safety mechanism that, should this be too threatening, as soon as the person starts to feel uncomfortable they can pass the leadership on to someone else. Also, when someone has been hogging the limelight for an excessively long time, it is possible to ask them to pass on to someone else in the group. The time an individual wishes to lead the group is as important as the actions they do. This amount of time very often changes in response to a group, meeting regularly over a long period.

As leader it is important to start the group going unless there is very obviously a participant who can begin the dance confidently, thus encouraging individual choice in the process. Remember that you must work slowly and in small stages. It is perhaps rash to over-generalise, but simple linear staccato movements, such as stretching right hand and arm out to full extension in slow small stages, tend to be easier for most groups to follow than large elliptical or circular movements, at least in the early stages of the process. Groups can find sideways rhythmic patterns particularly difficult early on. This is perhaps a result of the 'mirror effect'; that is instead of copying actions we tend, in the initial stages when facing a person, to mirror them.

It is also particularly important to be aware of individual efforts, particularly when working with people with physical disabilities. For one person, simply moving the limbs may be a great achievement, and negative pressure to 'copy' the exact action may be very detrimental. In contrast, for others the inability to copy may simply be laziness or lack of commitment. Coaxing may be helpful at such times and very often a slight movement made by the participant can be echoed or exaggerated slightly, drawing attention to the quality of movement or gesture. It is helpful not to intervene too early on, which can sometimes inhibit the participant by focusing on their 'inability' in contrast to their 'ability'.

The insights gained in this way can then help in the process of deciding who needs help and in what way: coaxing, pressure, stretching, etc. It is then possible to choose music suitable for Follow my Dance II or for the next session. In addition when leading it is possible to make the leader's dance include actions that stretch individual group members in a way that expands their movement vocabulary. Try to use music with a happy bounce during your first sessions of Follow my Dance I. Then try to choose music that meets the specific age and ability of the group. However, a choice of music can include works by a whole range of artists and bands: Bruce Springsteen, Bryan Adams, Fairground Attraction, Dire Straits, Incantations, Fleetwood Mac, Simon and Garfunkel, Mrs Mills (piano music), Art of Noise, R.E.M., Clannad, Gabrielle Roth, Eric Clapton and the Beatles have all been used very effectively.

Further examples of warm-up activities

Different ways to greet each other.
Sign your name in the air,
dance it as a pathway on the floor,
run with it, stretch it; do it backwards.
Walk on the out-breath, pause on the in-breath, change direction, repeat.
Running and dodging.
Follow someone, allow yourself to be followed,
follow without being followed yourself.
Dance with different parts of the body in contact; hands, wrists, elbows,
    backs.
Draw how you feel,
dance the pathways,
dance someone else's pathways.
Become fascinated by your own movements.
Change direction, levels, pathways and planes.
Pass objects and props to one another and play with them.
The head takes the body on a journey.
Repeat an action until something else happens.[7]

BODY AWARENESS

Almost all movement requires at least a limited awareness of how the body works. To a certain degree, each movement exercise helps develop an awareness of how the body moves. The activities presented here not only emphasise body movement but also help focus on body image. In addition, many of these activities allow individuals to experience the link between body image, body movement and emotional response. These represent practically the soma/psyche linkage that dancers know all too well and reinforce references to Dance as 'emotion in motion'.

So individuals may become aware of their full body potential, I feel it is important to help them feel comfortable with their surroundings, and gain greater awareness of the articulation of their body joints to enable them to start linking their kinesthetic actions to their internal emotions.

Electric Puppet

There are various ways of introducing this game, depending on the age and ability of the group, perhaps the most common is the idea of the electric puppet. Split the group into pairs and then introduce the idea of the puppet. Tell them that we will be working with a puppet that responds to a small electrical charge. Ask one member of each pair to be the lifeless puppet and the other to be the puppeteer. Then introduce the electric baton[8] that, in the hands of the skilled puppeteer, generates a small electric charge that is powerful enough to move individual parts of the inert puppet's body. Then demonstrate the workings of the puppet; for example, if the charge is applied to the right arm, it forces the arm quickly away from the charge and it returns slowly to its original position, and so on. Ask the puppets to stand as still as possible with their arms relaxed by their sides. The puppeteers then go to work to see how efficiently their puppet responds to the electric charge. After a while allow the pairs to change roles.

This, despite its dramatic framework, is in essence an exercise in body control. Always ask the puppets to close their eyes and concentrate on exactly where the electric charge touches their body, and then to move that part of the body quickly away from the charge, then smoothly and with the minimum of effort, as there is no more electricity left to power the muscles and thus the body part must work under 'gravity', back to its original position. This can be an extremely difficult exercise for some people. It is an exercise that requires a great deal of body awareness and control. Often the puppeteer starts with whole limbs, that is arms, legs, and moves to more specific areas for example little finger, big toe and more difficult directions. It soon becomes obvious to all involved that certain movements are impossible. Also, slowly the puppet learns to move away from the stimulus – often at the beginning people move towards it. This can be reduced by asking the puppeteer to leave the electric baton where it is *until* the puppet moves away from it.

This game can cause problems. As a leader it is important to be aware of people who like to 'poke' or tend to work at head level. With children, particularly those with emotional problems, it may be wise, at least at first, to limit the use of the baton to the torso, legs and arms and to use an index finger as the baton. If the puppet is relaxed and focusing on the sensations of the body, it is not unusual both to sense the 'charge' before feeling it and to achieve a 'meditative' state.

Magic Aura

This is a good game to follow 'Stick in the Mud'.[9] It is always helpful to try to find dramatic or imaginative frameworks to use with physical activities. This often helps to suspend disbelief by stimulating the imagination so that the whole body can be totally involved.[10] This game is no exception.

Split the group into pairs. Explain that on the word 'Zing' (or other suitable word, Abracadabra, Shazzam, etc.) a magic spell will take hold of the group. The effect of the spell is that one member will become a frozen 'statue' but the other person will have the power to free their partner. However, the power will only work if the 'healer' works slowly and goes as close as they can to their partner's body *without* touching, so they can feel the statue's body energy. If the 'healer' touches the frozen 'statue' they have to start again.

Start the statues off in a standing star shape. This allows for a large area to be 'healed'. Ask the statues to close their eyes and both members of each pair to try to sense the body energy – to feel the aura. Once freed, the pairs reverse roles. Once both have explored the sensations and have been both 'statue' and 'healer', ask them both to keep their eyes closed during the healing process. It is often during this part of the exercise that the healer can 'see' their partner's aura,[11] even though their eyes are closed. If the pairs have a good rapport, the process can be repeated using more difficult and convoluted frozen shapes.

Again, this exercise can be particularly soothing. It requires a slow and sensitive approach by the healer and a relaxed but fixed posture of the statue. Children at first tend to want to rush through this game. Along with the obvious benefits to be gained in terms of body schema, muscle control, etc., this is a valuable sensitivity exercise, with the selection of suitable pairs often being crucial to the quality of experience that individuals receive.

Ninja

The Ninja were a breed of warrior-assassins who were reputed to be able to perform such super-human feats as walking through walls, becoming invisible and breathing under water. All of these feats were generated as a result of their extremely disciplined training, which emphasised mind–body co-ordination and control. This exercise is adapted from Ninja training exercises, and variants of the exercises are found in many martial arts systems.

Everyone is spread around the room with space to themselves. Inform them that the floor is made of rice paper and that great care must be taken if the rice paper is to remain intact. Then introduce the following stages one at a time; allowing the group to progress to the next stage only after mastering the basics of the previous one.

1 *Point of 'absolute' balance.* Ankles shoulder-width apart so an imaginary line could be drawn from the centre of the heel to the centre of the armpit. Feet turned out 45°. Knees slightly bent, hips rotated to straighten spine. Back straight – imagine a straight line could be drawn from the centre of the Earth through the body up to the sun. Breathing in through nose and out through mouth. Weight can now be transferred easily in any direction *without* losing balance!

2 *Forward walk.* Weight slowly transferred totally on to left leg, so that ball of right foot is last to leave floor. Right foot is placed back on floor so that weight is transferred from *heel* to *ball* to *toe* until the whole of the right foot is on the floor. The weight is then transferred totally on to the right foot as the left is removed. This process slowly gains fluidity until the walker moves forward without consciously having to think about the movement. If 'stop' or 'freeze' is called during any of these moving exercises, individuals should be on balance and able to return to 'absolute' balance with a minimum of effort. Throughout the exercise, emphasise fluid and light movements – no jerky or heavy moves or else the rice paper will be torn.

3 *Backward walk.* This is the opposite of the forward walk. Weight is transferred to the left leg – the ball of the right foot is still the last to leave the floor *but* weight is transferred back to the right leg from *toe* to *ball* to *heel*.

4 *Sideways walk.* This should be done as if you were walking with your back to a wall casting a 4-inch shadow. Mastery of the sideways walk, done in the shadow of a wall, was one of the techniques that created the Ninja's famed invisibility!

Transfer weight on to left leg. Replace right leg *heel* to *ball* to *toe*. Transfer weight to right leg. Lift left foot from floor. Bring *behind* right leg and place back on floor *toe* to *ball* to *heel*. Fluidity is achieved by simultaneously shifting weight from right leg to left as left foot starts to 'grip' the floor.

5 *Half-turn jump.* Jumping up and turning on the '*in*' breath and '*out*' on the return to the floor. A very small jump is all that is needed to create a complete turn. Often energy is wasted trying to jump high or through not linking movement to the breath.

Once the basic movements of each component of this exercise have been mastered, then participants can be asked to keep their eyes closed and to 'sense' where other people are in the room. Also, it is important to get participants to try to synchronise their breathing with their movements. This reduces the amount of energy expended in achieving fluidity of movement, leads to participants being more relaxed and creates a more meditative inner awareness of the body's movement. Many students, particularly those who have experience of Eastern religions and/or meditation techniques, describe this exercise as 'a moving meditation'.

Besides the reflective aspects of the exercise, this is a great way for people to gain control over 'locomotive' muscles of the body. Once the group has gained a sense of confidence controlling the jump movements, you can add the release of explosively exhaling the word 'kiai' on the jump turn, as participants touch the floor.

GROUP AWARENESS

Parachute

Very little is needed in the way of equipment for dance/movement sessions; however, a parachute is a valuable piece of equipment to have around. The qualities of the material, the feeling of group contact and the sensation of movement to be gained from working with a parachute are quite unique.

There are many different parachute games, all for different purposes. This exercise is one linked to sensation. The group stands in a circle. If there are a number of individuals in wheelchairs, start by sitting in a circle. Everybody holds on to the parachute with both hands, if this is possible. Try to work as a group, raising the parachute as high as it will go and then letting it return to the floor. Work together to try to make the rise and fall of the parachute smooth and rhythmic.

When the group has achieved this rhythmic flow, ask each person to say a word or sentence to describe what the parachute makes them feel. Ask them to say this when the parachute is at the top of its travel. This allows that individual to make eye contact with other members of the group. Then ask the group to repeat the word or sentence as the parachute returns to the floor. Sometimes the feeling described is a simple emotion, for example, happy; sometimes the feeling described is a sensation evoked by the movement of the parachute, for example, light and airy. In this way not only do participants express the sensations they feel, but they are also exposed to new vocabulary. In addition to working on linking sensation to expression, the parachute is an excellent tool for extending physical limits.[12]

Reed in the Wind

This is often referred to as a trust exercise; however it is an exercise in sensitivity.[13] One person (the reed) stands in the middle of a circle formed by the rest of the group. The reed has its eyes closed, hands by its side and ankles close together throughout the exercise. The outer circle (the wind) place their hands gently on the reed. Slowly and smoothly they start to move the reed, who 'pivots' on its axis. Gradually the distance the reed is moved is increased. In this exercise it is important to remain as silent as possible and the wind should always keep their hands in contact with the reed. After the reed has reached its maximum point of travel (this need not be much – a few inches is quite enough), it is returned slowly to the central starting position. It is important always to begin slowly and not to fall into the trap of 'starting' from where the last reed stopped. The 'laying on of hands'[14] – the point where the wind touches the reed – is very important. Before any movement starts, and again after the reed's movement has stopped, there should be a time when there is a silent, non-verbal communication through the hands of the wind with the reed. The length of this communication should be dictated by the needs of the group – particularly those of the reed. At the start it is a time when the wind can reassure the reed, through touch, that they will look after him or her during the exercise. Occasionally the wind may want to hum a soothing tune quietly, for example a lullaby.

This is an exercise in which all the group is able to participate. Everyone who wants to should be allowed to be the reed. If group members feel hesitant, they *should* be encouraged to try being the reed but they must always have the option to pass – without being made to feel guilty about it, either by the group or the leader! In many cases the simple 'laying on of hands' is as valuable, if not more valuable, than the gentle swaying motion.

Change

This is adapted from a Marian Chace exercise. The game is based on group cohesion and following a leader as exactly as the group's capabilities allow. (Obviously, when working with a group whose individual physical disabilities are diverse, allowances must be made to acknowledge that certain movements may be impossible for particular individuals.)

The group stands, or sits, in a circle. Tell the group that you will do a repetitious action(s) which the group has to copy exactly. When everyone is synchronised, call 'change'. At this point the person on your left will be the new leader. Each time the new leader must subtly change the action(s) and then repeat it (them) until the group are following exactly, and then call 'change'. In this way the leadership passes around the circle. This game can be seen as a further adaptation of Follow My Dance I.

It is helpful to start this game without music. When the group has grasped the idea then add music. The music that can be used is extremely varied; almost any music will do. Again this game allows individuals to be spotlighted and works towards emphasising group identity. The group 'dances' created in this way are often every bit as fascinating as some of the tightest show choreography – and nowhere near as expensive.

DANCING

An individual's response to an internal and/or external stimulus is extremely personal. Often there is little structure that can be imposed, for there are no easily stated rules as there are with the dance/movement games. All that creates the urge to dance is the stimulus.[15] It is very important to have a wide range of stimuli available.

Music, photographs and painting

These can all be used to create a mood or to generate a response. The choice of a particular painting for the specific needs of the group is important. Having shown the group a painting, you can allow them to create a dance from the emotions engendered by the image. This may require choice of suitable music or may be better suited by silence.[16]

Dance in/dance out

This is a useful activity for groups with whom you will be working for long periods of time. It allows you a chance to see what the general mood of the group is before and/or after each session. Simply play a selection of music before the session 'proper' begins and after it is finished. Allow the group to respond to the music in any way the music 'takes' them. Asking them what sort of music they would like to hear at that time can be beneficial. It is very important to have a wide variety of music with you; however, after a few meetings the group will have a good idea of the range of music you carry with you. In later sessions ask the group to bring their own music selections with them to the dance/movement sessions.

Observation of this free-form movement activity can be used to supplement other information you have about group members. Your job is often detective work, trying to piece together a three-dimensional jigsaw full of emotion, where many of the pieces are lost or unknown. Any activity that allows you to step back and just observe provides a potential store of information in a much shorter time than most of the more directive activities.[17]

Feather Dances

For a long time I (BW) was stumped. I kept being asked to do workshops with youngsters with severe and multiple disabilities and I felt much of my material to be unsuitable. Then my assistant, Jane Newhouse, introduced me to peacock and ostrich feathers. From that day on I have been using these feathers not just with children with severe disabilities (where they often form the bridge to my other material) but with all groups.

For this activity I use one of three specific pieces of music: Allan Stivell's 'Renaissance of the Celtic Harp', Howard Davison's 'Music from the Thunder Tree' and the theme music to Paul Gallico's 'Snow Goose'. Ask the group to lie, or sit, comfortably with a peacock feather in their hand. In the case of children with severe and multiple disabilities I work one-to-one with an 'able-bodied' person cradling[18] and supporting them. When the music starts ask the group to follow the 'eye' of the peacock's feather[19] as it moves to the music. The feather often appears to have a life of its own and will 'take' the person holding it dancing.

With groups of children with severe disabilities, ask their supporter to work through stages. First the feather is moved so that the 'eye' catches the child's attention. This necessitates making very small and fluid movements. Once the child's attention has been caught, place the feather in the child's hand and manipulate the hand so that the feather moves. As the child becomes more aware that it is his body moving the feather, the manipulator slowly releases the grip on the hand until the feather is moving totally under the child's control. The children may drop the feather – if so, simply put it back in their hands.

Lastly, add a second feather, so that there is one in each hand. These three stages may be traversed quickly or may take an extremely long time and much patience on the parts of the supporters and the leader.

The ostrich feather is less of an 'attention getter' but it has a textural quality that fascinates many. The combination of peacock and ostrich feathers allows an extension of movement: a small movement with the peacock feather creates a huge and fascinating effect for a severely restricted child, and a sensual experience. The group can be placed so they work in pairs or, in the case of more able groups, they can freely interact. One word of warning: always be on the lookout for children who try to eat the feathers. It not only damages the feathers but can also severely injure the child. Finally, be aware of the other materials that can extend small movements of physically restricted individuals. Experimenting with different types of cloth, string, ribbons, etc., can often find the materials best suited to your group's needs.

Follow My Dance II

This is a variation on Follow My Dance I. It illustrates a way of taking a name game into a group dance and then into a partner or small group dance. It begins as a name game, develops into movement and transforms into dance. It also helps participants to experience the difference between movement as exercise compared with movement as dance: a felt act of communication – an emotional response; the former as a preparation for the latter.

The group makes a circle; this time individuals are asked to close their eyes and have a sense of how they feel in their bodies. What follows is a sequence of instructions to be given by the leader to the group that are aimed at enabling participants to switch off the 'little voice' in their heads, which continually gives instructions about what to do and how to think, etc. The purpose is to allow participants to listen to messages from the body instead.

Allow yourself to stand.
Listen to your breath (without changing it).
Become aware of any aches and pains.
Allow the body to balance around a central axis.
Feel the support of the earth.
Imagine a cushion of air between each vertebra, how does that make you want to move?
Your back is wide; allow it to support you.
Imagine an electrical field of energy around your body, how wide is it? Explore this field.
Say your name quietly to yourself and create a way of moving in your personal energy field, that is unique to yourself.

There are many ways of framing these questions, explore them and find ones which work for you and for the group. Now find a shape or gesture that expresses how you feel right now or allow the shape to find you.[20]

Each individual is then asked to share their shape with the rest of the group by saying their name and making the shape. The saying of the name can vary from coming at the beginning to coming at the end. After each shape and name the rest of the group echo that person's name and shape, finding a matching tone of voice and quality of movement.

At the end of this task, to help develop a movement memory in the group, the leader can walk round touching the shoulder of each person in turn. The rest of the group then say that person's name and repeat the movements in turn. This certainly helps to encourage a state of creative alertness in the participants as well as in the leader. The quality of movement, gesture and tone of voice will be very different for each person and the leader may wish to draw attention to any that have a special quality about them. These movements can often be developed into solo material.

Follow My Dance III

The leader splits the group into threes or fours, and asks each group to make a dance by putting the movements explored in Follow My Dance II together in any way that feels interesting or comfortable to the group. Each group is then asked to show their 'piece' to the others. Another idea is to ask the audience if the dance conveys any images, thoughts or feelings for them. This can be done at the end, or better still, after each dance, if there is the time. The dancing group may wish to incorporate this new material into developing their dance and this is the point at which the session can really develop. The leader may then suggest a series of ideas; or more appropriately perhaps, encourage each group to find their own way of developing what they have created. Some ideas may include:

One group providing a sound experience for a dance group using their bodies and voices to make a sound accompaniment.
Musical instruments could be used.
Merge the dance with another group.
Draw the dance on paper. Dance the drawing.
Discover an emotional quality or expressiveness to the dance; dance its opposite.
Find a moment of stillness in the dance.
Walk with the dance. Run with the dance. Take the dance on to the floor. Play with the dance.
The dance has an identity; give it a voice.
Write the story of the dance and let the story inform the dance.

The ideas and possible ways to explore each dance are endless; however the leader's confidence in trying out new ideas and new ways of moving is dependent on their, and the group's state of creative alertness. Other art-forms can be used, including poetry, music and sculpture to encourage this process of self-expression through dance.

Essences

The aim of this dance improvisation is to create a safe[21] enough and comfortable environment so that individuals can make a dance that is self-directed. What is more important perhaps, it is about 'stilling the mind' and 'climbing into the body'. This means 'turning off' the little voice in the head by becoming fascinated with one's own range and quality of movement expressiveness. The leader also gives permission for individuals to dance from a more self-directed place and experience of this quality of self-motivation is helpful.

The dance requires a warm-up period before starting, as in all creative work. It also needs an ability to be confident with the elements of dance and movement, for example changing directions, levels, planes, pathways and different dynamics, etc. Some assistance can be given by the leader during the dance to introduce these elements to further develop the improvisation, encouraging the imagination as well as a rich use of movement vocabulary.

The dance is created by individuals visiting four different places in the room, finding a shape or movement phrase at each place and then joining them all together. The dance created is then shared or performed with the group. The instructions are presented as movement ideas, images, questions and the ones given here form the essentials only. The leader will need to fill them out and present them in such a way as to enable the participants to feel confident and secure in their personal exploration. Permission is given to explore the images, questions and movement tasks in a 'safe' environment. Imagery is presented by the leader, and worked with by the dancer to create a satisfying and enjoyable experience. It is not possible in these pages to transform the movement experience into a complete written picture that will give the same result every time. If used with sensitivity, intelligence of feeling and in a spirit of adventure it is likely that 'Essences' will encourage further self-exploration through dance.

People who have worked with Essences have commented on its ability to enable them to 'free up' and dance from the inside/out[22] rather than vice versa. This means dancing from a different place of knowing, a place that has brought insight and clarity as well as the bodily experience. After the sharing or performance the dance is often shared with a partner when it is possible to talk objectively and subjectively about the experience, exploring its personal relevance and meaning, giving clarity and insight.

1 *Centring*: lie on the floor. Become aware of the breath without changing it. On the 'out' breath release your weight into the floor. On the 'in' breath rest.
2 *Images of*: opening in the back, spreading, lengthening. Feeling the wholeness of the back. Letting go of tiredness, releasing, opening.
3 *Questions about*: 'stilling the mind' to connect with the body.
  Find a place in the room where you feel most comfortable.
  Explore that place in a way that is most comfortable for you.
  Express that place in a shape or movement phrase.
  Move to another place in the room where you feel comfortable and repeat the experience.
  Move to the first place again and explore the transition.
  Move to the second place. Discover its essence.
  Repeat the movement phrase. In what way has it changed?
  Move to a third place and repeat.
  Move to a fourth place and repeat.
  Now return to the first place.
  Move between places. Exploring the different qualities of movement.
  The essence of each place, each movement, each feeling.
  What images come to mind? Dance with the image.

Create a movement phrase that is repeatable and made up of the four shapes or movement phrases.

With paper and soft pastels, draw the essence of the dance on paper. Quickly and intuitively. Write any words on the drawing.

Incorporate the image[23] into the dance. Use the words in the dance. Allow the dance to be witnessed or shared with a partner or the whole group.

Share the experience in words with a partner or with the group. Or with both.

The sharing can take a variety of forms. In pairs, threes or in a large group. In the process of allowing this development of personal creativity, many different ways of moving are possible. It is a dialogue between stillness and movement, between a form that is understood and a form that is emerging. There is complexity and simplicity and in the sharing of the dance these paradoxes will no doubt emerge. The task of the leader is to enable the individuals to dance in a way that is most expressive of themselves and then to reflect on the result of that experience. The task of the individual is to have a really satisfying and enjoyable experience with comfort, ease and enjoyment the main starting points.

Repeat at a different time in a different place. Enjoy the dance, creatively alert to new possibilities for self-expression, healing and renewal. If the reader wants to take this work further, then the publications of Fulkerson (1977) and Tufnell and Crickmay (1990) should prove very helpful in suggesting imagery and ideas for finding the inner dancer.

POSTSCRIPT

Dance offers individuals a path to developing a greater sensory awareness, while at the same time releasing restricting or non-aligned patterns as they appear in posture, everyday movement patterns and expressive gestures. Developing this sensory awareness enables people to begin to create their own unique dances; ones that can help to clarify, extend and define an emerging sense of self. This may in turn help to promote an independence of thought; bodily functioning; concentration; focus; and more spontaneous, less routine behaviour.

The expression through dance of our unique self is a momentary fleeting thing, one that cannot be fixed or captured. It can only really be sensed as a living entity and certainly not captured in print. It is a coming together of shapes, movements, thoughts and feelings, rhythms and sensations, all of which make up an emotional response, a response that brings together many seemingly disparate elements, without the use of words. There is no doubt, however, that working with dance creatively, as a way to explore space, shape, rhythm and our own bodies in movement, is a very fulfilling, enjoyable and challenging task.

Watching for those special moments of 'aliveness' when the individual is 'in tune' with him- or herself requires a creative alertness. Being creatively alert for the group leader means being alive to dance as a felt act of communication. However, it is also necessary to have an understanding of the overall framework within which dance/movement activity is taking place and how one's own dance group or session contributes to the overall picture. Also, keep in mind that the ideas expressed in this chapter are in no way fixed rules about what should be done. They have their history in what has gone before – movement and dance ideas that have worked in many different settings, and ones that have been worked with, changed and developed along the way. Always remember that you are working with other human beings, their emotions and their well-being, and not simply playing or performing.

Finally, dance allows individuals to gain in self-confidence and self-management by learning about their bodies, their minds and their place in the world. Dance affects everybody, from the very young to frail older people. It enlarges people's imaginations, extends their ability to communicate and increases their capacity for social action. Individuals can be valued for their unique contribution and thus help to increase their own sense of self worth. We hope that the material we have presented here, along with the suggested films and books, will provide ideas and a framework in which you may continue to expand and develop your work in dance/movement.

APPENDIX: MOVEMENT ANALYSIS

(This movement analysis based on the principles of Rudolf Laban is adapted from LUDUS Dance in Education Teachers' Pack for *The Thunder Tree*, edited by C. Thomson and B. Warren.)

The body is capable of a wide range of movement, but all movement can be broken down into five basic actions. This kind of breakdown is known as a 'movement analysis'.

The five basic actions are:

travel: redistribution of weight through space
balance: stillness in equilibrium
turn: rotation around an axis
jump: launching weight into the air
gesture: movement without change of weight

Further, the body is capable of three kinds of mechanical action: bending, *stretching* and *twisting*.

The quality of any movement can be described by four 'movement factors':

space	high–low	near–far
weight	light–strong	soft–hard
time	fast–slow	sudden–sustained
flow	free	bound

Actions and their movement factors can be described in many ways, as shown in the following table (Table 6.1).

Table 6.1 How you move

Actions			Qualities		
hop	rock	stab	gentle	wide	lingering
skip	crawl	stroke	weak	small	dashing
step	slither	cut	heavy	tall	hurrying
run	twizzle	pinch	firm	thin	
bounce	wiggle	throw	long	fat	
leap	shake	catch	short	flat	
fall	carry	hold	angular	stiff	
stand	push	release	spiky	floppy	
rise	pull	wave	bendy	delicate	
roll	kick	flutter	curved	floating	
see-saw	punch	tense	rounded	flicking	

Table 6.2 Basic descriptors

Body parts	Directions	Relationships
What you move	Where you move	How or with whom
whole body	up	with
head	down	against
neck	in	together
shoulders	out	copying
arms	backwards	contrasting
elbows	forwards	in pairs
wrists	in front	in threes, fours ...
hands	behind	in groups
fingers	left	following
back	right	leading
hips	into the middle	joining
bottom	out to the side	leaving
tummy	straight	passing
legs	sideways	taking turns
knees	zig-zag	containing/enclosing
ankles	circle	
feet	spiral	
toes		
eyes		
mouth		
nose		

As well as these elements, all movements involve one or more *parts of the body*, have a *direction*, and are executed in relation to other people or objects.

In addition to the words that describe movement actions and qualities, there are some basic descriptors, which may be useful in planning, running or describing your sessions (Table 6.2).

These ways of describing movement are fundamental to movement analysis. You can use movement analysis to help you recognise and note the movement capabilities of your group. For example, which parts of the body, if any, can they move in isolation? Can they travel? Balance? Can they travel, but only on the floor – that is roll, crawl – or can they travel only in a wheelchair?

Movement analysis, combined with your knowledge of the individual needs and capabilities of your group, will help you to decide on your movement aims and to structure the content of your sessions. In addition it enables you to describe and record an individual's 'behaviour' in movement terms, and to detail the changes that occur in your sessions over time.

ACKNOWLEDGEMENTS

I (RC) wish to thank the following professional colleagues for their work, their vision and for the influence they have had on my own work in this field: Mary Fulkerson, Wolfgang Stange, Hilda Holger, Joanna Harris, Marcia Leventhal, Penny Greenland, Janice 'Chic' Parker, Gabrielle Parker, Steve Paxton, Alison McMorland, Carola Gross, Jasmine Pasch, Gerry Hunt, Bonnie Meekums, Klaas Overzee and Christina McDonald. I would also like to thank Peter Brinson for his contribution to the Jabadao Conference, 'Dance in a Changing World', April 1992, in Leeds, West Yorkshire.

I (BW) wish to thank the following professional colleagues, some of whom I am lucky enough to count as my friends, for their work and vision and for the influence they have had on my own work in this field: Veronica Sherborne, Keith Yon, Kedzie Penfield, Walli Meir, Steph Record, Veronica Lewis, Jane Newhouse, Helen Payne; and particularly Lesley Hutchison and Chris Thomson for their support during my time with LUDUS Dance Company, and Sensei O'Tani who awakened me to the way of the circle. However, my greatest thanks go to Julie Ortynsky and to Dr George Mager for showing me not only the power of the discipline and art of dance but also the effect this art form can have on the lives of people with disabilities.

NOTES

1 This is a concept that applies to all performers. Authorities refer to it in many different ways – it can be thought of as commitment to the role, an engagement

or linking of emotion to action, or simply a focusing of emotion. The diversity of explanations regarding this almost universally accepted concept may simply reflect the problems human beings have communicating.

2 A state of *creative alertness* means being receptive to the immediate moment, *tuning in* to our sensations, our feelings and our own bodily responses. It means *tolerating ambiguity*, not holding on to an expectation of a particular end result. It is a 'waiting without expecting', as Mary Fulkerson (1977) so aptly describes it. The impetus to action or starting point can come from many different sources: from words, images, dreams, sensations, music and everyday living.

A creative alertness helps provide the means to *creating dances* from a different place of knowing; a place that is not relative to current social and cultural ideas or one that imposes an external technique which entails learning movement and dance by imitation. It is about encouraging each individual to find the dancer in him- or herself. This often can be described as a healing experience as we come to know and express our fullest potential. It is often accompanied by a sense of release, centring calmness and insight and it is an experience open and available to everyone.

As dance leaders we often look to others to give us our ideas and material usually in the form of movement tasks or games. When we run out of ideas we again look to others for more 'tools for the toolbag'. It is so exciting to discover that being creatively alert releases a dependence on others as we discover our own personal creative journey. We create our own questions, images to explore and material for dance exploration. This is not to imply that dance leaders do not need ideas or techniques suggested to them, certainly in the early stages. It is instead to suggest ways in which leaders can enter into a creative dialogue with their minds and their bodies which can naturally extend to encouraging this process with their clients.

3 A colleague, an historian by training and sociologist by profession, once advised that one should 'always expect the unexpected' – a useful rule of thumb for the creative arts specialist!

4 This relates to a belief that all human beings need to be the centre of attention, to be 'spotlighted', for at least a short period of their waking day. It builds on a number of other earlier theories and is discussed on p. 114.

5 'Diagnostic tool' is a term used here to describe any activity that, besides producing the explicit surface behaviours expressly desired as part of its structure, also produces an insight into the capabilities and/or feelings of the group and therefore allows the leader to build a picture of the individual which supplements and quite often contradicts the existing second-hand clinical reports.

6 Movement observation and analysis are invaluable tools for the dance/movement specialist. They allow the leader the ability to learn very quickly how confident individuals are at relating to each other, to the material presented and to their own bodies, etc. There are a number of formal and informal methods of analysing movements. A very rudimentary example, based on Laban Movement Analysis is provided in the Appendix to this chapter. This is no more than a starting point. For further information see North (1972) or Bartenieff (1980).

7 Repetition is a key idea for allowing movement material to develop in an organic way. The movement has some connection with what has gone before and a state of creative alertness allows the movement potential of that moment to be developed.

8 A garden cane with a circumference of slightly less than the size of a dime or an English new penny works well. At first it may be worth using larger sticks, particularly with groups who have poor muscle control or kinesthetic awareness.

9 See R. Watling in this volume.

10 This is not a plea for individuals to be 'consciously' thinking during kinesthetic activities; as all too often this leads to cognitive blocking of feeling sensation. However, in order for the mind to be engaged, switched on if you like, individuals must want to be involved. Often a suitable dramatic framework helps to do this.

11 There can be a number of explanations why the healers see their partner's aura. Some require a leap of faith, a belief in the existence of body energy fields. Other more pragmatic explanations rest on the concept of feeling body heat and creating a 'mind's-eye' heat-outlined picture of their partner.

12 As an example, in one session I (BW) was working with a young woman who had a cerebral palsy. As a manifestation of her condition she was unable to hold her head up for more than a minute or so at a time. She became so involved in the parachute activities that she maintained focus and control over her neck muscles and her head remained erect throughout the activity. Not only this, she was able to extend the reach in her arms, way beyond their normal extension. Professionals who had worked with her remarked on the fact that they had never seen her so involved in an activity and commented that she was doing things they thought she was not capable of.

13 All too often group leaders allow exercises such as these too become an excuse to 'scare' participants; to see if they will trust the group to let them drop almost to the floor. Instead use this exercise to reaffirm the group and to accentuate its sensitivity, care and concern for its members.

14 This exercise, carried out with a sensitive group, can practically illustrate the power of faith healers who are reputed to be able to 'cure' simply by placing their hands on people. The sense of well-being and caring generated by a supportive and sensitive group is very powerful.

15 It is true that many dance/movement specialists do use/teach 'technique' to their groups. For the well-trained ex-professional dancer, allowing the group to learn these techniques is certainly an legitimate option for you. However, people without this training should be extremely wary of attempting to teach 'technique'. All too often in unskilled hands it is synonymous with training dogs to jump through hoops and as such by-passes the emotions.

16 All too often music is assumed to be essential to dance.

17 As a cautionary note: it is very important to beware the 'This obviously shows . . .' trap! Although certain behaviours may indicate a particular emotion or state of mind, a single observation is *not* sufficient to enable *anyone* to make a definite statement concerning one individual's capabilities. Humans are extremely complicated beings, not easily willing to oblige linear cause-and-effect hypotheses!

18 Those unfamiliar with either the technique or the importance of cradling should read Veronica Sherborne (1990).

19 Please note that some children and adults can be extremely disturbed by this. If so, use an ostrich's feather.

20 This idea of allowing 'the shape to find you' suggests a non-directive way of working. As in 'waiting without expecting', this idea implies an allowing or waiting for a new movement idea to arise – one that is not consciously thought out or directed – another example of where a state of creative alertness can prove very helpful.

21 Creating a 'safe' environment is about the leader having the skills, confidence and experience to give the individuals permission to dance in a spirit of adventure with a shared sense of energy, trust, enthusiasm and commitment.

22 Dancing from the 'inside/out' is about allowing images, sensations, feelings to emerge from the individual as source material for dance which is different from

the imposition of a movement style or technique from the outside. This does not diminish the importance of what is traditionally understood to be technique, that is contemporary, ballet, jazz, etc. It does, however, suggest a way of moving which has equal validity, for the individual and the dance experience, without implying movement imitation. New Dance is one term used to describe this approach to dance.

23 This implies using the essence of the drawing to add to the dance, to take the movement journey on. The colours, the shapes, the words, the pathways in the drawing can all be worked with as new starting points for the dance. In a sense the drawing helps to 'clarify' the dance in a different medium and provide added inspiration. The meaning of the dance, too, can become a new starting point for further exploration.

SUGGESTED READING

Bartenieff, I. (1980) *Body Movement – Coping with the Environment*, Gordon and Breach, NY.

Bernstein, P. L. (1979) *Eight Theoretical Approaches in Dance-Movement Therapy*, Kendall/Hunt, Dubuque and Toronto.

Bernstein, P. L. (1981) *Theory and Method in Dance Movement Therapy*, 3rd edn, Kendall/Hunt, Dubuque and Toronto.

Caplow-Lindner, E. (1979) *Therapeutic Dance/Movement* [Expressive activities for older adults], Human Sciences Press, London.

Fulkerson, M. (1977) *Language of the Axis* Dartington College of Arts, Theatre Papers, 1st Series No. 12, UK.

Garnet, E. (1982) *Movement is Life* [A holistic approach to exercise for older adults] Princeton Book Co., USA.

Greenland, P. (1987) *Dance – A Non-Verbal Approach – (A Handbook for Leaders)*, Jabadao, W. Yorks Dance Resource, short paper to accompany video, Leeds, UK.

Hanna, J. L. (1979) *To Dance is Human – A Theory of Non-Verbal Communication*, University of Texas Press, Austin and London.

Harris, J. G. (1988) *A Practicum for Dance Therapy*, distributed by ADMT Publications, Springfield Hospital, London.

Hartley, L. (1984) *Body Mind Centring*, ADMT Publications, Springfield Hospital, London.

Haselbach, B. (1981) *Improvisation Dance Movement*, Magnamusic-Baton, St Louis, USA.

Heckler, R. S. (1984) *The Anatomy of Change (East/West Approaches to Body/Mind Therapy)*, Shambhala Publications Inc., USA.

Keleman, S. (1985) *Emotional Anatomy*, Center Press, California, USA.

Lamb, W. and Watson, E. (1987) *Body Code: The meaning in movement*, Princeton Book Co., USA.

Lange, R. (1975) *The Nature of Dance – An Anthropological Perspective*, Macdonald and Evans, Plymouth.

Lerman, L. (1980) *Teaching Dance to Senior Adults*, C. Thomas, USA.

Levete, G. (1982) *No Handicap to Dance*, Souvenir Press, London.

Levete, G. (1987) *The Creative Tree*, Michael Russell (Publishing) Ltd, Salisbury, UK.

Levy, F. (1988) *Dance Movement Therapy. A Healing Art*, American Alliance for Health, Physical Education, Recreation and Dance, Virginia, USA.

North, M. (1972) *Personality Assessment through Movement*, Macdonald and Evans, London.

Pasch, J. (1984) *Creative Dance with People with Learning Difficulties*, short paper distributed by ADMT Publications, Springfield Hospital, London.

Pasch, J. (1985) *Dance and Movement with Older People*, short paper distributed by ADMT Publications, Springfield Hospital, London.

Payne, H. (1984) *Responding with Dance*, ADMT Publications, Springfield Hospital, London.

Sherborne, V. (1990) *Developmental Movement for Children*, Cambridge University Press, Cambridge.

Torbert, M. (1980) *Follow Me*, Prentice-Hall, NJ.

Tufnell, M. and Crickmay, C. (1990) *Body, Space, Image*, Virago, London.

Videos

American Dance-Movement Therapy Association (1984) *Dance Therapy – the Power of Movement*, University of California, Berkeley.

Bernstein, P. L. (1975) *To Move is to Be Alive: A Developmental Approach in Dance-Movement Therapy*, Pittsburgh Guidance Center, Pittsburgh.

Jabadao (W. Yorks) Dance Resource (1987) *Dance – A Non-Verbal Approach*, Leeds.

Jabadao (W. Yorks) Dance Resource (1987) *Dancing for Celebration*, Leeds.

Sherborne, V. (1976) *A Sense of Movement*, Concorde Films, Ipswich.

Sherborne, V. (1982) *Building Bridges*, Concorde Films, Ipswich.

Chapter 7

Expanding human potential through music

Keith Yon

Why is music of such value to me that I feel others could similarly benefit? Simply, music lifts me: my feelings, thinking and spirit are extended beyond the strictures of ordinariness, paradoxically by taking me physically inwards to my body-centre. This is not mere escapism: self-absorption is as distinguishable from indulgence as self-centredness is from selfishness. Having a centre to 'hold on to' allows me to move between moods which are normally judged as opposites, e.g. happiness and sadness, the one to be hoped for and the other avoided. In view of the fact that feeling is the source of action, it cannot be so undervalued, especially for those who find it unmanageable. Rather, the body should exercise its means to accommodate all feelings with the ability for transcending those that prove unpleasant.

Immobility of body, mind, feelings or spirit can constitute handicap; but seeing that these aspects of an individual may be interrelated, the immobility, for example of body and mind, may be remedied, or at least alleviated through the potential of mobility in feelings or spirit. Physical, emotional, intellectual or spiritual preferences of musical experience evolve from personal need; I would like everybody to experience what happens to me in music: the spaciousness of Monteverdi, the self-statement of Bach, the form of Mozart, the sense of time transcended by Schumann, the vibrant silences of Webern, the jolt out of complacency by Stravinsky; and to confront, as in many modern compositions, the relationship between music and life: music or noise, animate or inanimate sound. But being involved in response to satisfying personal neuroses, musical taste must, in the educational interests of allowing others to function as individuals, be questioned in favour of underlying principles, directly related to the fundamental concern of individuality. This concern is to function within the pace, spaces and forms of society, which may be directly allied to the elements of music: rhythm, tune and texture. An infant exploring forms in space and time builds imaginative resources: an elderly individual is a treasury of images, needing only forms, time and space to be realised.

PRACTICAL ACTIVITIES

Throughout this chapter I make reference to several key ideas regarding both forms and structures. I make great use of the circle within my sessions. Circles allow for both containment and for the possibility of a group member to become an individual within the group, by moving into the circle to perform. It also provides the possibility for each participant to become a leader and possibly to be imitated by the group.

I also use semicircle formations; this opening of the circle 'longways' is a crucial learning experience: it is important as a midway point, comparable to the body opening from self-contained 'sphere' to other-aware erect, by way of 'demi', half-open and enclosed: animal alert, martial artist.

The area of play, i.e. the space within which to behave beyond the norm, may be defined by instruments, chairs, etc. Low benches proved useful as a 'cat-walk' into a 'circus' from the changing rooms, then angled to define a more manageable space within a large room.

Rudimentary musical experience can be described as the difference between *duplet* pulses, i.e. two even beats, e.g. X X, and *triplet* pulses, i.e. two uneven pulses, e.g. long–short, *X* X, or short–long, X *X*; or three beats, e.g. X X X. I make extensive reference to these two forms for transforming modes of communication in speech: *duplet*, giving information, generally controlled pulse stresses, as opposed to *triplet*, expressing feeling, expansive pulse stresses: a pulse = two or three beats, a stress = two or three syllables; as a 'physical' example of each form; running = duplet, skipping = triplet.[1] How this all works in practice is best demonstrated in the format of a typical session of mime: (I) greeting, (II) body-exercise, (III) sound-play and (IV) reflection.

(I) Greeting

The group, including myself, is seated in a circle on the floor, if possible. Some people may need assistance from a helper who can act as a physical and vocal extension and/or interpreter.

(1) Hello

A simple song to greet each member: 'Hello Sue, Hello Hamish', etc. 'Hello', sung, allows the 'lo' to be suspended as long as is necessary to gain the nominee's attention, which is then confirmed by naming: 'Helloooooooooo – Jim!' The suspension of the sound may be enlivened by repeating the 'hello' as a sustained and articulated phrase.

When it is possible for the list of names to be sung without suspending the 'lo', i.e. on one breath, an overall intention is set up; but it is more musical and structurally beneficial to phrase the names in groups of three or four similar to actions within actions, as in a story. The group, by pointing to each person in turn being named, might gain in concentration and focus, particularly in the case of those people unable to create sound.

(2) Absent

Having celebrated those who are present, it is sensitive to remember those absent.

Pe-ter, Pe-ter where are you, where are you, where are you to - day?

Pe-ter, Pe-ter we miss you, we miss you, we miss you to - day.

The absence of individuals from the group can be used as an occasion to acknowledge sadness and thus to extend concerns beyond immediate confines, raising the status of those present.

(3) Framing

The group members, in turn, name themselves; so that each name may stand out individually. However, the name needs to be framed, either by the vulnerability of a pause (providing an opportunity to manage silence) or by the group repeating the syllables of the name, and clapping them (keeping them lifted in silence and providing an immediate memory exercise) e.g.:

Joe X Helena X X X Herman X X Dot X etc.

resulting in an exciting rhythm.

(4) Gestures

Each individual sings his or her name accompanied by hand or facial gestures, which are imitated by the group either after or simultaneously with the singer e.g. Laughing *at* oneself, *with* the group is socially healthy. Simultaneity, e.g. mirror-image exercise, helps envisaging oneself removed; imitation from the side when touch or confrontation is impossible.

(5) *Good morning signed*

A more elaborate song accompanied by signing:

Good morn - ing, Good morn - ing and how are you, and

how are you, Good morn - ing, Good morn - ing and how are you to - day.

after which a contrasting coda is shouted, clapped and stamped:

Ve-ry well, thank you   O.   K.

the rhythm of a football (soccer) chant. Parrot-fashion learning is justified here because a football chant is social currency; it gives a sense of belonging (Chorus: David Ward). Gesture or signing, paradoxically by taking pressure off the eyes and releasing tension from upper body, allows fuller eye contact.

(6) *'Oh What a Beautiful Morning'*

This and similar popular songs may be sung to get body and voice moving together, swaying from side to side:

> 'Oh what a beautiful morning; Oh what a beautiful day;
> LEFT   RIGHT LEFT;   RIGHT   LEFT   RIGHT;
>
> I have a beautiful feeling; everything's going my way.'
> LEFT   RIGHT LEFT; RIGHT   LEFT   RIGHT.

Use familiarity with communal songs to balance rawer, cruder sounds of creativity. Though still the containing stage of the session, expressive elements may be introduced through slight modification of regular rhythm, suspended double beat to allow extended reaching, i.e. opposition of left and right sides.

L R L   R L R

Reaching arms and extending vowel approximation yawning: maximum longways stretch, anus to soft palate; and sideways, hand to hand, the most lifted sensation in the body which, sustained, is the basis of singing.

With some disturbed groups, repetition of familiar songs might be the extent of the session, i.e. confirming manageable space and working within it. However, a creative dimension (listening, play and formalising) is possible in exercising qualities of: loud–soft, far–near; song-dances exploring small–large circles; fast–slow, e.g. song sung at double and triple speeds; using major–minor keys to transform moods.

(7) Events

Songs need sometimes to be improvised to cover exigencies, e.g. a birthday, a cold, a hurt finger, new glasses, an intrusion, a visitor, etc. Use a simple song structure e.g. 'Who has, Who has, Who has come into the room.'

(8) Rocking: forwards and backwards

This song accompanies forwards–backwards rocking, first in duplet pulse

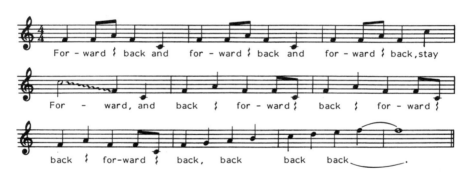

and then in triplet pulse (obsessional rocking, reflex motion, being accepted then extended):

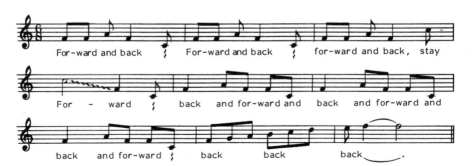

pausing long enough to allow the body to curl into itself enclosed in self-communication, humming an extra layer of 'smell'; allowing the body to fall backwards and straighten out, retaining self-assurance of curled-up sphere. If some people with disabilities are unable to rock on their own, work in pairs (with one person cradling the other) to feed in the duplet and the triplet pulses.

(9) Rocking: sideways

Sideways rocking movement allows 'limitless' reaching. Long lines of pairs can become ships: shipwrecks, underwater movement and sounds. The moment of overbalance in reaching is related to a suspended beat; of duplet becoming triplet.

(10) Pull the boat: push the boat

Modification of a favourite action song:

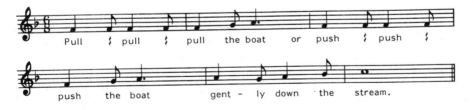

Exercising seesaw for two-way action of communication; distinguish 'push and be pushed' or 'pull and be pulled' from 'push and pull': reach–recoil reflex action of individuals who compulsively put objects in mouth extended to considered action.

(II) Body-exercise

Individuals of limited or no vocal means need to experience song in their silent bodies (as a self-recognising container and expresser of feelings, i.e. self-communication prior to other communication); the musical lift comes through the feet, if standing, or the bottom, if seated.

(1) Silent song

Sing and dance a song, then dance the song:

(a) without singing it outwardly,
(b) without using the arms, then
(c) without using the body or feet. Hear the song in silence.

(2) Humming

The group practises humming: 'Mmmmm', while curling themselves up; then, while stretching themselves out, they articulate the sound: 'Me-me-me', extending the vowel and possibly rising to the octave above. This is similar to singers tuning up; 'M' inward lip-movement; teeth kept apart for free jaw.

(3) Toe song

This song accompanies massaging appropriate parts of the body. It can provide the important sensation of simple syncopation between pulses on 'big' (or 'little', 'pink', 'brown', etc.), challenging rigidity of pulses; principle applies to time between striking instrument; motivation; compare vowel between consonants.

The last verse may be 'Oh there were ten fingers, etc.', in which case the word 'reached' may reach up the eight steps of the scale, with the hands trying to touch the sky and the body coming erect; then the cadence, instead of falling, remains open in a flourish of sound, after which the silent body tries to maintain the sense of flourish.

Contrast this with walking on pointed toes, 'lordly', and smooth heels, 'peasant', exercises high and low body-centres producing different qualities of sound, catering for individuals of different dispositions.

Also try this exercise in syncopated clapping:

duplet – step ^{clap} step ^{clap} step ^{clap} step ^{clap};

triplet – step ^{clap clap} step ^{clap clap} step ^{clap clap} step ^{clap clap}

(4) Body blues

The sad quality of this song is effective at a containing, turning-inwards stage of a session; song sequence: *upwards*, heels – knees – back – fingers, and *downwards*, sides – bottom, makes a satisfying arc.

(5) Tarzan song

A sequence of vocal sounds, duplicating those experienced slapping the body cavities:

Foot///:Calf///:Knee///:Thigh///:Belly///:Chest///:Neck///:Mouth (Yodel)

An alternative arrival at the top of the body is to roll the head around, humming in gentle triplet. This should ideally be experienced in the fast group-regulated version only after individual exploration of cavities' resonances.

(6) Rockets

Humming drones, as if 'engines' starting up, accompany hands massaging the thighs downwards to the knee, where they lift off; sounds duplicate their 'flight' to its apex, then sparkle, as 'fireworks', in a sustained cadenza, the hands, at length, returning to the knee-base and the voice to its drone. This can create a warming at body-centre; sense of centre reaffirmed from tension drawn downwards before lifting.

(7) Breath

Whether vocal or silent, individuals may exercise the three basic types of breathing: (a) breathe in and hold the breath till bursting; (b) breathe in and out regularly to counts, e.g. one in, one out, two in, two out, etc.; (c) breathe out for as long as possible.

(a) Held breath blocking tension in the muscle here exercised in fun normally to be avoided; uncontrolled release of energy in aggressive reflex action may be transformed into considered expression, e.g. expletives – sentences, grunts – songs, kicks – dance steps, hitting – gestures;
(b) Both shallow and deep breathing need exercise; avoid percussive in–out motion, raising tension: instead exercising rolling abdominal movement, i.e. inwards and upwards for exhalation and outwards and downwards for inhalation;
(c) Extending breath to spread thoughts and feelings out; self – prior to other – recognition.

(8) Sentence

Build a song based on repeated parts of a sentence, e.g.:

(a) 'Today' . . .
(b) 'Today I am' . . .
(c) 'Today I am feeling' . . .
(d) 'Today I am feeling very tired' . . .
(e) 'Today I am feeling very tired because I got up late.'

The principle of sentence is a thing (noun) activated (verb); also sentence structure is based on Who, What happened, When, Where, How and Why; and uses poly-rhythm of speech-stresses, i.e. mixture of two and three; the essential rhythmic expression in undemonstrative cultures.

Each phrase may be repeated until assimilated by the group, the breath between exaggerated with the lengthening phrases. Full breath release avoids frustration build-up.

Interlude

During the first part of the session the group should have experienced sounds ranging from very loud to very soft, indicating the parameters within which they may be expressive in the second part. The overall intention so far has been to treat the body as an instrument: as a group member, 'tuning it up' first to contain feelings, through close body contact, then for expression: individuals start to develop a secure physical base for creating sounds which allows them to venture beyond their bodily confines. An expression echoed by at least one other voice is the basis of communication; therefore, like an instrument, the body-voice has to be sympathetically 'toned' to respond effectively and appropriately.

Individuals concerned only to express themselves may be as wayward as suits their purpose; but when intent upon communicating, be it with an audience of one or many, they have to accept the necessity for agreed structures, e.g. the conductor's beat, being in tune, being in step and, in social dance, the agreed feet patterns (over which real communication is played through eye and upper body contact, etc.). This is how music is normally experienced and taught: the teacher presenting models based on accepted musical products within which individuals may choose to conform or rebel.

In contrast to this structured practice, music may be taught organically, beginning with the crude materials of sounds which, through a process of exploration, become realised in individual forms. The dilemma of whether the finished production of a piece of music is more beneficial than the process undergone producing it, a topic which occupies so much pedagogic discussion, is in practice dispelled: process is product in a state of transformation, whereas product is process suspended. Whether structured or organic, the means for helping individuals to create are only as effective as the leader employing them: ultimately I may communicate only the habit of conviction and motivation, i.e. what keeps me in one piece and what moves me to action: stillness and action. It is salutary to remember that infants reveal in their rudimentary language an intuitive sense of symmetry: 'da-da', 'ma-ma', etc. (The sequence of sound rebound couplet, i.e. 'uh-uh', 'ga-ga', 'da-da', 'ma-ma' and 'ba-ba' trace infant development from amorphous to self-identification.) Musical form is simply the dynamic of knowing that a sound will be repeated, and being surprised when it is.

The relationship between process and product is crucial when working with people with a disability who cannot manage the sharing of social 'products', i.e. cannot communicate and who, to ensure that their frustration may be alleviated, need to be provided with alternatives, forms of expression evolved from individual rudimentary sounds. It is essential for people with a disability to experience something of the repertoire of music and songs to increase their sense of belonging in their society. These received forms, articulated intervals, structured rhythms, etc., which are the elements of 'proper' music, some people may find difficult to accommodate, but through play they may in time assimilate them into their vocabulary. It must be remembered that the musical sounds normally heard are articulated, i.e. played on keyed or fretted instruments, or are formal speech syllables: the gaps between, being sufficient to cause disquiet or excess tension, are likely to be abhorred by individuals lacking the technique for managing discomfort. Therefore it is essential to fortify the ability to accommodate stimuli by having the experience of more readily acceptable sounds, e.g, unbroken, melismatic intervals, which abound in folksongs, jazz and Eastern music: a swanee (slide) whistle should be part of every leader's equipment. Even more fundamental is the experience gained from playing with free sound, i.e. unstructured rhythms, microtonal intervals and noise: humming, grunts, expletives, banging, etc. It is not uncommon to find individuals, not only those people with a disability, for whom the sensation of noise beating *at* their bodies, (therefore requiring no response) is more to their liking than the spaces of rhythm and interval, which demand exposure of feelings. Transforming noise into music is finding the lifting quality of sound. Sound being an extension of the body must also be three-dimensional (depth, vertical, lateral) and must reproduce the elements of the most immediate form of contact which it displaces: smell–touch.

1 *Depth*. Animal sounds evolved to establish territory, clothing the body in vibration like an extra *texture* of skin: purring, humming, hardly more than a more intense layer of reassuring smell; by this means the body may choose either to isolate or express itself.
2 *Vertical*. Changes in vibration produce notes of different intervals i.e. *tune*: the change from one vibration to another, producing a feeling of suspension in the spaces between the intervals. Lack of interval, however microtonal, is noise.
3 *Lateral*. Sound may travel where the body, for either physical or social reasons, may not: suspending itself in time, either sustained or kept lifted on articulating pulses, i.e. *rhythm*; which has the potential to behave with the dual characteristics of touch:
    (a) as if handling, giving information, the one-way traffic of expression, favouring the control of duplet-pulses; and
    (b) as if caressing, the two-way action of communication, sharing feelings, warmth oscillating in the space between bodies, favouring the expansive propensity of triplet-pulses. The spaces between the pulses allow the body to be controlled or to soar; over-insistence on the pulse of rigidity of beat is tantamount to noise. (A lawnmower, moved by muscular effort, makes sound-phrases nearer to music than the mechanical rigidity of repeated beats from one driven by a motor.) Rhythmic patterns seem to be the property of the primitive and young, whereas sustained melody seems to satisfy more mature natures.

The following sections isolate the elements of music, in an order which is perhaps more accessible to people with a disability: rhythm, tune, texture. They attempt to provide: first, scope for both structured and organic processes of creativity, which is to say, forms as the bases rather than the ideals of exploration; secondly, rudiments for developing from accommodation to assimilation and finally, group and individual involvement. Throughout, the essentials of creativity should be kept to the fore:

(a) listening going into oneself: is it sound or silence?
(b) play – sorting things out: is it noise (inanimate sound) or music? and
(c) formalising – moving into expression or action: is it relevant, animated?

Where I have thought it helpful, I have related the elements of music to other media; and because I firmly support the notion that instrumental sounds should be related to the body-voice, I shall continue to limit examples to the voice, hoping that their application to music generally is obvious.

(III) Sound-play

(A) Rhythm

This section explores the lateral aspect of music; breath or sound phrases conveyed over a period of time, either sustained (1 to 4) or articulated by pulses (5 to 11), allowing choice of being secure on the pulses or expansive between them. A breath phrase (a potential step, gesture or sound phrase) may be sustained or broken up, i.e. articulated with a build-up of excitement towards the phrase climax in proportion to the relationship of pulses. However, mechanically regular pulses or beats spell musical death, even within rhythmic patterns of social dance; a triplet should not be based on three even beats, but rather on the principles of the suspended duplet.

(1) Tennis

Pairs face each other throwing sounds across to each other, tracing the 'flight of the ball' with their hands and voices: transforming antagonism to co-operation; an essential 'developmental stage' for most groups.

(2) Ball of string

In a circle, individuals pass round a ball of string, humming and changing pitch as the string changes hands. When the string is substituted by sound being 'handed' around, the changing notes may be sung by the group, or individuals may hold on to their notes, budding a block of sound. The changing notes may simply 'climb' the scale: 1 to 8 for the diatonic, and 1 to 5 for the pentatonic.

(3) Star points

A piece of string is passed across the circle preferably of an odd number above five, to any but a neighbour. When the string is returned to its beginning the points of a star will have been created. If the group is numbered consecutively, the passage of the string, picked out on the numbered keys of, say, a xylophone, will make a 'star-tune' to which words may be added for example, to describe direction: 'To George . . . to Val', etc.

The string is best passed through the spokes of chairs, allowing the star' to be placed near the floor providing 'hopscotch' spaces, each space a different note; then, if moved up and down the spokes, the flat, two-dimensional figure becomes three-dimensional, among the shapes of which individuals may crawl, tracing the lines of string in sustained and changing notes. This is a two- to three-dimensional exercise in body image, essential for individuals who feel they are always on display.

(4) Star radials

One end of a large ball of string is secured to the floor in the centre of the circle. Each group member in turn is responsible for creating a radial, pointing in the direction he or she wishes their radial to go, and sustaining a note or gesture for the length he or she wishes the radial to be as the leader moves the string from centre until the sound terminates, i.e. the radial reaches its 'point'. The string is secured to the floor and returned to the centre for the next group member to create a radial.

(5) Support music (see also section B5)

The group sits in a semicircle, and its members make sounds to accompany individuals in turn travelling to a spot that may be defined by a large card on the floor; different textures of sound may be explored to parallel the walking, which build in intensity as the traveller nears his or her goal. When he or she steps on to the card, the accompanying group sustains a sound for as long as he or she chooses to remain on it: then they accompany his or her return journey. Distinction needs to be made between sounds that: (a) duplicate each step, and (b) (more profitably for extending halting walk) lift the gap between steps (syncopation), i.e. downwards action of step lifts body.

(6) Tile-dance chorus

Individuals choose a sequence of coloured floor tiles as a step pattern to be repeated as a dance chorus, e.g. 'Blue tile, blue tile, red tile, yellow; who is now a clever fellow?' Between the choruses individuals may improvise free steps and sounds.

(7) Stepping-stones

The 'banks of a river' are defined on the floor, and individuals, in actuality and in sound, try to cross in one go; the river is widened until stepping-stones – large pieces of card – are required to facilitate crossing. Travellers, accompanied by group chorus, may either:

(a) linger on each stone, to admire or reflect on the 'landscape' of sounds, the quality of which is different on each 'stone'; or
(b) move across with urgency, which will result in regular steps and the syncopated lift taking precedence over the step (creating a 'communication dilemma': to advance or reflect).

On reaching the other 'bank', the traveller, accompanied by the group, releases the tension built up in the crossing, in a cadenza of triumphant sound, particularly after the second mode of crossing.

(8) Football chant

Four cards are equally spaced in line on the floor; the leader maintains a regular pulse, singing and/or clicking fingers:

(a) the group, in single file, travel along the cards singing in time with the pulse, each beginning when the one before has completed the line, resulting in a continuous line of sound;
(b) another set of four cards is added:

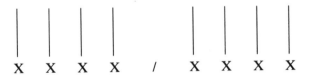

(c) card 3 of each set is halved:

(d) card 1 of set 2 is halved:

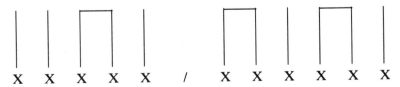

(e) the cards of set 2 are rearranged:

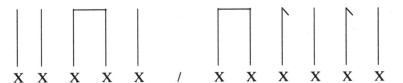

$$\text{X   X   X   X   X   /   X   X   X   X   X   X}$$

resulting in the rhythm of another popular British football (soccer) chant. Individuals may arrange a sequence of beats and half-beats for the others to attempt, either travelling, as described above, or clapping.

(9) Court dances

Step to a piece of music in 4/4 time, alternating left and right feet or sides of the body on the first beats of successive bars, which will result in the rhythms that formed the basis of court and social dances. Marching, pounding left foot presumably deadening right brain hemisphere, cf. Schumann March in 3/4.

(10) Sounds structured and free and silent

The group moves, claps and/or sings a repeated pattern of four beats. Experience of rhythms is better, through sideways movement, i.e. opposition than clapping:

(a) structured – on the beat for the four beats,
(b) free – over a period of four beats, and
(c) silent – for the duration of four beats. Repeat.

The free section will be anarchic; the leader will have to indicate the beginning and end of the silent section. Experiencing the 'electricity' in the silence after the free section reveals an individual's sense of control. Managing the contrast of feelings is dependent, ideally, on an ability to maintain a sense of centre, or for fast readjustment afterwards.

Groups of more able individuals have, individually, chosen difficult repeated patterns, e.g. five on the beat, three free and eleven silent, which when performed together resulted in a fascinating chorus choreography.

(11) Subdivision

A regular pulse is set up in foot-tapping, above which the voice and hands subdivide, exercising duplet, i.e. half-, quarter- or eighth-beats, and triplet, i.e. third- or sixth-beats, as much as possible playing off the main beats: syncopation.

That the presentation of this section might suggest a progression from individual to group rhythms is not to be interpreted as group member superseding individual; the progression could as easily be reversed from structured to free rhythm.

(B) Tune

This section exercises the vertical aspect of music: the pitch of interval, just as the important rhythmic sensation is time suspended between the pulses, so is the experience of space within the interval, i.e. the change of vibration from one note to the next, intrinsic to music.

(1) Plainsong

The group sustain a drone, above which individuals 'take flight' in sounds, words and hand gestures, contrasting free play of long and short notes with structured regular rhythms and coming to rest on the drone. To assist individuals who have limited sounds, the leader may have to pick up the pitch of the note and gesture and bring them to earth. The principle behind unaccompanied song or plainsong is that the drone is understood.

(2) Chords

The group sustains a note and feels the changes in the body as chords are changed below it, preferably sustained on the organ or accordion, first slowly then quickened. Chord changes may be gradual, e.g.

(a) I–III or VI, i.e. two notes in common;
(b) I–IV or V, i.e. one note in common; then
(c) I–II or VII, i.e. no notes in common.

Songs may be selected with these principles in mind, e.g. (a) Beatles songs, (b) almost any song, and (c) 'Drunken Sailor'. Predominance of I–IV–V chords, progression one note in common, is related to minimum of sustaining 'touch'; people with a disability might prefer the security of two notes in common.

(3) Major and minor

The group sings a song, in major and minor, and the leader inserts suitable verses in the opposite mode; accommodating change of mood.

(4) Blocks of sound

The leader conducts the group, who sustain notes, changing them as he or she indicates; or the leader may play them on the organ or accordion by superimposing as a listening exercise.[2]

(5) Support music (see also section A5)

After standing on a card, accompanied by a chorus, an individual may have the choice of two, three or four cards (of different colours) to step on to, to each of which the group sings a different (generalised) pitch, e.g. high or low, very high or very low, according to his signing. Or a group of five people sit at the piano: very low, low, middle, high, very high, and the leader-conductor, facing them, 'conducts' them.

(6) Soccer chant (see also section A8)

The original four cards may be 'pitched':

resulting in the final chant rhythm as:

An example of perfect intervals, essential components to vocabulary.

(7) Grunting

Exercise grunting at different pitches. Each group member grunts a note and indicates its pitch in the air, which is repeated by the group. Grunts may be repeated singly at first; then grouped in twos, threes or fours; finally as a whole sequence, phrased in twos, threes or fours. Related to building group sentences, one word each, or group stories, one action each.

(8) Articulated intervals

Certain musical intervals, e.g. octave, 5th and -3rd, are common in normal communication, and may be effectively exercised in isolation; limiting the pitch may be compensated by inventive use of rhythm and texture.

(9) Octave

Play with the sound of the octave, ascending and descending, by leap and step.

(10) Organum

Sing songs, some verses of which the leader sings or accompanies the 5th below.

(11) Thumb fifths

Using hand signs, thumb up = 5 and thumb down = 1, the leader improvises rhythmic patterns, e.g.

$$1\ ^5\ ^5\ 1\ ^5\ 1\ ^5\ 1\ 1\ ^5\ \ 1, \text{etc.}$$

for the group to imitate simultaneously, which creates great fun. Decrease in waiting for group to catch up, indication of reflex and involvement; hand-signs based on tetrachord: upper of scale 5th above lower half.

(12) Minor third

Play calling games utilising the natural calling sound of the falling -3rd.

(13) Within the interval

The group sings a song, but dwells on each word or note for as long as it takes them to be fully involved in it; then gradually the speed is quickened to normal but still intent upon keeping wholly involved. Take note that some people may be too slow or too deep to 'keep up'.

(14) Keening

Improvise a 'lament' by sustaining a note and ornamenting above and below it, sliding from note to note, with hand gestures to help. Perfect intervals ornamented, e.g. 8 by +7, 5 by −6, 4 by + 3 and 1 by −2, produce wild, sensual, 'archaic' mode, opposite to ascetic, 'dorian' mode: 8 −7 +6 5 4 −3 +2 1, favoured in West; range between 'archaic' and 'dorian' has greater subtlety than polarisation of major and minor.

(15) Ornamented folksongs

Sing a folksong and ornament it lavishly with melisma (a group of notes sung to one syllable), being aware whether the ornaments are melodic, or harmonic.

(C) Textures

Texture is the 'depth' element of sound against a background of silence. However terms such as 'high', 'low', etc. may not be helpful: a blind pianist describing how he learnt part-playing used terms like 'forward', 'back'.

(1) Tactile objects

Play with the textures and shapes of visual objects, lingering over a quality as long as is desired, looking at from different angles and height and trying to translate them into sounds.

(2) Percussive and sustained songs

Individuals stand near to slung cymbals to feel the effect of sound on their bodies, and respond to the different effects of banged and rolled sound (a percussive jolt accommodated by gradually increasing tremolo).

(3) Piano quintet

A group – of five at the most – sits in front of a piano, which has its front removed and the sustaining pedal depressed or is totally stripped down to the strings, to allow the different qualities of plucked or strummed string sounds to affect their bodies.

(4) Opposites

Explore materials of opposite qualities of texture, e.g. sharp–blunt, hard–soft, cold–warm, heavy–light, oily–gritty, rough–smooth, angular–curved, etc., and try to reproduce these qualities in movement and sounds: sustained–articulated, smooth–percussive, direct–indirect, etc., exercising slow–fast changes between qualities.

The opposite qualities of sound–silence may have been related to the negative–positive cutouts and remnants for a 'lilypond' (extension of B5, Support Music). Although given limited space here, the experience of listening is in some situations more relevant than activity.

(5) The elements

The floor may be divided into four areas: 'water', 'air', 'earth' and 'sky', which dictate the qualities of sound that individuals may make as they pass through them.

(6) Stereophonic sound

Groups of different sizes are placed around a room and make sounds producing stereophonic effects, concentrating particularly on feeling the silence between, and choosing between 'nice' and 'nasty' sounds with which to reply, i.e. individual experience of consonance and dissonance.

(7) Calling

Pairs and groups play with sounds of calling from far–near, related to the size of appropriate gestures, big–small. Confusing loud–near, soft–big, etc. causes great fun. Alternatively, the use of signing, supplementing speech, alleviates tension.

(8) Mirrors

Pairs face each other and move towards and away, attempting to make simultaneous sounds and gestures.

(9) Sound images

Make up sound images based on textures and qualities (rather than shapes) of, for example, wind, walking, tree, etc., or of characters, for example compounds of heavy, symmetrical, short, indirect, percussive, etc., which are repeated as refrains during the recitation of a story by the leader. Try allowing words to be sustained in near-singing to hold attention.

(10) Vowels

Explore rudimentary animal sounds, for example 'AH' – contented, 'EE' – screaming, and '00' – pouting; then modify them as human sounds, e.g. 'EH' – half-scream, and 'OH' – half-pout: constituting the structure of the five basic or cardinal vowels. Include continental 'U' = 'OO' + 'EE', and 'Ø' + 'EH' to exercise facial muscles.

(11) 'Big-bang'

The whole group, each with one sound, possibly played on piano or instrument, together make a loud noise and repeat their notes, individually increasing the length of silence between; this will need to be conducted by the leader from a prepared 'score', possibly on graph paper. This is an exercise in managing silences, sustaining climax: of chance composition.

(12) Name chorus

In a circle, the group sing their names (see section I.3, Framing), with choices of:

(a) high or low pitch, keeping to a regular pulse;
(b) long or short duration, each individual coming in immediately the one before has finished; and
(c) immediate or delayed entry, as soon as the individual before has opened his mouth to utter, resulting in a chorus of banked sounds and silences.

(IV) Reflection

The climax of the session will have been the creation of a piece of music; each individual and the group will have to some degree presented a bit of themselves and will probably be feeling excited and exposed. This is similar to the post-climax in Greek drama for teaching morality. However, just as children may tear up drawings after creating them, so they need time to come to terms after revealing themselves in sound. They will need to be taken back to normality. Try to include time before and after sessions, to take group from and return to norm; providing an opportunity for them to take something from the session, it is to be hoped, to help enrich their lives.

To help some groups of children with physical disabilities be more aware of floor exercise influencing their normal lives I kept them in their chairs, extending their activities until they felt they needed to move to the floor: being returned, they could recapture what they had done, particularly if there was the visual record of a 'map' of their wanderings (marked in individual colours) translated into songs and stories. With other groups, exercises were repeated in different positions, e.g. on the floor, half-erect and fully erect, or sitting, standing and moving, to reinforce their value.

(1) Memory

The leader recalls the events of the session, probably as a link for the following week, as a story (exercising sense of structure; story taking listeners out of themselves following a narrative and reflecting on the events) in recitative, encouraging moments of group participation, e.g. recalling in sounds the ways they had moved, songs from stories or to cover events, the weather, etc.

(2) Grounding

Sing songs of individual choice, gradually reducing the level of activity and sound to humming and silence.

POSTSCRIPT

I teach music both for itself and as a means towards social competence: the arts fill the space vacated by smell–touch. This direction came about as a result of being concerned for singers who could be competent projecting from the formality of a platform, yet in the 'give and take' of informal contact became tongue-tied. I found it difficult to go along with any form of training that allowed music to become a mask behind which individuals could retreat, sometimes never to re-emerge. I became concerned instead that individuals should explore their feelings through music, but only to the extent that they had techniques to express them, in the attempt to balance inner and outer life. Inhibition may be defined as lacking technique to express feelings; maladjustment, on the other hand, is lacking the physical means to contain and identify them.

My personal experience of feelings is like inner movement, self-understanding, continuously fluid. Words, on the other hand, seem like articulated sounds trying to make objective sense, first to myself, then for sharing. When the gap between 'fluidity' and articulation becomes too wide, a link is needed to transform containment into expression: a period of refreshment between self-assessment and managing social contact. Music, with its sounds faithfully reproducing both sustained and articulated movement, and its language, which uses the elements of words, i.e. feeling-vowel and articulating-consonant, is, rationally speaking, 'non-sense'. But, on the principle that animals sing, whereas humans may speak – speech being heightened singing – music provides an interim state allowing feelings to be revealed that may not be defined in words.

That it is possible to express without communicating is all too familiar in moments of maladjustment. Often the problem is being unable to accept the echo or comeback to one's own expression, whether from an audience of many or of one, or from oneself, in sound or silence. The sensation of hearing oneself is reflection after the build-up of feelings released in sound, e.g. banging an instrument, etc. When the habit of self-response is not inherent, individuals familiar only with the sensation of 'giving', possibly as a result of early experience of touch emphasising handling at the expense of caressing, may find it difficult to cope with the vulnerability of remaining exposed and receptive to possible comeback, after having expressed their feeling. To avoid this they might concentrate their energy before the expression in a sudden build-up of feelings, which, suddenly released in the violence of hitting, kicking or obscenity. removes the sense of responsibility after the act, not unlike the relief after banging one's head against a wall, or after inflicting pain to express affection. Music, because of its potential for free and structured sound, allows exercise of feelings being exposed gradually, at the same time involving oneself and others.

In a north London school in which racially opposed groups had no time or space for each other, I found that by placing the rival Greek and

Turkish, or black and white, groups side by side, they avoided confrontation, and could acknowledge at least the presence of the others; and having been encouraged to sing or listen to chosen songs, interleaving the lines of one group with those of the other, they had to experience silences alternating with sounds. The silences were initially antagonistic but, gradually affected by the music, could acquire a semblance of coexistence. The change in the children's normal spaces and sense of time produced a musical form more relevant to their needs.

Play with spaces, time and forms proved effective in other seemingly remedial situations, e.g. actors having to sing, musicians to speak, visual artists to move and dancers to make sounds. Over the years this has extended to communication therapy with second language casualties, mentally ill patients and prisoners, arriving at my present concerns, which involve exploring expressive alternatives with people with a disability. My work model is a matrix, one axis of which is a continuum from handicap to non-handicap, and the other from individual to group; the individual who cannot move within this matrix, in any sense, seems to me to be handicapped. Essentially my work involves expression – gradual rather than sudden, considered rather than reflex, but I have had to become more concerned for finding inner resources through music: increasing an individual's capacity for feeling to the extent that they are motivated to find, rather than be taught, their most effective means of expression. My role as reassurer, then catalyst, changes to reflector to help individuals evaluate their experiences.

Music is my discipline; but my subject, for the moment, is communication. Communication, in my experience, is fraught at the best of times, but being normal means being able to brave the hazards of making and sustaining contact, even contemplating failure, because of having expressive alternatives to alleviate any possible frustration. Making sense of words may prove difficult, but their sounds and supportive gestures provide me with alternative means for sustaining contact. These sounds and gestures, developed as music and dance, provide those people handicapped in speech with alternatives of expression. Alternatives of expression are integral to body structure: the body is a torsal chamber at the gut-centre of which stimulus is accommodated and feelings are generated, and through the outlets from which, i.e. the arms, neck, genitals and legs, feelings may be expressed in similar actions. References such as 'being centred' have physical foundation. A sense of centre in the gut places the arms, legs, genitals and throat in balanced and supplementary relationship to each other, conducive to spontaneity, like animals, which we basically are. Familiarity with this sense of centre is to be encouraged in those who may be described as functioning from higher and lower centres (e.g. very heavy in body with little feeling of lift, or so 'heady' as to be out of touch with reality), and as being limited in their expressive potential. Individuals who rely on the eyes for contact and expression, e.g. the partially hearing, individuals in wheelchairs, etc., are inclined to strain the upper body and stiffen the lower; excess tension at the throat produces harsh and unattractive sound, and stiff knees make for general discomfort. The enveloping vibration of music provides a sense of overall reassurance, and the pulse of music, probably more effectively than any other sensory means, gets immediate gut-reaction and sustains involvement in that crucial region.

Music leaves no record, which makes it unsatisfactory as the means for exercising self-involvement for those who need the security of handling or seeing what they are doing; but is ideal for those for whom having to manage only one sense at a time is enough. Music related to body movement and play with objects has proved effective for both these groups, particularly as an interim stage between self-involvement and human contact. Relationships presume 'give and take' and may need to be made familiar in stages, beginning with only 'giving' or 'taking' with inanimate objects to finding a balance. An individual playing with the shapes and textures of inanimate objects, e.g. toys, may dictate the length, position and modes of involvement. This one-way activity may be allied to experiencing noise, and to body movement, e.g. curling up as a self-contained sphere listening only to itself, as the basis of self-involvement. An extension of this is playing with animate 'objects', e.g. pets. This activity still accentuates the 'give' but the individual may 'take' the animal's response as they are able to. Such a reciprocal experience may be paralleled with 'animating' noise, e.g. banging or shouting through exploring its potential for rhythm interval and texture; moving the body between enclosed and erect forms, exercising the senses singly and in combination, fluctuating between solo and group involvement.

Throughout, rather than emphasising the specifics of musical language or appreciation of musical form, I have concentrated on integrating a sense of form into the body by experience to find a 'grammar' common to the arts, as an aid towards managing the morass of stimuli in life: a sentence is a thing (noun) enlivened (verb); a tune is a string of sounds animated by rhythm. Familiarity with this process of 'animation' may help to enliven the individual for whom the symbols of life have become stuck, including that of oneself as a cipher. Coming to terms with oneself as an individual functioning within society may be helped by the experience of singing or playing in a group:

1 the same thing at the same time: *tune, organum*;
2 the same thing at different times: *canon, counterpoint*;
3 different things at the same time: *harmony*; and
4 different things at different times: *?*

The form of a song or symphony is essentially a journey in which feelings are transformed. For many their source of transformation, awareness of possibilities, is restricted to television soap opera, which is limited both in the spaces of the imagination and length of involvement. Musical form, not limited by narrative, may take the imagination beyond its normal expectation and give the individual a greater satisfaction from having structured a period of time creatively. With my groups I try to induce a sense of extended form by means of the format of the sessions themselves, both (1) of the individual sessions, and (2) as stages within an extended programme.

1 That the session is experienced as a journey or story is crucial: all cultural groups use stories to reaffirm themselves. A story is a central event, an overall build-up, climax and release, sustained on a succession of subsidiary events, each smaller versions of the larger. So the 'journey' through the session progresses by stages of build-ups, climaxes and releases, through which the leader, like the storyteller acting beyond their normal body and voice, attempts to sustain a sense of overall caring.

It is worth making regular weekly visits to 'map' an inmate's time in an institution. These may be invigorated into a 'landscape' by exploring time, space and forms; rhythm, tune and textures. This is particularly important in those atmospheres of deodorant and Muzak, which as noise, effectively deprive the individual of his two main means of self-identity: body odour and sound.

2 The length of the programme must be agreed. Even if the group is unable to comprehend fully a time-span of eight or ten weeks, I still perform a ritual, from halfway through, of a weekly countdown, so that at the end they may not feel suddenly abandoned: the parting is prepared and mutual. Arts experience aiming to help accommodate pain should avoid inflicting it. The final session cannot be the climax of the programme, but a time to release myself gently from their environment.

A class of intelligent teenagers with a physical disability, conscious of their social prowess and the regard of their 'non-disabled' peers, found my sessions 'mad', and in order to be able to undertake the session, which presumably they wanted to, had to ritualise *every* meeting by protesting against what I asked of them. Responsibility for their 'madness' being removed on to me allowed them, within the secret of their classroom play space, to enjoy themselves and transcend their disability with impressive ingenuity and individuality.

The parameters of our relationship have also to be recognised. As leaders we aim to set up within the classroom an ambience of acceptance, and to provide a microcosm of society for individuals to test their personal and social expressive skills. But, in response to particular situations, we may need to limit our parameters to providing only as much time and space as those with whom we are working might be able to manage. In extreme situations, as helpers, we may need to become barely more than their physical parameters; actual body contact will allow us to become interpreters of their containment or expression. Within any learning situation, fluidity between the roles of helper, therapist and leader allows the artist which is in all of us to be revealed: to contest confinements, of body, society or sanity.

ACKNOWLEDGEMENTS

I am extremely indebted to the Carnegie UK Trust who generously funded the project based at Dartington College of Arts, Devon: 'The Arts in the Education of Handicapped Children and Young People', which made it possible for me to: study communication from the other side of normal; to work with Bruce Kent – who was so generous in sharing experiences relating visual art to movement and music, and David Ward – from whose music-making with children with a very wide range of disabilities I learnt much about the physicality of music and whose books are compulsory reading for anyone interested in this area of work; and to meet the many teachers, therapists, helpers and artists questioning the boundary between handicapped and non-handicapped people. Special reference must be made to Veronica Sherborne for the illuminating experience of her movement workshops from which many of the body exercises in this writing are adaptations for group and chorus work

NOTES

1 Alex, aged 19, who normally walked fast, noticing little, became excited by his self- and environment awareness, being held back by a strong wind; similarly changing duplet into triplet pulse to each step made him more open. Nigel, aged 29, though possessing an extensive repertoire of tunes which he hummed, only grunted isolated sounds. By encouraging the grunt rebound 'uh-uh' for a two-syllable word, e.g.

'Daw-lish'

then extending to three, e.g.

'E-xe-ter',

I could use the third sound of the triplet as the first sound of a new stress, e.g.

X   X   X

'O-ver   there'.

An initial sound, sign or mark may be comparatively easily prompted; the problem is encouraging the individual to react to it to make the second: keeping him alive during the gap.

2 'Modern' sound justified by modern composers. Neil, aged 16, having defined his territory on the piano with toys and spit, banged relentlessly on two adjacent white notes, i.e. −2nd nearest to noise on the piano requiring limited response; I tried to join in playing the same notes further down the piano, i.e. less vibration, and grouping in two and three, i.e. opening space, without success. Moving his hands one note, i.e, two white notes with black note between, i.e. +2nd, presumably because of increased interval space, caused him to pause; through gradual play he managed to assimilate this sound; I would have liked to develop this principal working down the intervals of the harmonic scale, i.e. −3rd, +3rd, 4th and 5th, but we lost contact.

SUGGESTED READING

Alvin, J. (1975) *Music Therapy*, Basic Books, New York.

Bailey, P. (1965) *They Can Make Music*, Oxford University Press, Oxford.

Feder, E. and Feder, B. (1981) *The Expressive Arts Therapies*, Feder Publications, Sarasota, FL.

Gaston, E. T. (ed.) (1968) *Music in Therapy*, Macmillan, London/New York.

Michel, D. E. (1976) *Music Therapy: An Introduction to Therapy and Special Education through Music*, Charles C. Thomas, Springfield, IL.

Nordoff, P. and Robbins, C. (1965) *Music Therapy for Handicapped Children*, Steiner Publications, New York.

Sherbourne, V. (1990) *Developmental Movement for Children*, Cambridge University Press, Cambridge.

Ward, D. (1973) *Music for Slow Learners*, Oxford University Press, Oxford.

Chapter 8

Drama

Using the imagination as a stepping-stone for personal growth

Bernie Warren

For many people drama is something that happens on a stage; a stage that separates the performers from the audience, and establishes as skilled 'craftsmen' the people presenting events to the people watching them. Yet this presentation of 'imagined acts'[1] on a stage is simply one facet of dramatic activity and although it is perhaps the most generally accepted view of what 'drama' is, it is not necessarily the most important. It is this misconception in many people's minds, that drama is only a presentation on a stage and thus the sole property of skilled and talented individuals, that has created blocks for individuals seeking to achieve their full creative potential, and in some cases even prevents their imaginations from coming into play at all. It is against this often self-imposed wall that professionals in the fields of developmental drama, personal creativity and drama therapy have been chipping away for more than two decades.

The origins of drama are to be found in storytelling[2] and in ritual.[3] In most cases, spontaneous actions precede ritual. In the creation of ritual these spontaneous actions, which are seen to have meaning for the well-being of the group, become transformed into a symbolic act. It now becomes essential for the original spontaneous actions to be carried out in a set order and with a particular style. This specific pattern is believed to be essential to the ritual 'working' and, as a result, spontaneity is lost.[4] This is a similar process to the one most people have, consciously or unconsciously, pursued with their own creativity. They have lost contact with their source of spontaneity and have fallen back on external frameworks that impose boundaries on the imagination and, more disastrously, often totally remove any emotional reaction and substitute it with conscious control.

Drama rarely, if ever, occurs in isolation. Individuals may occasionally indulge in isolated dramatic actions[5] but, for drama to occur, more than one person has to be present. Drama is an example of human interaction. It is concerned with human beings communicating with one another; verbally, physically and emotionally. Most importantly, this dramatic interaction is part of our everyday lives. Many role-theorists have pointed out that we are constantly shifting roles. Earlier in this book (Chapter 4), Rob Watling elaborates on the way in which context and function affects traditional material. In a similar way the roles we take are influenced by their context – that is where we are, who we are talking to, etc. – and their function. Thus the roles we take are often dictated by circumstances beyond our control.

Perhaps the most important external influences on our often unconscious role-playing are the people with whom we interact. In everyday interactions it is not just what we say, but how we say it that conveys not only our meaning but also our feelings, and preceding every action there is thought, sometimes subconscious, which in turn is inextricably linked to our imagination. Our every action, nuance of inflection and gesture are recorded, sometimes subliminally, by the people with whom we communicate. They then calibrate[6] their actions and the roles they take accordingly. I believe that the essence of drama is encapsulated in this process.

For me, drama is about the process whereby 'imaginative thought becomes action'[7] – in word or deed – and is particularly concerned with the way that this 'dramatic action' affects other people's actions. In essence, drama can be thought of as the communication of our imagination, through our action in a way that affects our inter-actions with others, whether this be on stage or in our daily lives.

Daily one of our biggest problems is communicating what we mean. Every one of us spends a large part of our day talking at but not necessarily communicating with others. I often draw the analogy of human beings as transceivers (transmitter/receivers). We all have our own 'radio station', which is created by, among other things, our previous experience, our vocabulary and our world map.[8] I feel that we all transmit on a 'wavelength' specific to us. Although we can transmit only on this single wavelength, we are able to vary the quality and the intensity of the signal by careful choice of language and by the role we are in, in a similar way to adjusting the tone, volume and balance on a stereo. However, we have the capacity to receive an incoming 'signal' on almost any wavelength. The problem is that all too often, in our struggles to communicate, we are not tuned in properly; we are not quite 'on station' – so we pick up only some of the incoming signal. Frequently we are not listening because we are too busy working on our next 'broadcast', on what we are going to say. As a result, we miss the point or lose the feeling of what the person talking to us is saying.

This process relates to all human communications. As I sit writing these words, displaced both in time and space from you reading them, I am struggling to find those words that will best convey my meaning to you. I am well aware that what I write, on the basis of my language system and world map, will have to be interpreted by you and that every reader will have a widely differing, unique background. So, as I write, I call on my imagination, trying to be aware of who will be reading these words, what their backgrounds are and what, if any, common ground they share. I am at the beginnings of the dramatic process. I am struggling to communicate and my imagination is *affecting* my actions. I am searching for the mode by which I can be heard by as many readers as possible, and in the process I am having to review the roles I have taken to transmit my meaning in my past.

Drama is concerned with communication between people. Many of the people we work with have difficulty communicating. Much of this results from an inability to change roles or respond to an alteration in external circumstances. This lack of role-flexibility[9] may be a result of a number of interrelated factors, for example, poor language use, inadequate body control, emotional blocks, poor social skills, etc. These factors often conspire to maintain an individual's inability to respond to external changes.

Through drama, individuals can not only be allowed to use their imaginations, but can also be encouraged to enjoy using them. Through games, improvisations and theatre scripts, different roles[10] can be taken. It is through this role-play and character-work that individuals can start to imagine what it is like to *be* someone else. These imaginative leaps can, through enactment and discussion of well-known job roles (for example, teacher, farmer, lawyer, policeman, etc.), engender a greater under-standing of social roles, or through similar enactment and discussion of more personal material lead to a greater awareness of one's self and one's relationship to family, friends and past life.

It is through dramatic process, by playing[11] other roles and through engaging imaginations and emotions, that we can increase our role-flexibility, develop our powers of communication and learn to interact acceptably in the society in which we live.

PRACTICAL ACTIVITIES

Like all the arts, drama is a personal activity. Developing your own personal style and making the material used your 'own' – so it fits your way of working – is often as important as the material itself. My own style is generally light, particularly in the early stages of a group's life, and my role is that of actor/facilitator.[12] I place a strong emphasis on humour as a vehicle for engaging other emotions. I place great store on gaining my group's trust and confidence through humour, laughter and enjoyment. My work as a clown and a comic actor obviously stands me in good stead for this. My reasons for sharing this with the reader are twofold. First, readers can look at my style of presentation and try to relate it to their own, but, what is more important, I share this information because I feel that without an element of fun, enjoyment and spontaneity many of the other benefits will not be reached. Engaging the interest of individuals in the group precedes gaining their confidence. Without their confidence and trust, no matter how much training and experience you have, they will be extremely reticent to share their world – with all its hopes, fears and emotions – with you. So no matter what your style, a primary concern is to engage and keep the group's interest. It was with this in mind that I chose the following material. All the material is 'track tested' and requires little or no equipment. I have divided the material into three sections: Name games, Awakening the imagination, and finally Creating character(s).

Name games

In the beginning an individual's name is perhaps the most important thing taken into the dramatic arena. For some of the people I work with their name is the only thing they can share with the group and some find even this too much for them. Our name is our identity. It tells others who we are and reaffirms our own existence. Name games allow the group to get to know one another and establish a sense of group spirit. I generally play a name game at the beginning of each session, just to re-establish the group. This is particularly important if the group meets once a week or less. Name games also allow each individual to be spotlighted,[13] that is, for a short time individual participants are the centre of attention. A name game sets the tone of 'we as a group are here and we all have names, personalities, feelings; we are all individuals'.

Simple name game(s)

Initially this game and its many variations are best played sitting in a circle. Start by saying your name. Then ask each person to say their own name in turn around the circle. This saying of names can go first to the right and then to the left of the leader, all the way round the circle.

A variation is for the leader to point at the person who has to speak – this can sometimes be threatening, particularly with a new group. Another variation is for the leader to walk around the inside of the circle, stopping in front of each group member and saying 'My name's Bernie, and what's your name?' On the reply, e.g., 'My name's Susan', the leader and Susan would shake hands. This continues until the leader has been introduced to all of the group.

Mr (or Ms) Engine

Mr Engine is a variation on shaking hands. It is a children's game I learnt from Bert Amies that is full of sound, ritual and enjoyment. The group sits in a circle with the leader standing in the centre. The leader is the engine of the train – known as 'Mr or Ms Engine'. As the engine moves it makes steam train noises, e.g., 'Choo choo choo choo, Choo choo choo choo'. When the engine comes to a halt in front of one of the group members, it goes 'Woo woo', making an action as if pulling on a lever. There then follows a ritual exchange. The engine starts 'Hello, little girl'; hopefully the girl replies 'Hello, Mr Engine'; leader 'What's your name?' The girl replies 'My name is Sue'; leader to rest of group 'Her name is Sue', to Sue 'Would you like to join my train, Sue?'; reply (hopefully) 'Yes, please.' At this point Sue 'joins the train' by standing behind the engine and putting her arms around Mr Engine's waist or on Mr Engine's shoulders. Slowly, the number of 'cars' behind Mr Engine increases, each linking around the waist of the car in front. When the engine has cars added, the name of the new person is said by each member of the train with the last car saying that name to the rest of the group. So if the train with two cars stops in front of Brian, the ritual goes like this: engine to first car 'His name is Brian'; first car to second car 'His name is Brian (pause). Would you like to join our train, Brian?' In this way the person's name is passed down the train and the greater the number of cars the train has, the more times the name is said. This repetition of the person's name acts as a form of spotlighting and the extended repetition in some ways compensates for being one of the last cars to join the train. However, it is very important that the last people to join are made to feel part of the group.

The structure of the game allows for full group involvement at all stages of its development. There are ritual chants with all the group accompanying the leader on the 'Choo choo choo choo, Choo choo choo choo' and on the 'Woo Woo, Woo Woo'. The group members can physically become the moving train and when the whole group is part of the train, a song can be sung as the train moves around the room, in and out of the furniture. One of my favoured songs is 'Chattanooga Choo Choo'. This is a great game to get people involved, out of their chairs and moving. If you have the luxury of volunteers,[14] try to intersperse them between the people who might need assistance. Occasionally people will refuse to join the train but a little gentle persuasion is often all that is needed. In the case of someone obstinately refusing to join the train, try *not* to spend undue time attempting to coax them because you risk losing the attention of other members of the group. After moving as a unit, the train can uncouple one car at a time; again this can be accompanied by a song or a group chant. This game is a good way of separating and mixing group members.

Dracula

This is one of my favourite and most theatrical[15] games. It is also one that is asked for repeatedly by groups of all ages and abilities. Over the years this game has changed quite considerably, mainly as a result of the groups who have played it.

At the start of the game the group sits in a circle with the leader standing in the middle. I ask the group about vampires and Dracula. After a very brief discussion, I tell them that I am going to be Dracula, one of the 'undead', and that they are all in the land of the living. I tell them that Dracula can return to the land of the living only if he can find a victim to take his place. Dracula does this by means of an 'instant blood exchange' through placing his fangs (Dracula's index fingers) at the back of the victim's neck. The victim then becomes the new Dracula. Sometimes I tell them that Dracula's spirit is always in need of a new host body to avoid the ravages of time – this adds to the blood exchange idea.

However, Dracula doesn't have it easy! As Dracula walks towards his victims, finger fangs outstretched; the intended victim makes the sign of the cross (by crossing index fingers). As soon as the sign of the cross is made, the rest of the group shouts the victim's name. If they are successful and call the victim's name before Dracula touches his neck, then Dracula must go in search of another victim. If Dracula gets there first, then the victim and Dracula change places and the group has a new Dracula.

Once the group has the general idea of how to play the game, extra rules can be added. Here are *some* examples:

(a) Dracula can be given a 'handicap', for example he has to walk with a limp, take baby steps, close one eye, count to three in front of the victim, etc.
(b) Victims have to direct their 'cross' at *one* member of the group who then has to call the victim's name.
(c) Adding to (b), if that one member of the group is too slow, it is he, not Dracula's victim, who becomes the new Dracula.

This is a great game for generating eye contact, group feeling and emotional response. Some important points to watch: young children can occasionally be scared by Dracula; always play a simple name game before Dracula; beware of violent Draculas (poking in the back of the neck can hurt!); be prepared to allow Dracula to 'suck blood' from the victim's knees, particularly important for Draculas who use wheelchairs.

My final point about Dracula concerns equipment. I play this game with the added extra of a cape – Dracula's cape – a black one with a scarlet red inner lining. This has really added to the game. It allows Dracula to gain added movement by using the cape's material, it seems to enable the more reticent individuals to 'become' Dracula and it allows for a social exchange between Dracula and victim. At the point of transformation when Dracula has caught a victim, the old Dracula helps the new Dracula on with the cape before sitting down as a member of the land of the living. This Transylvanian valet service is often one of the comic highlights of the game.

Tarzan

This is another one of my favourite and most asked-for games. It is often the first name game I play with a new group. I always tell a story before the game, about Tarzan swinging through the jungle and filling it with the sound of his own name. The story can take a number of turns and has a number of explanations for the famous Tarzan call with the explanation changing to meet the needs of the group I am working with.

The basic game is as follows: go round the circle and ask each person's name. Then I tell the Tarzan story and say that we are going to fill the room with the sound of our names. Then go round the circle, stopping at each group member, who says their name. This is then echoed by the rest of the group shouting that name while beating their chests. This goes all the way round the circle until everyone's name has filled the room, and finally we all beat our chests and shout the Tarzan call.

This is a great game for spotlighting individuals. Even the shyest person's face lights up when they hear all the group shouting their name and that sound filling the room.

These are but a few examples from the huge array of simple and dramatic name games available in the literature. Often a group will have special, favourite name games. These may be ones you have introduced or, more likely, ones they have adapted or created.

Awakening the imagination

Many of the people we work with have been actively discouraged from using their imaginations. Programmes that emphasise socially acceptable behaviours and the facing of reality – in the programmer's terms – cause the often fertile imaginations of individuals in our groups to atrophy! I am not suggesting that individuals should not be helped to face the realities of our often inhumane and alienating industrialised society; what I am suggesting is that there are many ways in which this can be achieved. One of these is through the individual's imagination. I feel that in order to help them grasp a sense of the socially accepted norms of reality, we must first gain a sense of how they imagine the world, and attempt to see the world through their eyes so that we do not always transfer or project our world view on to them. Our understanding of their perceptions of the world, gained through imaginative exercises, can provide a framework in which to initiate a change to more socially acceptable behaviour. The first three games deal with awakening and engaging the senses, and the others in this section focus on the act of creating *something from nothing*, and on the imagination taking a concrete object and transforming it into something else.

Keeper of the Keys

A variation on a traditional children's game. I tell the group a story about
a pirate who amasses great wealth and keeps this in his house. However,
the pirate is often away from his home and needs someone to guard his
house and treasure. He is told of a blind person whose hearing is so acute
they can hear a pin drop in a crowded room. After an embellished
preamble, one of the group sits on a chair in the centre of the circle, closes
their eyes and becomes the Guardian of the Treasure. The rest of the
group is seated in a circle around the Guardian. In front of the Guardian
are the keys to the treasure; for children this is often described as a huge
store of candy or chocolate. The rest of the group try, one at a time, to
take the keys without being heard. When the Guardian hears a noise he
or she points in the direction of the noise, saying 'Get out of this house.'
If the would-be-thief is pointed at, he or she has to go back to their seat.
If the thief captures the keys without being spotted, he or she becomes the
new Guardian.

Added complications can be to give the Guardian a gun (extended index
finger) the verbal taunt now becomes 'Get out of this house, bang!' This
adds the dramatic element of a theatrical death. The thief can be required
to get the keys from under the Guardian's nose and back to the thief's
seat; or a group of two or three thieves can work as a team to get the keys
from the Guardian (this can be very unsettling for the person playing the
Guardian and should not be tried early on).

This game is extremely good for accentuating auditory skills. It is also
an exercise in control for the thief, who must try not to be heard, and for
the rest of the group who must remain quiet and still.

There is a tendency for Guardians not to keep their eyes totally closed;
however, I am reluctant to use a blindfold. My own experience is that
many individuals are scared by wearing a blindfold. The return to trust –
trusting the individual to keep his or her eyes closed requires patience and
a liberal dose of turning a blind eye in the initial stages. Slowly, individuals
will be less scared of closing their eyes and will become totally engaged in
the game. Pushing and cajoling them to close their eyes will probably only
aggravate the problem.

Male or Female?

This game is a regular favourite. I have found it particularly good when
working with groups of long-stay institutionalised people, especially
seniors, as it seems to provide that essential element of acceptable human
contact so often lacking from these people's lives.

The group sits in a circle with one member of the group sitting in the
middle. The person in the middle has his or her eyes closed. One at a time

other members of the group go and gently touch the person in the centre, who then has to guess whether he or she was touched by a man or a woman. I never force anyone either to sit in the centre or to get up and touch the person sitting there. I let the game continue until everyone who wants to has had a go.

This game provides a fascinating experience. When you are in the middle it is extremely difficult to discern if the touch is that of a man or a woman; *however,* it does force you to be aware of other factors, for example pressure, warmth, sound – particularly breathing and smell. After a while, when working with a group over a long period of time, I can generally pick out exactly who is touching me by the sounds they make coming towards me, their breathing pattern, the way they touch me and so on. As an observer, the ways that people approach the person in the middle and then make physical contact can be particularly informative concerning the dynamics of the group. Often, individuals hide their feelings behind the words they use to communicate; in this exercise these feelings are made concrete, often in very subtle ways.

This activity can also be used as part of work on sex roles and stereotypes. Often, when working with teenagers, a discussion is an essential close to this activity. Other groups, particularly those involving people with developmental disabilities, often turn this game into a competition and some individuals get bitterly disappointed if they guess incorrectly. This disappointment needs to be dissipated either through group support or a 'success' in another activity, or whatever means is appropriate to that individual in your group.

This is generally one of the first physical contact activities I use with a group as it gives me a rough gauge of how individuals in the group respond to being touched. It also gives a pointer to who will or will not work well together. This activity can lead into more directed activities dealing with emotion and physical contact.

The Magic Box

I often carry with me a large magic box. On the outside, painted in large letters, are the words 'Bernie's Magic Box'. This box has a practical purpose, as it enables me to carry with me all the equipment I ever use – tape recorder, tapes, parachute, etc. However, it has another far more important function and that is to serve as a focus for group members' imaginations.

The magic box is an extremely simple tool. It is one of those timeless dramatic activities. Stanislavski used a version of the magic box for training actors, and many noted drama specialists have some form of magic box exercise. In essence the magic box is a projective exercise. All I ask as leader is 'What do you think is in the box?' The group then responds by projecting from their imaginations what they think is in the box. The responses of the group can then be directed or shaped by the leader in a number of ways.

First I generally employ a *free association* approach – where I simply allow the group to come up with as many ideas as possible. When using this approach I try not to make judgments, although I do make mental notes of who said what. Also, I attempt to provide an environment that allows the group to imagine as many things to be inside the box as they want to tell me about.

Sometimes I am slightly more directive, taking a *theme-based* approach. Here I tell the group there is food or treasure or unusual objects inside the box. This is an approach I take with youngsters with developmental disabilities. I still allow the group to free-wheel, but within a given framework. This can provide the necessary grounding for individuals who are 'paralysed' by a completely open-ended task.

Sometimes I break with a free-wheeling or free-association approach and take a *question-based* approach. Here, as soon as an individual has a particular idea about what is in the box, I ask questions related to the object they have described. For example, if they have suggested there is a purse in the box; I might ask, 'What colour is it?' 'How large is it?' 'Is it soft?' 'Does it have writing on the outside?' and so on. As a result of these questions, often a clear picture of this object can be created in a very short space of time.

Once the group has created objects, there are a number of ways of working with the ideas. Here are two basic approaches. Having created a variety of objects to be found in the box, take the 'imagined' objects from the box one at a time and pass them round the group. Get the group to take the time to feel each object's texture, weight, etc. At some point I might ask one of the group to describe the object to the rest of the group.

Another technique is to use two or three objects that the group created that might link together. For example, one group told me that in the box, among other things, were a bloody hand, a sword and a dragon's tooth. I then asked the group to tell me how the objects got there. In this way, from the objects a group creates, a story can evolve, which can then be 'acted out'. The magic box then, in common with other activities described in this section, allows the group to use its collective experience as the basis for the dramatic activity. I will pursue these ideas through description of other activities in this chapter. The magic box can also be used to reinforce the magical qualities of objects that are taken out of it, such as the Magic newspaper.

Magic Newspaper

This is one of my 'old faithfuls', which I use at some point in my work with every group. This game is both a starting point for mime and a diagnostic tool.

I produce from my magic box the magic newspaper. I tell the group that this may look like an ordinary newspaper, but it is in fact magic. At this point most of the group is, to say the least, sceptical. I say that the magic of the newspaper is that, by working with it, the paper can become anything you want and that, without telling anyone, the group will immediately know what it is. I then create a telescope, someone in the group says 'telescope', I reply 'See, magic works every time', and we're off. I then might show a few more examples of the newspaper's power and then the paper is passed around the circle. Each person has a chance to work with the 'magic'. The only rule is that you cannot pass twice. So if you cannot think or make something first time round, you must do something the next time.

The way that individuals respond to the magic newspaper is fascinating and it is for me, as already mentioned, a very valuable diagnostic tool. From the way individuals use the paper I can gain information that enables me to make observations about the way that each person's imagination functions. In general terms, there are three basic ways of working with the magic newspaper – moving from the concrete to the abstract use of imagination. First, people work at a concrete level. The focus is on *making* the newspaper into something. Here the paper has to be an actual representation, for example a hat, an aeroplane or a newspaper. What work the individual does with the paper is related to origami. Further along, people reach a stage where they are less concerned about what the object looks like and more concerned about how to use it. The focus is on *using* the newspaper as something, for example a paint brush, a baseball bat or a fishing rod. This marks a mid-point between the concrete and the abstract uses of the newspaper. At the most abstract level, the focus is on the newspaper being *part of* a larger imaginative picture, for example, the newspaper is the lead for a dog being taken for a walk. The focus is now on the dog *not* on the lead. The shift of focus on the newspaper is from making into, to using as, to being part of something – it is a shift from the concrete to the abstract use of imagination. The way the individuals use the paper can serve as a guide to the level at which other imaginative exercises might best be started.

Although the way in which people use the newspaper is a clue to the way in which they use their imaginations, it is by no means a direct cause-and-effect relationship. People who are able to function at the highest abstract level are often intimidated during the first sessions of the magic newspaper and appear to function only at a concrete level. Also, some people appear to be functioning at a higher, more abstract level than would at first be expected. There may also be some who can only copy others. All of these pieces of information should be made note of and used to help fill out the three-dimensional jigsaws that are the individuals within your group. No single piece alone can complete the picture but every little piece of information helps.

Magic Clay

This is an extension of the magic newspaper. Again it can be a starting point for mime work. I was first introduced to this exercise early on in my training as part of a mime workshop. The workshop leaders introduced this as an exercise which allowed the Mime to 'produce' objects on stage with a minimum of fuss and effort. Magic Clay is my reworking of that simple exercise.

I tell the group that I have a ball of magic clay and that when I work with it I can create objects. I then stretch the clay, drawing it out and shaping it, perhaps into a bouquet of flowers that I then present to someone in the group. When we have completed our transaction, I mould the clay back into a ball and pass it to the person next to me. The clay is passed around the circle with each person *consciously* creating something, using and demonstrating it so that the group understands, and returning it to the shape of a ball. In this stage of the exercise the ball is being consciously shaped and manipulated by the group member holding it.

Another way of using the magic clay is to ask the individuals holding it to close their eyes and let the clay move them. The sceptics among my readers will argue that something that does not exist cannot move the individual not holding it. In a sense they are right, yet what is being asked is for the person holding the clay to try to suspend the cerebral override that we all employ in almost any task and let the subconscious take over. The need is to do, without thinking about what to do. The results can be fascinating. I ask individuals to describe their experiences as they are happening telling the rest of the group of what they experienced (the colours, shapes, weight, textures, etc.) when working with the clay. I always emphasise that there is no need to describe or label what has been created, as the end of the process does not have to be something known or tangible.

When the individual lets go of conscious control of the clay, the emotions and the feelings take over. There must be no criticism or judgment of the creation – this is not a work of art, this is a work of emotion, colour and form. The effect of the experience on the individual varies immensely, depending on their emotional state and the degree to which they allow themselves to go with the clay. In most cases, people describe it as a relaxing, refreshing and pleasant experience. For others it can act as a stimulus to open the floodgates for troublesome or unresolved experience. It is essential that you are aware of this possibility and timetable Magic Clay so that there is always time to explore anything that comes up as a result of the exercise and you do not simply close the session with the activity. This activity integrates well with various visual arts techniques, for example 'painting' the experience with the clay.

Tennis–Elbow–Foot Game

The group sits in a circle. The idea is to throw a soft ball from one person to another. As the ball is thrown, the thrower says a word, for example 'tennis'. The catcher must then respond with the first word that comes into their head, for example 'elbow', simultaneously throwing the ball to another person as they do so. The game is based on an instant response to the word that went before. There should be no time to pre-plan because you never know what word you will have to respond to. If there is a break in continuity or if someone pauses before responding, blocking has almost certainly occurred.

This is an extremely interesting and often entertaining game. It is an excellent exercise to work against blocking and as such to promote spontaneity and creativity. It forms a good springboard for storytelling exercises. It can give valuable clues about individuals within the group in much the same way as the magic box. When working with people with a developmental disability or young children it is often best to start with a theme, such as colours. So the task would then be to say the first colour that you think of. Again, it is important to cross-reference information. For example, if a child is stuck with the response 'yellow', certain questions need to be answered. Do they also repeatedly choose yellow in art work? Do they describe their house as yellow? If they do, why? Is it the only colour they know? Some more deep-seated reason? It is important to gain as much first-hand information as possible, but it is also important to cross-refer experiences with the other professionals who work with that individual.

In Chapter 2 and 3 I have made reference to the importance of the contract between the leader and the group. If the contract is a 'therapeutic' one, then the leader will want to make note of the *pattern, repetition* and *blocking* of responses for, based on the information from this and other activities and sources, an 'intervention' or 'strategy for change' can be planned. In the context above the *pattern* is the sequence of words exchanged between group members, for example 'on top', 'underneath', 'blanket', '*bed*'; *repetition is* where an individual is stuck with a particular word or limited response, for example, 'purple', or only using words related to touch; and *blocking* is what occurs when an individual is unable to respond to a particular word or topic, such as 'love'.

The reasons for the patterns, repetition or blocking can be many. One aberration that should be considered when looking at the pattern is whether individuals were responding to the penultimate word. This happens when the game is being played fast and the group members are new to each other.

Repetition is usually an individual problem and may simply be a language deficiency; this is particularly likely for people with developmental disabilities. However, with a more 'verbal' group the repetition *may* be psychological in origin.

Blocking is far more complicated and highlights the problem posed by evaluating the group's responses. Certain words or topics, for example, sexuality, may be blocked for a number of individual or collective reasons. One of the most obvious is that individuals feel a lack of trust and confidence in other members of the group. The reasons for this lack of trust may be a key to the direction a strategy for change should take.

In general terms, it is unusual for a group of post-pubescent people not to mention sex – covertly or overtly – at some point in the game. However with adolescents, given a supportive and creative environment, the pattern may be predominantly concerned with sex. This can lead to very interesting discussions after the game.

Guided fantasy

The term 'guided fantasy' is one that is used loosely to describe a leader relating to an individual or group a pertinent tale, anecdote or similar stimulus. At its simplest, the guided fantasy has been the stock in trade of all good storytellers since humankind first started telling stories. At its central core is the need to engage individuals in the events of the story. Therefore there is a need to choose material that is specific not only to the group's needs but also to their way of viewing the world.

As already mentioned by Rob Watling earlier in this book (Chapter 4), traditional material with its store of wisdom and knowledge may often be a suitable starting point for a guided fantasy. The way a story or stimulus is used by a leader can take a number of directions, with the direction often being dictated by the nature of the intended outcome of the exercise.[16]

In a guided fantasy the leader's role can be directive or non-directive, and the participants may be actively or passively involved. In a *non-directive* approach the leader simply provides a loose framework – suggestions to stimulate the imagination. In a *directive* approach the leader makes statements that give step-by-step instructions – literally guiding the imagination. These styles are often mixed, so that statements, such as 'You walk down the road and come to a big house. You walk up to the front door', may be interspersed with questions. 'What colour is the door?' 'Is the door open?' The leader may even leave the end totally open for individuals to supply the conclusion that satisfies their needs.

The participants in a guided fantasy may be *passive*; that is relaxed, lying on the floor, eyes closed. The leader may use terms such as 'imagine you are looking at a large cinema screen' – suggesting that the story is happening there and then on the screen, or reference may be made to an environment: 'You are in a garden full of flowers – brightly coloured, beautiful, sweet-smelling – take time to smell the flowers, feel their texture, look at the colours.' The emphasis may then be placed on action or sensation or both.

In a guided fantasy where the participants are *active,* they *do* what the story suggests. Thus, if the story calls for the heroine to ride into town, the participants act as if they were riding into town. If it calls for the heroine to pick a magical flower, the participants act as if they are picking that flower. When participants are active, they are like actors responding to the instructions in the script – they are wide awake and respond in their own creative way within the restrictions imposed by the script.

Sometimes a guided fantasy may be both active and non-directive; when used with a group this is often referred to as a community exercise. Guided fantasy, as with so many other creative activities, is often a stepping-stone to the discussion it creates as a result of participants being engaged in the activity. This discussion is often as important as the activity that preceded it.

Creating character(s)

The creation of characters, through both storytelling and the act of becoming someone else, are the natural extensions of awakening the imagination. It is this dramatic awakening, the linking of words to emotion, that also forms the backbone for many of the verbal forms of individualised counselling and therapy. In the act of suspending conscious control, in the removing of those blocks that prevent us from being truly creative, we regain contact with the raw emotions, past experiences and inspiration that are the source of the personal creative statement – the unique creative thumbprint that only we as individuals can make. These blocks are the death of personal creativity. We all have them and we all employ them. They allow us to hide behind a wall. They also act as barriers to social performers acting on the stage of everyday life, fully creating the roles that allow them truly to communicate. In my work I have identified what I believe to be three major blocks to being spontaneous and creative. I feel they are present in all of us and are in many ways a necessary defence in certain social situations. However, they are often more apparent in people who have limited role-flexibility and communication skills. I call the three major blocks, 'the wall', 'the censor' and 'playing the crowd'.

(a) *The wall.* Here, conscious control is so great and people are so desperately trying to be creative that they cannot do anything. A common response is 'I had many ideas but when it was my turn to do something, my mind went blank.'

(b) *The censor.* Here, people are able to do something but it is feeble, half-hearted. If questioned, common responses are 'I thought that was what you wanted' or, what is more important, 'I didn't know what others would think.'

(c) *Playing the crowd.* Here, the exhibited behaviour is of someone frantically creating. It is, however, surface behaviour – attention-seeking. The individual will use any means of being the centre of the group's attention. At the extreme, there is *no* censoring behaviour; often 'taboo' subjects are played up, with emphasis on cheap laughs and crowd reinforcement.

In exercises or games where the awakened imagination develops a story and later creates characters, these three blocks are particularly prevalent. The skilled leader can make use of the blocks, first, by making note of them and later, often in the same session, providing material that allows a chance for the individual to overcome them.

The characters created and the stories they tell often provide a three-dimensional map of where individuals have come from, where they are going to and, sometimes, where they stopped along the way. The construction of the sentences, the inflection used, and the body posture assumed are every bit as important as the content. The leader must be all eyes and ears, sensing the sub-text of what is said both in and out of character. In carefully listening to, observing and developing the events during the session, the leader is able not only to establish a creative environment, but also to help individuals regain contact with themselves and thus start to increase role-flexibility and communication skills.

To Be Continued (group storytelling)

This is an excellent way to create a script or story that has significance for the group. The story created can be recorded by means of a tape recorder. It can then be written down and used as a stimulus for other activities, and can be used as a guided fantasy, a theatre script or a starting point for developing reading and writing skills.[17]

The group sits in a circle. The leader starts a story going, for example, 'Once upon a time in a large city lived a small cat called Boots.' This first sentence is then built on, a section at a time, by each member of the circle, one at a time, contributing to the story – a word, a phrase, a sentence or whatever seems appropriate. Slowly the group introduces new characters and situations, which develop the action. The focus may shift dramatically as a result of characters and situations introduced by the group. What is important is that each group member is actively involved in creating the story – it is an expression of their shared, collective experiences and imaginations.

To spice the activity up, with a group who have had experience in creating their own stories, I take a soft ball and ask individuals, when they have added their section to the story, to throw the ball to someone else. This makes contributions more spontaneous because you never know when it will be your turn.

Another variation is to have someone in the centre acting out the story as it is being created. I have a rule that they can sit back in the circle at any time and choose who will replace them. Again, you never know when it will be your turn to be in the centre of the circle. The 'actor' often decides to swap with a 'storyteller' when the addition to the story is difficult for them to perform. This forces the 'storyteller' to take their own medicine, normally to the great amusement of the rest of the group.

It is important that less verbal people are allowed to contribute at their own level. For some people with a developmental disability this may require the leader asking questions, some of which a court of law might view as leading the witness, so that each individual can participate; other individuals may require the leader to intervene to prevent one person controlling the story for an extended time. This person is an obvious candidate to be 'the actor' when the time comes to act out the story.

Liar's Tag

The group sits in a circle. The leader starts miming an action, such as brushing his teeth. Number two, the person on his left, asks 'What are you doing?' The leader then has to lie, for example: 'I'm riding my bike.' Number two must then mime riding a bike. Number three then asks number two 'What are you doing?' The reply might be 'I'm taking a bath.' Number three must then mime taking a bath, and so on.

The person performing the action must tell the questioner a lie, and the questioner must then act out that lie. Again, this is an excellent game for most groups. For some groups with slower than average cognitive skills, the leader must be patient and allow time for the group to work at their own pace and within their own limitations.

I'm Sorry I Must Be Leaving

This is a standard acting improvisation, which is often a riot to watch. I start a scene with one person in a given situation, such as watching TV, a second person enters and chooses his character, and a scene starts to develop through improvisation. At some point in the scene a third person joins the action. At this point the first person must find a legitimate excuse to leave the scene.

Each time a new 'actor' joins the scene the first person in the scene must leave. Thus, when number four joins the scene; number two must leave and when number five joins, then number three must leave and so on. The effect is a continuously changing non-stop scene with each new actor choosing his character and how he will react to the people left on stage.

A variation on I'm Sorry I Must Be Leaving is to start number one with an action, for example washing windows. When number two comes in, he takes number one's action but changes it slightly into something else, such as grooming a horse. Number one and number two then interact by number one joining in number two's activity until number three joins the action. Number one must now find an excuse to leave and number two must find a way of joining in number three's actions. Thus number three might now be conducting an orchestra so number two might pick up a violin and be conducted. It is important for the development of the game that *the last person in is always in control of the scene.*

Again there is a fast-changing, free-flowing improvisation being played out for the audience. This is an excellent game with almost any group. Obviously, for groups whose cognitive skills are slower than average, the game moves more slowly and may need more direction from the leader, *but* having played the game a couple of times, people slowly gain an awareness of the rules and create some fascinating scenes and scene changes.

Who Owned the Bag?

This is a projective exercise and has many similarities to the Magic Box. I bring in a battered and aged bag. I have two I use regularly. One is an old-fashioned leather briefcase and the other is a hold-all made from alligator hide. I tell the group that it is a very old bag and has had many owners. I then ask the group to tell me who owned the bag. When someone tells me they know who owned the bag, I ask them to tell me about the owner. Normally the first piece of information concerns the owner's job; for example 'It was owned by a doctor.' Once the group member has started to tell me about the owner I start asking questions, for example 'What's the owner's name?', 'How old is he?', 'How tall?', 'What colour is his hair?', 'How much does he weigh?', etc. Slowly, the person is building a physical picture of the bag's owner. Then I can start asking questions about the owner's lifestyle, the sort of house he lives in, his favourite foods, etc. Once I have done this with one person, then the group can be involved in asking subsequent informants about other owners of the bag.

In using a simple stimulus, an old bag, as a focal point, the group is able to create characters. These characters can be used in other exercises. Owners of the bag can act out the exchange of the bag from one to another. Scenes can be played with the bag's owner as the central character. The character can be used in a situation that is yet unresolved by his or her creator and so on.

The leader can always ask questions about the bag's owner that help the person describing him. If the description is very concrete, questions relating to emotion can be asked, such as 'How does he feel about his job?' If the description is very abstract, the leader can ask questions that 'anchor' the group member, for example 'What size of shoes does he wear?'

It is important to let the group member describing the bag's owner know that they are always right. They cannot say 'I think he is 5 feet 6 inches', for they are creating the character. The way the individual creates the character, the points they describe, the ones they avoid, particularly those dealing with the character's emotions, can be very valuable clues to completing the three-dimensional jigsaws I have spoken about throughout this chapter.

POSTSCRIPT

In this chapter I have described some of the ways drama can be used with people to awaken the imagination and create characters. I have tried to emphasise throughout the close link between imagination and dramatic action. Many groups are thought of as being incapable, unable to take part, and yet my experience is that in almost all cases this belief is unfounded. There are many with whom the process is a long, hard one but when the results occur, when someone is able to allow their imaginative thoughts to become action, to participate in dramatic activity, the wait and the effort all seem worthwhile.

In working with any group, the only real limits to an individual's taking part in dramatic activities are time, patience and the limits of the leader's imagination. It is within the power of the human imagination to overcome mental restrictions, physical limitations and emotional barriers, and, in so doing, truly to move mountains.

ACKNOWLEDGEMENTS

I wish to thank the following professional colleagues and friends for their advice, encouragement and inspiration over the years: Bill Morris, Dek Leverton, Gordi Wiseman, Sue Jennings, Derek Gale, Nancy Breitenbach, Tony Jeffries, Paul Johnson and Ian McHugh, and I must give special thanks to Derek Akers for all his help and advice; to Rob Watling, with whom I have shared so many of my successes and failures; and above all to my first mentor, the late Bert Amies MBE who is the single most important influence on my way of working and my current profession.

NOTES

1 Beckerman (1970) suggests that drama occurs when 'one or more human beings, isolated in time and space, present themselves in imagined acts to another or

others'. This definition, although primarily based on theatrical performance, does emphasise the importance both of the imagination and of communication between people.

2 This area will be discussed in detail by Cheryl Neill in Chapter 9, this volume, on storytelling.

3 Ritual is an extremely complicated concept, but at the risk of oversimplifying one can think of ritual as: consistently repeated actions (words, movements, sounds, expressions, etc.) that possess specific meaning for a particular group (tribe, subculture). Often rituals started as spontaneous random acts, which only later on acquired significance for other members of the group.

4 I do not mean to confuse this loss of spontaneity with lack of meaning. It is when the group loses contact with, and understanding of, the purpose of the ritual that the ritual loses meaning and becomes 'dead'. See Chapter 4, this volume by Rob Watling.

5 Dramatic actions in this case could be viewed as speech or movement that is not simply functional but excessively expressive or dramatic. Often these dramatic actions are socially unacceptable and are often exhibited by people who become our 'clients'.

6 Calibration relates to the mutual response process in which all human beings are continually engaged, in their attempts to communicate their feelings, beliefs, ideas, etc. – to others. See Gordon (1978).

7 Courtney (1980) p. vii.

8 Each individual's specific and personal way of viewing the world, which forms the basic grid by which all incoming stimuli are processed, categorised and stored.

9 Role-flexibility can be seen as both a change of 'social role', e.g. from husband to teacher to shopper to father to son, etc., but also it can be seen in terms of a change in 'social status' – dominant, equal or subordinate. In any set social role we may be required to change status not only frequently but also rapidly during interactions with others. Role-flexibility is an essential skill for actors, but is also invaluable in facilitating everyday communication. See Johnstone (1981) for a different perspective on status interactions in relation to theatre.

10 Role and character are frequently used interchangeably in the literature. However, when I speak of role-play, I am referring to improvised dramas created by the meeting and interaction of set role types, for example student and teacher, traffic cop and motorist. The responses of the types are left to the imaginations of the individuals playing the role, but are based on experience and their general perceptions of that social role. However, the more information that is given about the role, for example name, age, favourite colour, gender, marital status, occupation of parents, etc., the closer one gets to a character with a known past history and probable emotional responses to any given situation. The greater the detail, the more the individual must respond 'as if' they were that character. This is, in essence, the basis of naturalistic acting.

11 Playing is integrally linked with dramatic activity. As my great friend and mentor, Bert Amies, often pointed out, whether children are playing 'cops and robbers' or even if you are playing Hamlet or Macbeth, it is still play – something that is often forgotten by some people.

12 The person leading a drama session can take many roles as leader, but in essence these are but facets of being a play leader – in the widest sense of the term. However, there are three basic sub-roles that a play leader can assume. There is the role of the *actor* – where the leader is *actively* involved in the group and, apart from suggesting starting points, is almost totally non-directive.

Then there is the role of *facilitator* where the leader steps back a pace or two from the group so as to gain some objectivity. In this role the leader is *passively* guiding the group by asking questions, making observations that allow the group to make its own decisions and direction changes. Finally, there is the role of *director* where the leader directs the group, providing a strong structure in which they must react and create. All play leaders exhibit a mixture of role types within their leadership style. Many switch roles as appropriate to the surroundings in which they work and to the people with whom they are interacting.

13 Activities that spotlight need to be set up so that they are non-threatening and supportive, so that those involved may gain a positive reinforcement of self-image and feel secure within the group's limelight.

14 Extra helpers, whether volunteers or paid aides, can be a great help, but they can also be a pain in the – ! Often, so much time is spent helping the helpers understand a particular way of working, or an individual's specific needs, that the moment is lost. However, sensitive or well-trained helpers who support those in greatest need without becoming too obtrusive can make the leader's job so much more simple. Volunteer help is essential when working with individuals with profound disabilities, and much of my time is spent recruiting and educating voluntary help from janitors and kitchen staff as well as the more obvious professional colleagues and students.

15 When a player enters the circle, they enter a space where anything can happen. When they become Dracula they transform the other players into both participants in and spectators of the dramatic action. The game involves a costumed player creating a character that involves the emotions of all other participants; as such, this game demonstrates many of the quintessential elements of theatre.

16 This is discussed in detail in Cheryl Neill's chapter on storytelling (Chapter 9).

17 From the recording of the group's story a story book can be produced. This book can be used for people to read from. It can also be produced with large script and with lots of space between each word to allow the person to copy the word. This is not new educational practice, but the material the person is learning from has been created by them and this can affect the motivation to learn. Good results have been achieved using this method with adolescents from inner city areas who are street-wise but 'learning disabled'.

SUGGESTED READING

Amies, H. T., Warren, B. and Watling, R. (1986) *Social Drama*, John Clare Books, London.

Barker, C. (1977) *Theatre Games*, Eyre Methuen, London.

Beckerman, B. (1970) *The Dynamics of Drama*, Drama Book Specialists, New York.

Courtney, R. (1980) *The Dramatic Curriculum*, Heinemann, London.

Gordon, D. (1978) *Therapeutic Metaphor*, Meta, Cuperdine, CA.

Grainger, R. (1990) *Drama and Healing*, Jessica Kingsley Publishers, London.

Jennings, S. (1973) *Remedial Drama*, Pitman, London.

Johnstone, K. (1981) *Impro*, Eyre Methuen, London.

Landy, R. (1986) *Drama Therapy*, Charles C. Thomas, Springfield, IL.

McLeod, J. (1988) *Drama is Real Pretending*, Ministry of Education, Victoria, Australia.

Shaw, A., Perks, W. and Stevens, C. J. (1981) *Perspectives: Drama and Theatre by, with and for Handicapped Individuals*, A.T.A., Washington, DC.

Spolin, V. (1963) *Improvisations for the Theatre*, Northwestern University Press, Evanston, IL.

Warren, B. (ed.) (1991) *A Theatre In Your Classroom*, Captus University Publications, North York, Ontario.

Way, B. (1969) *Development Through Drama*, Longman, London.

Films

Breaking Free (1981, directed by Chris Noonan).

Feeling Good Feeling Proud (1981, directed by Richard Heus).

Chapter 9

Storymaking and storytelling
Weaving the fabric that creates our lives

Cheryl Neill

INTRODUCTION

> A hero ventures forth from the world of common day into a region of
> supernatural wonder: fabulous forces are there encountered and a
> decisive victory is won: the hero comes back from this mysterious
> adventure with the power to bestow boons on his fellow man.
>
> (Campbell 1990: xvi)

There are really only two kinds of stories; those that we tell to others and
those that someone else tells to us. While all stories are true (in the sense
that all are a reflection of different states of the human mind), stories are
also metaphors for life experience; for they are mirrors in which we see
facets of ourselves. Good stories, like our dreams, are full of symbolic
images where different aspects of the psyche are highlighted. Our subconscious often recognises these symbols while our conscious mind does
not.

Many people (including some famous ones such as Einstein and Ben
Franklin) have reported new insights or breakthroughs on problems they
have been trying to solve after a particularly vivid dream. They say that
the answer just 'appeared to them' in a flash. There seems to be a well of
knowledge and awareness that is ordinarily inaccessible to us while we are
conscious. Stories, the good ones, speak directly to this inner mind through
symbolic picture language and can provoke the same kind of dawning
insight to occur.

When working with people in health care, rehabilitation or special
education settings, traditional methods of healing and therapy can be
greatly enhanced by storytelling and storymaking. Many of these individuals
have a preconception of the world, a rigid set of unconscious 'truths' which
can stop them from moving forward. The unconscious mind is very difficult
to reach by rational argument alone.

A reason for this is that opinions and views of reality are extremely
well guarded by what William James referred to as the 'Sentiment of
Rationality'. This is the feeling of 'rightness' given to an opinion that then

becomes the only one accepted as 'rational'. Although other opinions and explanations may exist, the one chosen is the best liked and is defended against all others. Since it is best liked, it is rational. Here is a simple example: 'I am overweight because my mother overfed me as a child.' Other obvious arguments could be put forward such as I just like to eat, but because I like my argument I will rationalise it and defend it.

This is what happens to some individuals who believe that the way they view the world and their behaviour is the only 'rational' way of seeing or behaving. Arguing against such a view usually only causes them to cling more stubbornly to their opinion. In fact, this 'Sentiment of Rationality' is very resistant to 'logic' and 'rational' talk.

Herein lies the value of stories. Stories do not tackle these barriers head on; they circumvent them by appealing directly to the unconscious. Stories are also non-threatening since on the surface they seem non-invasive. After all, at any point in a story, listeners can decide that the story is not about them! Even when the conscious mind has made such a decision, the unconscious side may not agree.

Stories work on two main levels. One level appeals to the intellectual, 'rational' left side of the brain that absorbs the plot and the spoken language, dream imagery and symbols. This side is not interested in moralistic principles and 'rational' arguments. It is also not swayed by interpretive language, rather it has an instinctive vocabulary and is the least guarded against new ways of 'seeing' or outside 'help'. This phenomenon and other aspects of story will be examined in this chapter as well as how to choose, prepare and tell stories to others.

THE BEGINNING OF STORY

In the beginning of all things
wisdom and knowledge were with the animals,
For Tirawa, the One Above, did not speak directly
to man. He sent certain animals to tell men
that he showed himself through the beasts,
and that from them, and from the stars and
the sun and the moon, man should learn.
Tirawa spoke to man through his works.

(in Curtis 1907: 96)

I was working with a group of 11-, 12- and 13-year-olds in a storytelling session last spring. I had just finished a tale that described the great Greek pantheon of gods – the one that speaks of the birth of Athena from Zeus's head and gives details of the magical hall of the deities on Mount Olympus.

I had no sooner finished when a young man, a serious thoughtful boy spoke up.

'Now that makes sense to me', he said excitedly, 'A god to look after different areas of the world.'

'What do you mean?' I queried, knowing somehow where this was leading.

'Well', he answered enthusiastically, 'how can one god look after the whole world and the universe too? I've always thought that there was something wrong with that! It makes much more sense that there are lots of gods – each of them having their own specialty – wind, sun, grass, animals – you know?'

'Yes, yes', chorused others in the group. 'That does make a lot more sense. It's too big a job for one god.'

The discussion went on a while longer and I thought of the phone calls from disturbed parents I would be receiving as a result. To my surprise (and relief) this never happened but still, I was struck by the struggle of these modern twentieth-century children, this enlightened progeny acquainted with 'new science', computers and cellular phones, trying to understand, to make sense of their 2000-year-old mythology. It reminded me of a quotation that came from the Gnostic period: 'The trouble with Yahweh [god] is he thinks he's god.' Obviously, these children had come to the same conclusion!

One might not think that in today's modern world anyone is much concerned with these 'spiritual' matters but it has been my experience, working in storytelling sessions with both children and adults alike, that symbolic material, myths and legends in particular are not only firm favourites but they seem to feed a real need, especially as people feel more and more cut off from nature, society and self.

Participants in my storytelling classes consistently choose to tell American Indian and Eastern myths when given the assignment to prepare a story of their choice to tell for others. Given the wealth of folkloric material available to them, I found this curious. Then I realised that there was something about these particular stories that 'grab' both teller and listener. In both traditions there are many 'spirit' gods, some not quite anthropomorphised, others in animal guise. There is a wonderful respect for nature. These are in high contrast to our own heritage that stresses the superiority of man over beast, sees a singular 'god' as being outside the world and of mankind and favours the taming of nature rather than the nurturing of it. A totally different civilisation and way of living are experienced when the informing myth presents nature as 'fallen' (as in the Garden of Eden story) or is seen as a manifestation of divine presence on earth.

It seems that in these trying times, for people who are struggling to reconcile lifestyle with spiritual concerns, storymaking and storytelling that includes some mythological material that points to the revelation of divinity in nature, may help individuals to find a path that puts them in accord with their surroundings.

Diane Wolkstein has suggested that 'to tell stories is to be human'. It has been an expression of humankind's wonder at the mysteries of existence, not just for centuries, but for millennia, for storytelling is as much a part of the human experience as waking and sleeping and as necessary to the psyche as food to the body.

The goal of all mythologies is to instruct the members of a given society on their role throughout life; to put people in accord with the nature of life, death and the universe. The basic motivating factors that govern the behaviour of human beings have not changed since early times. The life crises of birth, initiation, marriage, separation and death are the same ones that have been faced by humanity since time immemorial and these are still the main motivational forces today in all societies despite historic modifications and differing social systems (see Eliade 1974: 5)

Mythology helps individuals to identify not with particular isolated incidents but with the universal images that transcend time and place them in accord with all those who have gone before and all those that will follow. These rites continue to elevate the ordinary individual to the status of warrior, bride, widow or priest. These roles (and the accompanying rituals such as weddings and wakes) are manifestations of the archetypes of myth. By participating in the ritual, we are participating in the myth.

Down through the ages the custodians of the traditional, instructive material of myth and legend have been the storytellers. They have held positions of great awe and reverence and were counted upon to remember the past and reveal the future. They were often thought, as in the case of the Shamanic traditions found in many places in the world (including the American Indian and Inuit in North America) to walk amongst the very gods and to have power over life and death (Eliade 1991: 26)

In all cases, in primitive times, the storyteller was not an ordinary individual and the stories were not told for entertainment but for instructional and transformational purposes. Myths were definitely not created by ordinary folk. They were the result of visions experienced by select individuals who had gone through a psychological crisis or collapse, most often in childhood (Jungian therapists often report the same images in the dreams of patients suffering from psychosis today. The difference is that we put these people in mental institutions!)

Their stories refer to psychological insights governed by natural environmental factors. The images of virgin births, great floods and resurrections are found in most mythological traditions and seem to be examples of what Jung refers to as a 'collective unconscious'. Keep in mind that these are symbolic images and are not to be taken as literal fact. To concretise the symbol is to lose its message. Mythology is a picture language and its goal is to transcend history and to let the mind open to the great mysteries of life and the universe. An example would be an initiation rite or baptism in which one 'dies' from a former life to 'resurrect' as a new being. You don't have to die physically of course. It is a spiritual death and one is reborn to a larger and hopefully more fulfilling way of living. We have seen examples of people who get caught in the symbol and end up sacrificing themselves or others because the symbol has been read literally.

One of the great problems of the Western mythic tradition is that we have concretised the symbols. Our myths have become euphemisms, dying from allegations of lies, our technology proving for example that sacred events such as Jesus rising bodily to heaven (even at the speed of light he would not be out of our galaxy yet) or our view of the earth as being the centre of the universe (Copernicus put this to rest in 1543 when he published his vision of the heliocentric universe), are emphatically false when viewed historically and has left our traditions mutilated, humbled minimised and/or condemned. In fact, from the nineteenth century onward mythic tradition fell into such disfavour that the public need for spiritual material went into a kind of 'underground' (Eliade 1991: 11)

Mythic symbolism was disguised in many pieces of literature. T. S. Eliot's *The Wasteland* (a reworking of the Grail legends from the twelfth century), Robert Browning's *Childe Roland to the Dark Tower Came* (towers are found in all mythic traditions, usually representing the central axis of the world) and James Joyce's *Ulysses* (a familiar mythic frame to express 'modern' and personal feelings) are all examples of archetypal images disguised as profane literature. There are hundreds more pieces that could be categorised in this vein. Even today, our novels and films abound with symbolic imagery – the search for paradise, the 'perfect' man or woman, the hero's quest, slaying the monster and life after death.

We can see that mythology still plays a dominant role in our lives and material that is rich in symbolism needs to be sought out and rediscovered. The question is, why do we need to tell these stories when television and film can do it for us?

First, a story told orally allows listeners to imagine the hero, the monster, the tower, in their own way. The symbolic figures will be painted according to the needs of the individual. How disappointed I remember feeling when the filmed version of a beloved tale did not match my own imagined one.

Second, there is a personalised feeling one receives when listening to a real person tell a story. There is a human connection; a thread sustained by eye contact and motivated by the audience's mood or reaction to the material.

Third, there can be audience participation. In the old days most of the stories were known by heart and the crowd was encouraged to join in on key phrases or on parts that were sung.

Fourth, many stories are meant to be shared orally and do not lend themselves well to the visual medium. I am thinking of those where 'gods' are represented or supernatural events occur. Sometimes the special effects of film are so 'special' that the symbolism is lost in favour of the effect!

Personally (as more and more people are channelled into sitting in front of computer screens) I feel the need for the oral tradition becomes almost imperative. Many of our children see more of teachers than they do of parents, and 'new technology' is making even this human contact less and less possible.

Storytelling has fallen on hard times and it will take great effort to restore it to its rightful place. When trying to resurrect the art, we must search for material that will hold meaning for today's audiences. The wonderful thing about most mythic stories is that they distance listeners from themselves and allow the symbols to work on the unconscious level. The listener identifies with the hero or heroine and can learn vicariously from the triumph over great obstacles and hardships that are experienced or the tragic ending that some characters face.

CHOOSING STORIES

> Men really need sea monsters in their personal oceans. . . . An ocean without its unnamed monsters would be like a completely dreamless sleep.
>
> (Steinbeck, quoted in Larsen 1991: 23)

Choosing stories is one of the most challenging tasks facing a teller. This is particularly true if the objective of the telling is work in special education, rehabilitation or health care settings on personal development or self-healing. I will endeavour to help identify some 'meaty' material and its uses in the next section.

Teaching stories

There exists in almost every tradition a body of instructional material known as 'teaching stories'. These have existed both in oral and written form for thousands of years. Examples that the reader may already be familiar with are Sufi, Zen and many Christian and Hasidic stories. These works are not to be confused with parables or fables, which although instructional in nature, tend to be more openly didactic with moralistic principles and values. True teaching stories do not preach. Their distinctive feature is that (although appearing to be simply entertaining) their inner content stays with you long after the story is done. Also, in some cases, the listener may not even be aware of external significance at all, until an event in their lives parallels the story in some way.

For this reason, using teaching stories tends to be a little like learning the procedures for fire safety. We review what to do, and this information is stored in order to be prepared in case a fire breaks out. However, fires do not happen every day. The knowledge of fire safety stays dormant in the brain until the need for it arises. The same applies to teaching stories. When something in life triggers its memory it gives insight into human behaviour and thought, and often points past the individual human act to a greater and deeper truth. They may be thought of as a kind of pattern of human response. We can hold them up against our own lives and get some sense of what 'fits' and what doesn't. Most teaching stories are very 'lean'. They do not make superfluous points or add unnecessary characters. They are pure protein for the inner mind. No fat, no cholesterol.

It is not the goal of teaching stories to give rational explanations for human behaviour. There is also no right way of interpreting these stories. No right answers. When working with a group, comments on the story should be confined to personal interpretations only – there should not be any commenting on other people's comments. All individual reactions are valid for the person who has them; all interpretations or feelings, true. It is often interesting to help participants in these sessions to look for patterns in their responses. For instance, similar reactions to similar characters or behaviour in a number of stories may point to the way in which the participant holds the world. The more opposed the reaction is, the more certain we can be that we have struck an important note.

It sounds as though teaching stories are extremely powerful tools. The job, then, is to identify teaching stories from other kinds of material.

Finding the story

First, there are books that are labelled teaching stories. Good libraries and bookstores can be helpful to find them.

Second, look for traditional material; this includes myths, legends and folktales. Generally speaking, the older the tale, the richer the inner content. If it were not so the tale would not have survived for so long. A good example of the kind of material that works well on both outer and inner contents is the 'trickster' tales of various traditions. Coyote, for instance, in North American Indian legends is a 'trickster' character. He is portrayed as a powerful, godlike figure one moment and a snivelling coward the next. The same kind of figure is also found in the Turkish stories of Nasreddin (there are various spellings). He also appears at different times as both a wise man and a fool or as a teacher or a student. Two other popular 'trickster' characters are Loki of the Norse mythology and Jack of the Appalachian mountains in the United States. Perhaps, in all of these characters we find the dualism found in ourselves and this is the reason these stories have remained so popular.

Another source for teaching stories is folktales. Not all are as rich as some of the above material. However, some stories do strike a chord. You can identify such a story if it stays with you after a few readings. Again, look for stories that do not preach but seem to speak of some inner truth.

Myths

Of course myths come under the heading of teaching stories as well. Some of these stories can be quite gruesome (witness many of the Greek myths as an example). However, in most cases there is a certain satisfaction in the fact that the characters in myth who show distinctive character flaws (greed, vanity or disobedience) receive what they deserve. These stories can spark great debate over whether the 'punishment' meted out was too severe or not. It is interesting that in the Greek tradition, as well as in many stories from the Christian faith, obedience is the main factor for punishment in the story. This is contrary to other traditions, such as Celtic, Norse and Germanic myths where disobedience often helps the character to grow in wisdom or strength.

Think of stories where there is a door that must not be opened at all cost. Yet the hero is placed in the position where *the door must be opened* in order for the kingdom to be saved or the elixir to be retrieved from evil hands. Telling a variety of myths from many traditions is a good way to find out with what basic belief system we identify.

Legends

Now, when speaking of legends, I am referring to stories that are usually based on historical figures in specific time periods. These characters are larger than life – these figures have been endowed with almost super-human qualities and are able to transcend ordinary human possibilities. Again they are essentially tutorial in nature and most often contain the same symbols as myths. The Grail legends of Sir Gawain and the Green Knight, King Arthur and Lancelot come to mind; also, tales of Robin Hood. It seems to matter little if the ultimate conclusion of the story shows the hero gaining a kingdom, a princess or some other reward. The final success is the culmination of a spiritual quest in which the individual (Robin Hood, for instance) against great odds (the Sheriff of Nottingham and his men) earns a sense of himself in terms of self-integration, wisdom and spiritual realisation (Robin becomes a man and takes his rightful place as leader of his people).

All of these sources are good ones for 'meaty' stories. The reader is encouraged to discover material from a variety of traditions and to choose from as wide a selection of stories as possible. Once you begin reading you will find that even some newspaper stories parallel the teaching stories you have been reading and are also excellent to use. Sometimes the line between life and art is indeed a very fine one!

Simple folk and fairy-tales

Now, some of the same symbols contained in myths and legends can be found in simple folk and fairy-tales. These stories are told primarily for entertainment and are not purposely designed to instruct the individual on matters of living with the order of nature, society and the universe. Most of these tales end happily and were the pastimes of simple folk whiling away the long days and nights long ago. Nevertheless, one can still discern mythological motifs within them. An example would be a character venturing deep into the forest who suddenly hears a voice or meets a 'helper' sometimes disguised as a bird or animal who points the way out of the woods.

These stories now are primarily for children, and can be looked upon as a form of children's mythology. Many of the tales are about initiation into adulthood expressed by killing dragons, crossing dangerous thresholds or getting past a place where one is 'stuck' in childhood (Snow White is an example of this – the little girl goes to sleep until the prince comes and awakens her womanhood).

Since these tales are not looked upon as 'real' events (Little Red Riding Hood is not a 'real' girl for instance) the symbols inherent in the material are able to do their work and can leave important subliminal messages for the psyche.

Many tales contain vestiges of primitive beliefs and customs. Super-natural tales, tales of animal magic and those fairies, gnomes and giants were all once contained in the myths of the past.

In his Commentary on *Grimm's Fairy Tales*, Joseph Campbell (1972: 863) states

> The folk tale is the primer of the picture language of the soul. . . . The tale survives furthermore, not simply as a quaint relic of days childlike in belief. Its world of magic is symptomatic of fevers deeply burning in the psyche: permanent presences, desires, fears, ideals, potentialities, that have glowed in the nerves, hummed in the blood, baffled the senses, since the beginning.

There are timeless images that we recognise, the young man going off to seek his fortune, the little girl pondering life while tossing a golden ball, the mother waiting for news of a son called to war, all these and more speak of the eternal cycle of life and of concerns that swirl in the deep waters of human memory.

Readers will find their own favourites. One can recognise a good story for telling when it calls to you repeatedly. These are the ones that need telling as, if they call to you, you can be sure they will appeal to others as well.

Telling teaching stories

As a rule, teaching stories should be repeated as faithfully to the original as possible. This is because the wording has been mulled over and perfected countless times to maximise impact. Try to stay with the vocabulary that is used and avoid improvising new situations or dialogue for the characters.

Another distinct difference between telling teaching stories and 'regular' stories is that teaching stories should be told with as little personal inflection, emphasis or judgment on the part of the teller as possible. The teaching story is told slowly so that the listeners are encouraged to work on personal insights without relying on the teller for clues. This takes a little getting used to as most of us want to make our tales lively and full of personality. This will work against the material in this case.

A cautionary note about these particular stories is not to tell too many in one session. They were originally designed to be told one at a time so that there would be ample time for reflection. I would suggest using only one or perhaps two in an hour session.

Home stories

Those who lived long before our day
Did not know how to store their words
In little black marks as you do
They could only tell stories
And they told many things
And therefore are not without knowledge
Of these those things which we have heard told
Many a time since we were little children.

(Rasmussen 1921: 16)

As mentioned before, there are two types of story, 'theirs' (teaching stories) and 'ours' (home stories). There are those that are carried in the myths, legends and folktales of a given society and there are those that are familial – told to us by parents and relatives. It is the latter 'home stories' – a term coined by Barton (1986) that we will deal with here.

Home stories form a substantial body of largely unconscious material that provide the framework for what we may recognise as personal identity. These are made up of an interwoven set of stories, rituals, customs and rites that shape our world view, often causing this view to be held uncritically, and give a sense of meaning and direction to our lives.

These informing myths, as Sam Keen calls them, have the power to propel individuals forward with confidence in their ability and a healthy perspective on their place in the world or they can stifle feelings of self-worth and leave people feeling powerless to change their fate. Home stories can give the illusion of 'no choice' for what is simply a judgment call.

We begin to receive these messages as children. Our ideas on self-worth, race, colour and creed are all a part of this body of knowledge. We learn whom to recognise as the good guys (our family, our country, our church), who are enemies (foreign leaders, politicians, big business), what is right (look before crossing the street, eat everything on your plate, love your mother), what is wrong (hitting, communism), who to fear (the boss, the law), and whom to imitate (daddy or mom). This information is absorbed and stored away in our unconscious and is called upon when important decisions need to be made. Statements such as 'That is the way it is', or 'You can't change things', or 'Welcome to the real world', are a reflection of such a perspective on the world. So is 'It's not like it was in the good old days.'

Of course the 'truths' of one family may not be shared by others. Dysfunctional families, for instance, often share an inherited view of reality that would seem abnormal to most. This view is very difficult to overcome in the face of other 'normal' situations since 'reality' is always shaped more on an unconscious level than a conscious one. The illusion of 'that's the way it is' is very strong and difficult to change.

As well as these family truths there are also the larger societal ones that help to form a larger accepted view of the world. Ours, in the Western tradition, assumes that values such as free enterprise, democracy and competition are fundamentally right. This largely unconscious assumption promotes both obedience and action without discrimination within this framework.

Thus status quo and time-worn 'truths' become sacred, almost holy. It can be seen that, unless there is a radical forced change to lifestyle, such as a world war or depression, society will stick to the proven path, even when change can be shown to be needed. (A good example of this is the struggle to revamp the educational system – a large segment of the population is still clinging to the 'back to basics' movement.) Marshall McLuhan refers to the phenomenon as 'a walk into the future while looking through a rear view mirror'. This picture is further complicated by the media of television and film.

People are bombarded psychologically by ideals. Fashion is dictated by soap operas and rock stars, eating habits by commercials. Heroes may be created and villains exposed. Sometimes, as in the case of dealings with foreign countries, people may be convinced that foreign leaders are the essence of evil one week and our trusted partner in the global village the next. This picture, obviously, can be very muddy and confusing to people struggling to find their identity and role in society.

Consider also the names of our main streets: everywhere we see examples of famous historical conquerors, generals, politicians and statesmen. Our informing myth of competition and hierarchy is very clear. There are very few poets, painters, musicians or storytellers on this list. One can understand the disillusionment in many young people when it begins to dawn on them that the Great North American Dream of fame, money and power is but an illusion for most and they are left awash in a sea of media-induced wants and needs.

It becomes increasingly clear as we reflect on the above, that stories (particularly those of childhood) need to be put into a kind of perspective in order to be dealt with objectively. For as Bernie Warren suggests 'From the day we are born our lives are enmeshed in story. The way we talk about ourselves and the way that others talk about us creates the story of our lives.'

James Hillman stresses the great significance of story awareness in childhood.

> To have had stories of any sort in childhood puts a person into a basic recognition of, and familiarity with, the legitimate reality of story per se. It is something given with life, with speech and communications, and not something later that comes with learning and literature. Coming early in life it is already a perspective on life. One integrates life as story because one has stories in the back of the mind (unconscious) as containers for organising events into meaningful experiences. The stories are means of finding oneself in events that might not otherwise make psychological sense at all.
>
> (Hillman 1989: 43)

So childhood conceptions are brought forward into adulthood and operate within our daily lives. I have been concerned, as an instructor of storytelling and storymaking, with uncovering these lost or buried pieces of the puzzle. In order to deal better with external struggles, it is often very helpful to understand the internal ones. This can bring new meaning to the term 'know thyself'.

The activities that I use to uncover lost stories are designed to shed light on otherwise forgotten material and the new or rediscovered insights to be helpful, eye-opening and often produce a feeling of nostalgia, empowerment and well-being.

TECHNIQUES FOR LEARNING AND SHARING STORIES

> From some point here, goddess, daughter of Zeus,
> speak and begin our story.
>
> (Homer 1967: 67)

We have previously discussed the telling of teaching stories, which has a separate technique from most other material. The next section concentrates on looking at the components of most other stories and gives some exercises to help develop skills to tell them.

General characteristics of story

Shape

All stories (with the exception of some North American Indian myths which have no real ending per se) have three basic sections; the beginning, middle and the end. Each has a specific function or goal.

The first section or 'act' establishes the setting for the story, introduces the main character, outlines the situation that propels the main character into action and sets up the outer motivation of the hero/heroine – what is to be achieved by the end of the story.

The second section builds the obstacles, impasses or conflicts that the main character must overcome. It is also the section where character development takes place. The last section contains the highest moment or climax of the story. The ending should also resolve whether or not the hero/heroine has met the objectives set out in section one.

Roughly speaking, the first section takes up about one quarter of the story, the middle section about half and the ending about one quarter. If you are telling a 10-minute story, then 2 minutes would be spent on the objectives of section one, 6 minutes on section two and 2 minutes on section three.

A visual image of this is shown below:

```
___1_____2_____3__
Establish     Build tension and characters     Resolve
```

Conflict

All stories have problems, conflicts or hurdles that the main character must face. Each of these must be made to seem greater and more difficult than the previous one. If the teller makes the first obstacle as overwhelming as the last, most difficult hurdle, without any break in the tension, the other obstacles become a land of anti-climax. The idea is to make each challenge a little more insurmountable than the last so that the tension of whether or not the main characters will reach their objective is maintained. This is represented in the graph on page 146.

Pacing

The momentum of the story must build steadily as the main character progresses towards the climax (usually the last most difficult obstacle of all). The pace must accelerate. This is done in two ways.

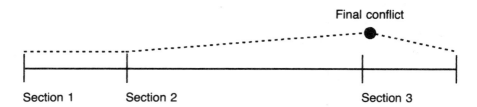

First, the gaps between hurdles or conflicts must become shorter and shorter. There is consequently less time for the listeners to 'catch their breath' ('catching breath' is very important and is discussed later).

Second, there should be an increase in the speed of delivery and an increase in the intensity of the voice. This is sometimes accompanied by a shortening of sentences which gives the illusion that the story is going faster.

Now, in order to maximise the impact of the final climax it is absolutely imperative that the listeners understand what is going on in the story. It is disastrous to have to stop and explain how the hero/heroine got into the mess in the first place. If this happens, it is usually because not enough attention was spent on section one. The accelerated pace will not be maintained if explanations are necessary at a crucial moment so be sure to emphasise the story set up and tell it slowly and carefully!

Creating highs and lows

A story told from beginning to end in a highly emotional tone will leave the listener emotionally uninvolved. This is because there is only so much emotional investment a person can give at a stretch.

Highly emotional moments must be balanced by ones with less emotional impact so that the audience has a chance to take a breath. Failure to do this creates a situation of over-stimulation where the audience becomes desensitised and emotionally distanced from the story. A plot where there is non-stop violence, for instance, becomes monotonous, even boring, if there is no break in the action. Think of each intense moment as needing a set up, a punch and a breather. The idea is to maximise each emotional segment and ensure the listener's emotional involvement. A roller coaster is a good image to remember here.

The finale

The climax of the story is that scene, usually found in the third section, where the hero/heroine meets the greatest obstacle. It is the highest emotional point of the story. It must be unambiguous to the listener. The hero/heroine either succeeds in achieving the goal or doesn't. Many beginning tellers writing their own stories spend a great deal of time developing the story line up to the highest climactic moment but fail to provide a satisfactory ending because the main motivation of the hero/heroine has been left unresolved. The audience must know at the onset what the character visibly or physically hopes to achieve or accomplish and this must be resolved satisfactorily and decisively at the end. This does not mean that all endings must be happy ones, it means that the audience needs to be clear as to whether the character met the objectives put forth at the beginning of the story.

Credibility

All stories have a kind of rule structure that must be adhered to in order for it to be believable or logical. Even stories of gods with super-powers have limitations within their unique universe.

The teller must make sure that the world where their characters reside appears to have a plausible structure. A character can't be dead one minute and alive the next, as an example, unless it is clearly spelled out that this is possible within the boundaries of the character's world.

Characters must talk and act within the limits of their powers and abilities and situations must appear logical. There must be compelling reasons why characters act as they do or the listener will disengage from the story or will not stay in emotional accord with the character. This is why it is critical to outline the setting and the abilities of the characters early in the story. Remember, even Superman has his weakness and this is what makes him an engaging and sympathetic hero.

The story in pictures

I find it helpful to 'see' the story as a series of snapshots. I make a set of pictures in my mind that gives me the order of the scenes. Then it is quite easy to flesh out the action around each picture. I also list words or phrases that I associate with each picture or episode and create an outline for each story; creating enough to jog the memory. The idea is to keep this outline short so that remembering it does not become more of a chore than learning the story! I most emphatically suggest that with the exception of teaching stories, the teller *does not memorise* the story. Memorising can be disastrous since a forgotten line or phrase can make the mind go completely blank leaving the teller truly at a loss for words. The teller should also be free to add details to the story, as previously shown. This is what makes storytelling such an appealing form. The story is new each time the teller begins.

However, I do suggest that the first line be memorised (just to get the teller started with confidence) and also the last line (many tellers find it difficult to end a story satisfactorily). In this way, the teller is able to bring both personality, style and response to the audience, to bear on the body of the tale.

Physicalising the story

One interesting way of practising a story is to work on it as though it were a physical exercise. The objective of the following exercises, based on Laban's (1975) principles for understanding the quality and range of the body's movement, is to make the storyteller as fluent and flexible in the use of body and voice as possible. Laban's techniques, which involve looking at human movement along the continuums of time, space, force and flow, are widely used for the training of dancers and theatre students.

Below are some adaptations of these exercises to help tellers visualise the 'motion' found within the story.

Time

All stories happen within a certain time-frame. As an example, a story may take place over the space of several hours, days or years. The story has a specific entry point where we meet the hero/heroine and a specific destination or ending point.

We want to maximise impact in certain sections (the hurdles or conflicts referred to previously) as we go along, and we also want the plot to move at an accelerated pace as the hero/heroine meets the final climax and proceeds to the final moments of the story.

Try the following exercises and keep in mind a story you are presently working on.

1 Walk at a normal pace around the room. Notice that your heartbeat is steady and regular. Your body should feel relaxed, unhurried. Increase the pace slightly and notice the feeling even this slight step up in momentum gives the body. Build up speed until you are moving as fast as you can without running. Notice the tension in your arms and upper body.
2 Now stop and start with quick, sudden bursts (it is a good idea to have one participant use a drum beat to indicate the stopping and starting). What sensation do you now feel in the body? What effect does this type of pace have on your heartbeat?
3 Return to normal pace and then slowly decrease your movement until you are going at the slowest possible pace without stopping. What kind of feeling are you now experiencing?

Keeping these exercises in mind it can be seen that combinations of a sustained or increased pace in your story possibly using intermittent pauses or slowing down can dramatically affect the body's involuntary response to it.

Try doing the same exercises vocalising a nonsense syllable like 'aah' as you move. As your pace increases let the volume of your voice become more intense.

This kind of variation is what the storyteller is trying for within the story. Remember that the teller's body language, the signs that this is a stressful moment, is 'read' by the audience and is as important as the words themselves. As for when to use a sustained or increased pace refer back to the section on the shape of a story.

Space

Another concept directly related to that of time is that of space. All stories take up a certain amount of space. Some move along directly to the point with a sparse amount of extraneous detail as though in a rather narrow band and others tend to meander, picking up threads of other characters, using detailed descriptions of settings or objects and sometimes recounting 'asides' or adjunct stories about the main characters that may add to our understanding of their motives or actions.

In order to physicalise this try the following exercises. It is always up to the teller which technique will be used. No matter which one is chosen, both need to be well under control.

1 Pick a point in the room. Focus on it ignoring all other objects around it. Go there directly without losing sight of your objective. Do not let anything else catch your interest.
2 Now, try going across the room to a new point. This time, however, allow your eyes to be caught by different objects or colours. Focus on this for a little while, even moving towards the new focus before returning to your objective. Take your time and don't feel that you are being rushed.

Some stories, those with a moral, for instance, often have a very narrow focus both in the meaning itself and in the language used to propel the story. It is like the first exercise which is very controlled and purposeful. Some other tales, such as those from the Irish tradition, are the opposite. The story seems to 'meander' off the point now and then as we learn more about the 'root to Paddy's problems' for instance or as details are added in order to keep the story from advancing too quickly. Do not be fooled into thinking that the meandering technique is an excuse to just improvise instead of planning the story carefully! Just as you would have to 'map' out the route you took in the second exercise in order to repeat it the storyteller too must carefully plan all 'asides' or added information. Any extraneous material must be designed to add to the impact of the story.

Both techniques take practice. Remember that too much meandering can obscure the hero's motivation and the point of the story can become lost.

Force

Every story needs to be considered in terms of force. By this I mean the impact of the story on the listener. Is it subtle and light, like the touch of a feather, or blunt and heavy.

Much of the control of this has to do with the teller's body language and use of voice. Is the teller conveying the tension in the story by lightening their own voice and muscles or is the body and voice in 'neutral'?

To get an idea of the difference try this.

1 Try tightening your muscles slowly to the slow beat of a drum. As the drummer increases the pace, tighten more. When the drummer produces one final loud beat, crumple to the floor allowing the tension to flow from your body.

   This is how the set up, 'punch' and breather mentioned previously works. The set up includes an increase in tension in both body and voice. The tension and intensity of voice rises to a peak or climax and then decreases once the climactic moment is passed so that the listeners are allowed to rest. Remember the roller coaster ride!

2 Try moving around the room now as if gravity were of no concern. Picture yourself physically rising up on each step. Think of the air in your lungs and arteries turning to helium. It rises up through the top of your head to escape. If you give sound to this you will probably notice the sound is centred in your head somewhere behind the eyes. There are stories where a 'far away' feeling is needed either for characterisation purposes or as a way for the teller to speak in a detached manner. Visualising this exercise may be helpful while telling in order to recreate this feeling of 'lightness' both for yourself and the audience.

3 The final exercise under *force* is to explore strong, firm, slashing motions. Move around the room taking great strides. Notice your body's commitment to each stroke and the abrupt end to each movement. Add sounds to the strokes. Try to see where this technique might be used to enhance the movement of a story. How could it be used in a fast-paced action story with lots of excitement for instance?

Flow

The last of the four areas to explore is that of flow. This element is very much connected to the qualities of space and force and time.

I like to think of flow as the kind of control the teller exercises on the other aspects above.

Consider these two polar opposites.

1 *Bound flow*. Remember the exercise of crossing the room directly, without distraction? Try this same exercise but imagine you are doing so while balancing a tray of very expensive glasses filled with champagne. Even though your ultimate focus remains the same and the time it takes to cross is roughly equal, the control of the body is very different. Without the tray, it is quite relaxed as you cross, arms swinging at your sides perhaps. As soon as the tray is added, tension is also added.

2 *Free flow*. Contrast this above exercise with this: try turning the body, slowly at first, in a circling motion. Increase the speed until you feel the impetus of the outward pull on the body. When the energy is at its peak allow the movement to run out until it is spent or is stopped by something else (such as the wall or if you spin downward, the floor). In free flow, the movement is not controlled as in bound flow. Try adding sound to these two exercises.

The teller must decide which kind of story they are telling. Does it need the teller to appear very controlled from beginning to end or would a seemingly more improvised style (as though the story has a momentum of its own) be better? I like to think of the first one as a kind of precision march and the second as a dance. Generally, myths and many folktales require the first while fantasy stories and humorous stories especially with chase scenes require the second.

All four of the above elements are important, particularly with beginning tellers. Vocalising the exercises is also very good, since many people are timid about using the range of their own voices. Exercises help to break down these barriers in an 'acceptable' format where no one is being put on the spot.

Gesture

A further area that I would like to mention is the teller's use of gestures. The teller must bring to life all of the characters, the setting and plot and theme for each story. Marie Shedlock, one of the great old tellers, speaks of the teller as reproducing a miniature theatrical production. When looking at a telling in this light, it is obvious that gestures would be an integral part of the overall effect of the story. Gestures must be used to enhance the story and should not detract from it. Nervous groping at buttons, tapping of feet or pacing and fidgeting while telling can draw so much attention that the actual story is lost. Be aware of body language and the use of the hands. Let gestures arise naturally from the story. Some tellers are more animated than others. This should not be stifled but should be under control.

These are a few of the components that make for a successful storytelling experience. These can be mastered by the reader and then shared with their own groups of beginning tellers. The main caution is to go slowly and enjoy the reactions that occur when a story is well told. Each success will encourage the teller to risk longer and longer stories and with a little practice a fairly extensive repertoire can be built up.

Storytelling is an art but with a little dedication it is accessible to everyone.

> Bow bended, my story's ended;
> If you don't like it, you may mend it.
>
> (Old ending for fairy-tale)

Techniques for sharing home stories

> The life of a man is a circle;
> From childhood to childhood;
> and so it is in everything where power moves . . .
> Everything the power of the world does
> is done in a circle.
>
> (in Neihardt 1961: 198)

One of the great causes of difficulties for people today, I feel, is brought about by our emphasis on becoming something other than what we already are. It seems that we are never good enough, smart enough, rich enough, beautiful enough or happy enough. There always is more that we must do or be in order to attain personal fulfilment. Consequently, the value of our lives as they are, the experiences we have had, are often viewed as rather dull or, at best, not terribly 'significant'. Countless times I have asked beginning storytelling groups, particularly teenage and young adults, to share a little about themselves only to receive the 'my life is really dull' or 'nothing exciting has ever happened to me' or 'I have nothing to tell' response. This seems to me to be extremely significant. How can one find meaning in one's life if one doesn't see anything of significance or value in it?

One of the great importances of sharing home stories is to bring to light the experiences that shape us and to *give them significance* and hence meaning. Home stories also promote, as shown previously, a new understanding of these stories as the foundation of a unique view of the world, our own personal sense of 'reality'.

Beginnings

When beginning with a group about to examine home stories, I try to establish a trust level and intimacy that will allow for more personal material to be shared. I do this in two ways: first, by sharing one or two of my own personal stories, usually in a lighthearted vein to show that even the leader is human!; second, by encouraging participants to share details about themselves that, while very low-key and non-threatening in detail brings about a personal knowledge of each member. The following activity, popular with many storytelling animators, is a good one to begin with.

I am

We all receive a name at birth and this is a great place to start telling home stories. Perhaps we are called after uncle Herbert, our mother's favourite brother, or the doctor who delivered us. Maybe our name means 'strength' or 'steadfast' or 'one who loves horses' in another language. It could be that a middle name is a former last name of a grandmother or great-grandmother. Finding out about and sharing information about names and family gives all members of the group both something in common and something unique to share with others.

There is something very special about knowing personal details about someone. It seems that by sharing, a bond is established. Perhaps this is because we only share information about ourselves with those who are meaningful to us in some way. The following activities lay a foundation of acceptance and belonging for later work.

1 To stimulate interest and to help those who have no access to such information, bring in books of name definitions – both given and surnames. Allow time for research and informal sharing. Later, let each person relate what they learned or already know about their names to a partner. This may further be increased to groups of four, each person telling about their partner, rather than about themselves.
2 Individuals may also bring in a family heirloom or an object that holds significance of some kind for their family. Again, these may be shared with a partner or in small groups (no more than five).
3 A third activity is to try to find out a little about their family history – the country of origin for instance or an anecdote about a grandparent. (Remember that we are keeping it simple at this point, no need to write a lengthy tale or make it 'perfect'. We are only trying to build a sense of sharing within the group.)

In all cases keep these little beginning story fragments short and confine the sharing to one to four people – whole-group sharing can be very intimidating to first-time tellers especially those who feel isolated or powerless in their daily lives.

Now, there may be some members of the group who do not have (or cannot share for some reason) any history of their names or family or find it difficult to talk about themselves at all. Perhaps their background is so troubled that they need to develop confidence to face it themselves. In these and all cases, participants should not be pushed to share information if they are not ready to do so. In these first activities it is sometimes enough for some just to look up their name origins in the book and to share the information. The more accepting the animator is of the individual's freedom to choose what is to be shared, the sooner these participants will feel safe enough to reveal more details about themselves.

My house

One of my favourite means of uncovering details of stories to do with the past is based on an activity I discovered in a book called *Telling Your Story* by Sam Keen and Anne Fox.

This involves giving each person a very large piece of squared paper and asking them to draw a floor plan (the inside) of the very first house they clearly remember living in.

It should include doors, windows, closets and cupboards. They are encouraged to remember the kind of furniture wallpaper and floor coverings that were in this house as well as any other details that made the house 'special'.

Many people also include the garden and garage if there was one as well.

Here are some questions that will stimulate memories while doing this activity.

1 What was your favourite room? Why?
2 Did you have a favourite hiding place?
3 What room if any was 'off limits'?
4 What window gave the best view?
5 What room do you associate with 'family' activities?
6 Did you have a best friend? Where did you play?

Each person writes down snatches of ideas as they spring up right on the paper after the floor plan is complete. This activity may take one session or may be worked on over a series depending on the interest of the group. The result is a rich supply of story fragments that may be shared in small groups or with the group as a whole. Some of these may be developed into a longer story for sharing as well.

I have seen participants become so absorbed in this 'house collage' that they actually research pieces of wallpaper and textures of materials on sofas and chairs and bring in samples to accompany their drawings. Others cut facsimiles from old catalogues and paste them in place. No matter how it is rendered, this activity always sparks a wealth of personal stories and it is gratifying to watch as some hidden or obscure memory suddenly surfaces and a group member eagerly shares an insight into the past.

School days

For most of us, the first formal introduction into the *laws* of our society comes when we enter school for the first time. It is here that Personal Freedom often takes a back seat to the Common Good and we learn to rate our performance in the light of that of other people.

Most of us have both good and bad memories of school days and these tend to be quite vivid as they represent the first dealings with 'outside' authority figures, new exciting experiences, fears and frustrations and formal routine. Much of who we turn out to be and how we view education in general stems from this time.

Some of the attitudes of older participants can also be clearly related to this period. 'If it was good enough for me, it's good enough for my child', or conversely, 'I hated school. I want my children to enjoy it.' Some see it as a kind of initiation that must be endured in order to reach adulthood. 'I got the strap lots of times when I was in school, but I survived it.'

I like to bring people back to their earliest recollections of school. With some groups, I use the same technique as in the House activity, having them create a map of their school, their route home, favourite game to play on the way to and from school, etc. A floor plan of one particular school room is also an interesting place to begin as is a physical description of a teacher who stands out in their minds in some way (either because they were exceptionally mean or exceptionally nice).

Here are some questions to help focus the group:

1 Do you remember the first time you were in trouble at school?
2 Who was your favourite teacher?
3 Who was the meanest teacher?
4 Did you ever 'skip' school in favour of another activity?
5 What games did you play during free time?
6 Who was your best friend?
7 Were you ever picked on by others? Did you ever pick on anyone else?
8 What rules do you remember from this time?

There is usually a great deal of discussion around this topic and these story fragments are once again very rich in detail. Some people elect to write those memories down in a kind of diary and these in turn often trigger other remembrances as well (such as vacation times, after-school activities and field trips).

Heroes and villains; friends and enemies

Many of those figures whom we consider to be heroic or villainous are a consequence of a kind of societal consensus as we have seen. Still, it is often quite revealing to go back and look at who was held up to us by our family as either a pillar of society or as an example of evil.

We may often gain insight into our value system, beliefs and prejudices (either conscious or unconscious) by examining our past.

1 Who did your parents hold as examples of good citizens?
2 Who did they discourage or forbid you to play with?
3 What causes or ideas were championed in your house?
4 Do you remember any incidents that involved prejudice of some kind?
5 What behaviour was frowned upon? (Either by members of the family or by neighbours, friends, etc.)
6 Who was your hero/heroine?
7 What qualities did you admire in them?
8 Does this still hold true today?
9 Who was your best friend?
10 Who was your enemy? Why?

There are many topics under Home Stories that could be examined in the above manner. These include Religion, Fantasies and Dreams, Fears (superstitions, strange events, first public performance, first time away from home, etc.), initiations (first dates, dares, forbidden places) and deaths (pets, relatives).

When dealing with Home Stories, it is not really important that they are told 'the right way'. The emphasis in fact is in the discovery process and on the personal insight that comes from uncovering the hidden story. It will be less inhibiting to both the teller and the listener if the structure for sharing the tales remains loose and above all non-judgmental in format. The stories should be allowed to flow freely for their own sake.

Sometimes tales of surprising clarity and quality are brought forth and, of course, these are a welcome gift; but it is the spirit of the tales that bind the group, leaving everyone with a sense of discovery and insight into the complex forms of human nature and behaviour.

Stories just for fun

They all lived happy
and died happy,
and never drank out
of a dry cappy.

(Old Arabian tale)

We have seen that stories have great power. They point to connections between the past and the present and can inform us of our innermost feelings, fears and hopes.But what about telling just for the fun of it? This is probably the best reason of all to share stories!

Here are some of the activities that I have used in my own sessions for no other reason than to share 'em.

The tall tale

A tale is an exaggerated story that is intended to make the listener laugh. A good way to give beginning tellers the idea of how a tale might grow out of proportion is as follows. Ask three volunteers to leave the room.

Have the rest of the group seated in a circle and tell the following little story:

> Once there was a man who was not used to country living who came to visit a cowboy way out west.
>
> One day he was out for a walk when he came upon a snake pinned down by a boulder that had rolled off a cliff. He released the rattler (for it was a rattle snake) and won its eternal gratitude. It followed him like a pet dog everywhere he went and even slept at the foot of his bed at night.
>
> One night, the man awoke with a start, feeling something was wrong. The snake was missing from its accustomed place. The man went out to the kitchen, feeling a draft from that direction. Sure enough, the window was open and there was the snake with its body tightly wrapped around a burglar, with its tail hanging out the window, rattling for help!

Ask one volunteer to come back into the room. Let someone who just heard the story retell it. The first volunteer then retells it to the second volunteer who has been brought back into the room and then the second repeats the story to the third volunteer. The third volunteer tells the story a final time to the group.

It is interesting to notice:

1 how different each version is from the last and whether details are altered;
2 the choice of words each teller uses;
3 whether the teller uses a dialect to embellish the story;
4 if the punch line stays the same in successive tellings.

Liar, liar, pants on fire

This activity encourages the participants to really exaggerate the details of their stories. The idea is to take a perfectly normal activity such as getting up in the morning or eating lunch and to exaggerate it all out of proportion.

I usually ask the participant to recount either that morning's activities, something that has happened to them recently or something they saw happening to someone else. There is no particular order to the tellings; each volunteer begins where the last person left off, trying to connect the story in some way to the previous one.

For example, if the last tale was about a really bad start to the day, the next teller could begin by saying, 'Hah! you think that was a bad morning? Listen to this', and then tell the tale. In this way, the tellings become a kind of collective, flowing from one story to the next.

The tellers should also be encouraged to have a reason for telling the story. For instance, it might be to make the audience feel sorry for them or to make them laugh or to make them believe they have super-human qualities!

Super Man, Wonder Woman

Ask the group to tell what attributes they associate with super heroes. Share these informally in round-robin fashion. Each person should now imagine a super hero of personal choice and 'become' that person. He or she may be in disguise during the day as an ordinary individual, but at night or in times of crisis turns into . . .

Give them one of the following situations to build the story around (they could also make up their own if they wish).

1 There are thieves breaking into a bank in the middle of the night. Tell how you foil their plans.
2 There is a damsel in distress. She is floating down a fast-flowing river on a log. There is a waterfall around the next curve. Tell how you bring her to safety.
3 There is a giant earthquake or volcano eruption and the government call on you to stop it. Tell how you save the day!

I knew her when

Tell the following little poem:

> There was a maid on Scrabble Hill
> And if not dead she lives there still
> She never drank, she never lied,
> She never laughed, she never cried.

Ask participants in small groups of three or four to do the following activities:

1 Write down what they know about the maid. These are facts they can glean from the poem.
2 Write down what questions they might have that are not answered in the poem.
3 Write down who might know the answers to their questions (i.e. neighbours, relatives, friends, etc.).
4 Now ask one person in each group to become the person they would

most like to question. Let the rest be reporters, historians, police officers or someone else who might be interested in the maid. Let each group have about five or six minutes to question their 'witness' then elect one person to report their findings to the group.

5 Each group can then prepare a group telling of what they think is the real story behind the poem of the maid. They should do this in a round-robin fashion where each person tells a portion of the completed tale. These tales are then shared with the whole group.

It is fun to work with existing dialogue, script or printed material and then to find the hidden story lurking just underneath the surface. The same technique as that used above works well with portions of novels. I try to take a section from a book that leaves lots of questions unanswered. It can be right at the beginning of the story or at the climax. There is no right or wrong of course. The participants are free to tell the story based on the story fragment in their own way. It is often interesting to go back and read the original book to see the author's version!

POSTSCRIPT

Be what you is, cuz if you be what you ain't,
Then you ain't what you is
(Epitaph to a Gunslinger, Boothill Cemetery, Tombstone, Arizona)

Throughout this chapter on storymaking and storytelling I have tried to show the great value, even the need, of sharing stories, both our own and those of others.

We live in interesting times where technological advancements and artificial intelligence make it difficult sometimes to remember our humanity.

Through the reawakening of the inner mind, through storytelling, we participate in our common heritage and come to sense the fundamental mysteries of being, in which we all share. The activation of our imaginative life, the life that is inside, is one of the most challenging tasks open to us, both personally and professionally.

If our technology is an expression of our intelligence then our stories are an expression of our soul.

The balance lies somewhere between.

SUGGESTED READING

Anderson, H. C. (1861) *Danish Fairy Legends and Tales* (translated by Caroline Peachey), Henry G. Bohn, London.

Arkhurst, J. C. (1964) *The Adventure of Spider: West African Folk Tales*, Little Brown and Co., Boston.

Barton, B. (1986) *Tell Me Another*, Pembroke Publishers Ltd., Markham, Ontario.

Bettelheim, B. (1989) *The Uses of Enchantment*, Random House, New York.

Campbell, J. (1949) *The Hero With a Thousand Faces*, Bollingen Series XVII, Princeton University Press, New York.

Campbell, J. (1972) 'Folkloric Commentary', in *The Complete Grimm's Fairy Tales*, Pantheon Books, New York.

Campbell, J. (1990) *The Hero's Journey*, Harper & Row, New York.

Chase, R. (1943) *The Jack Tales*, Houghton Mifflin Co., Cambridge, MA.

Curtis, N. (1907) *The Indian's Book: An Offering by the American Indians of Indian Lore, Musical and Narrative to Form a Record of the Songs and Legends of Their Race*, Harper & Brothers, New York.

Eliade, M. (1974) *The Myth of the Eternal Return*, Princeton University Press, New York.

Eliade, M. (1991) *Images and Symbols*, Princeton University Press, New Jersey.

Erdoes, R. and Ortiz, A. (1984) *American Indian Myths and Legends*, Pantheon Books, New York.

Feldmann, S. (1965) *The Storytelling Store: Myths and Tales of the American Indian*, Dell Publishing, New York.

Gersie, A. and King, N. (1990) *Storymaking in Education and Therapy*, Jessica Kingsley Publications, London.

Grimm, J. and Grimm, W. (1972) *The Complete Grimm's Fairy Tales*, Pantheon Books, New York.

Hamilton, E. (1942) *Mythology*, Little Brown and Company, Boston.

Hillman, J. (1989) 'A Note on Story', *Parabola*, iv(4): 43.

Homer (1967) *The Odyssey* (Lattimore translation), Harper & Row, New York.

Keen, S. and Fox, A. (1989) *Telling Your Story*, Tarcher, Los Angeles.

Laban, R. (1975) *Modern Educational Dance*, MacDonald & Evans, London.

Larsen, S. R. (1991) *A Fire in the Mind: The Life of Joseph Campbell*, Doubleday, New York.

Neihardt, J. G. (1961) *Black Elk Speaks*, Nebraska Press, Lincoln, NE.

Opie, I. and Opie, P. (1974) *The Classic Fairy Tales*, Oxford University Press, Oxford.

Perrault, C. (1957) *Fairy Tales of Charles Perrault* (translated by Geoffrey Brereton), Penguin Books, Harmondsworth, Middlesex.

Ransome, A. (1968) *Old Peter's Russian Tales*, Thomas Nelson, London.

Rasmussen, K. (1921) *Eskimo Folk Tales* (edited and translated by W. Worster), Glyldendal, London.

Rosen, B. (1988) *And None of It Was Nonsense*, Scholastic Tab Publications, Richmond Hill, Ontario.

Sawyer, R. (1970) *The Way of the Storyteller*, Penguin Books, New York.

Shah, I. (1979) *World Tales*, Harcourt Brace Jovanovich, New York.

Shedlock, M. L. (1951) *The Art of the Storyteller*, Dover Publications Inc., New York.

Steinbeck, J. (1982) *The Log of the Sea of Cortez*, Mount Vernon, Appel, New York.

Wilson, B. K. (1989) *Scottish Folktales and Legends*, Oxford University Press, New York.

Zipes, J. (1983) *Fairy Tales and the Art of Subversion*, Weldman, New York.

Chapter 10

Creating community
Ensemble performance using masks, puppets and theatre

Wende Welch

Anyone who has ever worked in the theatre will say that the experience is anything but private. Creating theatre involves many people working together, ultimately to communicate something to someone else. Theatre cannot exist for and of itself; it is only complete when it is performed for an audience. It depends on human interaction.

In this way, theatre can be seen as a microcosm of life itself. Just as we weave in and out of the events, crises and victories that occur in our lives, so too does the theatre artist. The agents of these events comprise the many relationships we are constantly building, maintaining or destroying throughout life's journey. Though the relationships between characters in a play may seem contrived, this should not lead us to believe that they are any less valid than our real life relationships.

The appeal of the theatre lies in the desire to witness and experience the mystery of human survival in extraordinary circumstances. The actors commit to the playing of their parts for an audience who wants to see them succeed. The pursuit of human achievement, reaching and perhaps surpassing one's potential, offers the participant and the spectator an opportunity to unite and celebrate the joy of life. In this way, theatre demands a sense of community for its success. It requires the joint effort of individuals coming together to pursue a common goal.

The arts serve this purpose by enabling an individual – or group of individuals – to express themselves, to communicate their ideas through whatever medium they choose. Providing the opportunity for this self-expression places responsibility on the community to expose individuals to the various forms of art. The chance for individuals to enrich their lives through artistic endeavours not only stimulates personal growth but also builds confidence through a sense of achievement. The result is a community that benefits from such capable and functioning members.

Theatre is a medium that can be used to create an environment where 'integration' can occur.[1] The collaborative nature of theatre lends itself to the exploration of artistic expression as a collective. This is what many theatre artists refer to as 'ensemble'. Ensemble means 'together'. The spirit of ensemble implies an unselfish support for the others with whom one works in harmony. The strength of a group is only as strong as its individuals. When integrating persons with disabilities into a theatrical environment, I have found that creating an ensemble proves both a necessity and a boon for all involved.[2] Under such circumstances, the combined efforts and talents of the collective ideally balance out to involve, as well as serve the immediate needs of, each individual within the group.

Ensemble theatre can be used effectively in an integrated setting as an aid to increased self-expression, and therefore self-awareness. In addition, imagine how such exploration might affect the individual's involvement in the greater community in which they live.

MASK AND PUPPETRY

Masks and puppets can be any inanimate object brought to life through human effort before an audience.[3] They both belong to a family of theatre animation that has existed for centuries in many different cultures. The dramatic function of mask and puppetry is not unlike any other performing art form. Essentially, it strives for communication between performer and audience: the actor, musician, dancer, singer or puppeteer shares something with the spectator, who in turn responds, thus reinforcing the will of the performer to communicate. This creates a constant cycle of exchange that unites the performer and audience. The success of a performance depends on the degree to which both performer and audience are willing to accept and commit to this interaction. The result is a shared human experience on many levels: intellectually, physically, spiritually and emotionally.

However, where some performing art forms might achieve this experience based on a subjective approach, mask and puppetry choose an objective presentation to fulfil the same function. For example, an actor playing a character in a play will elicit a different response from each audience member simply because human beings see other human beings differently. Their responses to the actor's appearance, the sound of his or her voice, the way he or she uses his or her body, and how he or she makes use of these to play the character will naturally vary according to personal taste. However, a mask or a puppet has one expression; it intends to capture the essence of an emotion or character trait. The audience immediately distinguishes the 'good' character from the 'evil' character. Mask and puppetry operate on less sophisticated principles, thereby making the theatrical convention easier to accept. This is directly responsible for the success of mask and puppetry with both children and adults.

The art of mask and puppetry mirrors that of the theatre, but adds another level. Discovering the reality of the inanimate object – the mask or the puppet – goes beyond using only one's body and voice to communicate with an audience. The performer must develop a relationship with the mask or puppet to breathe life into it. This should not be mistaken for 'hiding' behind the mask or puppet, using it as a crutch, transferring the responsibility for any action or thought on to the object itself. It is up to the performer to explore fully the potential of the mask or puppet: what is it capable of doing, feeling and saying? The answers to these questions lie in the ability of the performer to objectify the emotion of the character. Only then will the mask or puppet speak and delight its audience; when bond between actor and mask or puppeteer and puppet is an organic one, and therefore imperceptible.

Theatre with mask and puppetry can aid in building a sense of ensemble in an integrated setting. The first step involves learning to relate to an inanimate object. For those with certain developmental disabilities, this may come easier than having to relate to another human being. For others with severe physical disabilities, such interaction may only be possible with the help of other members of the group. Through 'playing', relationships begin to form as communication occurs between the individuals and the masks or puppets. Discovering the character of the mask or puppet requires the individual to explore imaginative ways of using their body and voice. This may lead to increased self-awareness and the confidence to express oneself. In an integrated group setting, participation fluctuates between doing, helping and observing. A sense of ensemble grows as individuals begin to trust and support one another. All of this work must ultimately serve the final step – the performance. Such a challenge rewards each individual with pride in their achievement. The discovery and realisation of the individual's contribution to the whole has involved the group in reaffirming the need to create community.

WORKSHOPS

The following are suggested activities designed to 'warm up' the individual's voice and body, in preparation for the creative work to follow. The warm-up should be a group activity, as a sense of ensemble must be implemented from the beginning. In an integrated group setting, all workshop activities may require assigning individuals to assist those with a disability. In such cases, the focus of the exercises become an investigation of how to help one another to perform the given task together.

Voice[4]

When warming up the voice, try to incorporate exercises that stimulate the body as well as the mind. For our purposes in the theatre, and specifically with mask and puppetry, emphasis should be placed on breath support, amplification of sound using the various vocal resonators, and the articulation of thoughts and feelings organically. The voice is inside the body; we release it when we feel the need to express ourselves.

Breath support begins with an awareness of the body. Ideally, the skeleton acts against gravity to support the body, relieving the muscles of that duty, leaving them free for movement. When this occurs, the breathing musculature responds freely, providing a more efficient support for the voice. Try rolling up and down the spine. Roll the head, shoulders and arms; raising and releasing arms, elbows and wrists – all with an increased awareness of the breath moving freely in the body.

Allow those with limited physical capabilities to work within their own range of movement. If they require assistance, encourage one or two other members of the group to help guide that individual through the exercises by gently moving the head, shoulders, arms and wrists for them. Working together in this way should only be attempted with the consent of the individual and if there's no risk of jeopardising their physical condition. Avoid rolling down the spine; similar results can be arrived at by having someone cradle the back of the individual's head and jaw in their hands, while another supports the upper arms. Gently lift the head and arms straight up, allowing the spine to 'hang' and the muscles around it to relax. Note increased awareness and freedom of the breathing muscles.

Humming provides a gentle means for waking up the resonators in the body, face and head. Feel the voice rumble, buzz or ping in various parts of the body while collecting vibrations on the lips. Then open the mouth and release the sound. Use vivid images that excite the mind and involve the voice and body in play: animals, insects, vehicles, industrial noise, carnival sounds, etc. Encourage interaction during these exercises.

Articulation implies clear speech. However 'correct' pronunciation won't move an audience without clear thought behind it. This point proves doubly vital for mask and puppetry, where articulation governs the animation of the mask or puppet. Effective communication through a mask or puppet requires precise speech and movement. Developing a sense of rhythm can help achieve this. Singing, preferably accompanied by some movement or dance, offers a comprehensive warm-up and unites the group. Here, you may choose to divide the group into smaller groups of twos, threes or fours, creating a less awkward and crowded environment for the sake of integrating with those individuals with a physical disability or those who have a visual disability. Singing in rounds offers an ideal warm-up for an integrated group and could prove a less threatening activity for those with developmental disabilities who need extra encouragement.

Body

A gentle stretch should precede and follow any physical activity. Animating a mask or a puppet for the first time may painfully awaken muscles one never dreamed one had. Pay particular attention to the neck, shoulders, arms, wrists, hands, fingers, waist, lower back and calves. Again, offer physical assistance to those who ask for it, within their range of movement capability.

The following simple playground game is a thorough actor's warm-up in disguise. It sharpens listening and memorisation skills, stimulates the body to respond to changing circumstances, builds concentration, hand–eye co-ordination and physical stamina – and is fun!

Water babies[5]

For this a soft ball, approximately 10 cm in diameter is required. In a circle, each individual in the group calls out a number, beginning with one. This number becomes theirs for the game and they will need to remember it, as well as those of the others. (If you chose to use this game in an orientation session, you may wish to substitute names for numbers.) To begin the game, one individual stands in the centre of the circle, throws the ball straight up into the air, and calls out a number (not their own). The individual whose number was called must now catch the ball: if they catch it, they throw the ball back into the air, calling out a new number; if they miss it, they must first retrieve the ball and then call 'freeze'. When someone has missed the ball, the others in the group must flee to the perimeter of the defined play area before that individual calls 'freeze'. Once 'freeze' is called, the others must stop and remain motionless. Fixed to the very spot from which they called 'freeze', the caller must now throw the ball at one of the 'frozen' others: if the ball touches someone, that someone is given a 'water baby' and must begin the game again from the centre of the circle; if the ball touches no one, the individual who called 'freeze' is given a water baby and must begin the game again from the centre of the circle. Once an individual has received three water babies, they are out of the game. Water babies are also given to an individual who calls the number of someone who is out of the game or who calls their own number.

Water babies can be adapted for an integrated group. Have those who have a visual disability play the game hand in hand with a seeing individual, sharing the ball-tossing and catching responsibilities. Those with physical disabilities may require an able-bodied partner to aid in tossing and catching, as well as moving around the circle. Using eye contact and calling the individuals' names (instead of numbers) may succeed in involving those with developmental and/or learning disabilities. The group dynamic becomes a network of support, with everyone eager to coach any individual through the game, as long as they need help.

The creative work now begins by building performance skills. The following exercises incorporate mask or puppetry dramatically in an improvisational context. The group leader should come prepared with several masks and puppets for use in the workshops. At this stage of the work, it is important to inspire the group with well-made, three-dimensional puppets that are large, colourful and full of character (see Astell-Burt 1981: 44).

Journey through the body[6]

The group begins by lying on their backs on the floor (those who use wheelchairs need not lie on the floor). With their eyes closed, encourage the group to relax every muscle in the body (guide them though this). As they begin to relax, remind them to pay attention to their breathing rhythms and placement in the body. Then ask each individual to imagine their ideal mode of transport. It can be anything from their past, present, future or fantasy life. Allow them to learn everything they can about their chosen 'vehicle' (ask questions pertaining to size, age, colour, interior/exterior, speed). At this point, inform them that they are going on a journey through their body, using their vehicle. However, their vehicle will only run on 'breath', so they must stay aware of their breathing to make the journey. Ask the group to put themselves in their vehicles and then either guide them through the journey or leave them to make it in their own time (allow 10–20 minutes for this).

You may need to pair certain individuals with developmental disabilities with a partner for the duration of the exercise. Avoid closing the eyes and lying on the floor. The partner should keep the individual's interest in the exercise stimulated by constant questioning and sharing of information about their vehicles and their journeys through the body. Making drawings or using toy vehicles may prove necessary.

When everyone has completed their journey, ask for volunteers to share their experience with the group. They must do this dramatically, using either a mask or a puppet. This means relating to and through the mask or puppet to engage the group in a storytelling experience. Focus initially on developing the relationship between actor and mask or puppeteer and puppet. Once this has solidified, then gradually encourage interaction between the mask or puppet 'character' and the group. Speech need not be the only form of communication, here; other forms such as song, mime or dance may be used effectively in conjunction with mask or puppetry. Remember, in an integrated group there will always be those available to help individuals with a disability to animate a puppet or to share the experience with them before the group if this is necessary. This should be done dramatically, to support the individual and to collaborate creatively in the telling of their story.

Blind drawing[7]

Part 1

Scarves for blindfolds, large newsprint paper, charcoals, 'wet ones' towels will be needed. Begin with the group comfortably seated at a table or on the floor. Ask each individual to tie a scarf around their head, covering their eyes. Do not insist on the blindfold; those who aren't ready to trust this concept may either close their eyes or focus anywhere but on the paper in front of them. Then, hand each individual a sheet of newsprint paper and a piece of charcoal. Next, give the group a word that will inspire them to draw whatever they associate with that word. Stick to abstract words like love, anger, depth, or music, as they tend not to have a single representational picture. Once they 'see' a picture in their mind's eye, they may begin to draw it. No peeking! Once a drawing is complete, remove the blindfolds and share them. Before doing any more drawing, hand out towels to clean the charcoal off hands, fingers, arms, faces, etc.

Those with limited upper body mobility may require a partner, to hold the paper for them, support the arm and/or hand as they draw, or even to draw for them. If the last is chosen, have the individual rest their hand on their partner's, moving with them as they draw.

Part 2

For this you will need 6 foot × 4 foot cotton drop(s),[8] high-intensity flashlights, sheets of thin cardboard, markers, exacto knives, scissors, fishing wire, garden wire, paperclips, rivets and scotch tape.

Divide the group into smaller groups. Have each of these small groups review the drawings and choose one they all agree on. Then give the groups some time to explore moving in a way that the picture suggests to them. Introduce the concept of shadows by giving each individual a chance to move between the cotton drop (held by two individuals) and the flashlight (held by one individual). Taking what they've just learned from using their bodies to make shadows, have each group build a shadow puppet capable of moving in the same way. They will quickly understand what the cardboard, markers and wire are all for and begin tracing and cutting away with great enthusiasm. Allow ample time for this phase, for here the notion of ensemble is put to the test. The groups are thrown into a situation where they must work together, sharing ideas and coming to agreements every step of the way, to produce the final product. They must also learn to integrate by delegating roles and responsibilities based on the individuals' capabilities. Be available to answer questions and offer technical advice, but try to let the groups do any problem-solving themselves. Finally, have each group present their shadow puppet and give a demonstration of what it can do (relating back to the original drawing).

Sock puppets

You will need socks with toes cut horizontally for the mouth; felt-covered cardboard oval shapes for the inside of the mouth; needle and thread or glue gun; assorted odds and ends for facial features; and hair – buttons, felt shapes, yarn, etc.

Sock puppets offer a friendly incentive to communicate and interact with others. They are easy to build and fun to animate. Most sock puppets have mouths used for speaking, but they are also used for grabbing, tugging, lifting, holding, throwing, catching, plucking and digging, among other things. They can rejuvenate a group and bring focus back to the work at hand.

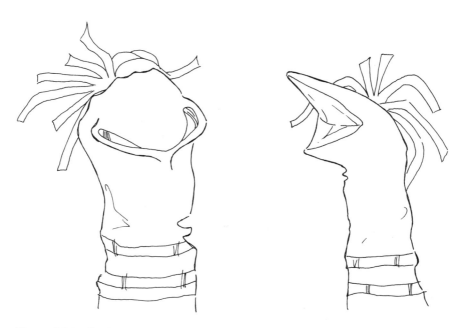

Figure 10.1   Sock puppets

Sock puppets also provide an enjoyable means for developing articulation and rhythm skills.[9] Bring in tapes of popular music that the group can all relate to (the Beatles are always a safe bet). Place a group of puppeteers behind a makeshift story board[10] and have the rest observe as audience. Watch how the puppets' lip sync the lyrics and dance to the music. Give everyone a chance to perform and to observe.

Where the puppeteer positions their body in relation to the puppet becomes an important consideration, especially when changing direction. Working behind a story board makes everyone sensitive to the spatial relationship between bodies, especially when there are puppeteers who use wheelchairs. Encourage the group to adapt by learning to share space and making room for everyone.

NEUTRAL MASK[11]

Essentially, neutral mask technique attempts to wipe the slate clean, so that the actor is left with a neutral base upon which to build a character. Neutral mask is not an end in itself; it is a process. At a glance, the exercises themselves seem fairly straightforward. However, once the expressionless mask covers the face, any extraneous, idiosyncratic movement becomes glaringly apparent. The goal here is not to move like a robot; it is rather to strip movement down to the bare essentials necessary to complete a given task. This requires that the individual think about each step they make, and its intention. This moment-to-moment concentration on the present toward the future is the actor's thinking process, and must be developed for the sake of ensemble performance.

The workshop leader should come prepared with at least two neutral masks. It is much easier to make them than to buy them; the leather Sartori neutral masks, made in Italy, would cause a pronounced deficit in most budgets. The masks I use are an adaptation of the Sartori masks. I built up a papier mâché form over a three-dimensional styrofoam mould covered with petroleum jelly. I then reinforced the papier mâché form with plaster of Paris gauze strips and secured an elastic band at both sides.

Figure 10.2 A neutral mask

There are several schools of thought surrounding the actual 'putting on' of the mask. Some recommend a period of contemplation, studying the mask for an increased understanding of every layer of its character, before putting it on. Others prefer to work with the mask on right from the start, allowing the character to unfold as the body takes on the rhythm and energy of chosen images. Once the mask is on, some insist on working in front of a mirror, whereas others may rely on the impressions and comments of the instructor or director. Either way, it really comes down to a matter of personal preference, based on training, experience and appropriateness for the group in question.

Once the mask is put on, a visible (to the audience) and tangible (for the actor) transformation occurs. Those who have worked with mask will often speak of the 'energy' or 'personality' of the mask and it's no wonder, as a lot of imagination has already gone into the creation of the mask. Perhaps several actors have already 'put on' the mask, adding to its own personal history with their creative energies. The mask is a powerful tool for communication and should, therefore, be handled with care and treated with respect.

You will undoubtedly encounter those in the group who either fear the mask or won't wear it. Never force the issue of the mask. Rather, encourage those individuals actively to participate by observing others in the exercises and giving constructive feedback afterwards. Watching others tackle the exercises first may give some the courage they need to try the mask themselves. Or, you may find it necessary to pair individuals in the exercises. The same principles of neutral mask would apply; only now there's the added benefit of two actors, learning to communicate with and be aware of each other in the work.

There may also be those in the group who haven't full control of their motor skills and for whom it may appear impossible to exercise any economy of movement. Neutral mask is a mental and physical challenge for everyone, regardless of disability. Part of integration involves learning to appreciate an individual's movement as a reflection of who they are. Why deny anyone the right to express themselves or the chance to develop a keener understanding of how their body can serve them creatively?

The first set of exercises allows the individual to discover their neutral base through improvising in a given situation. Feedback on the exercises serves to make the individual aware of what they may be consciously or unconsciously communicating with their body. It may be clear in the mind of the individual what they are doing or feeling, but are they making it clear enough for an audience to understand? The second set of exercises gives the individual the opportunity to begin building on the neutral base they've achieved in the first exercises. Here, the individual learns to tap into their physical resources by calling upon the body to explore the different rhythms and energies suggested by certain images.

Participation must obviously be limited to the number of masks available. More than four individuals at a time makes it difficult to watch what each one is doing. The defined play area ('stage') may only be used by those participating in an exercise, the rest of the group must observe the exercises from the periphery ('audience').

First exercises

Ask those participating to assume a comfortable resting position either by lying on the floor or by totally relaxing in their wheelchair, on stage with the masks on. In their own time, they are to do the following:

1 Get up, look at the horizon, then resume resting position.
2 Get up, look at the horizon, see an object (real or imaginary) before you, take it, use the object, place it back where you found it, look at the horizon, resume resting position.
3 Get up, look at the horizon, see your bus before you, move as quickly as you can to try to catch your bus as it is pulling away, watch it drive away, turn and move back to your original position, turn and look at the horizon, resume resting position.

Give everyone in the group a chance to do an exercise before moving on to the next one. Ask those participating to remove the masks once everyone on stage has completed the exercise. At this point, encourage those observing to give constructive comments based on what they saw.

Second exercises

Begin the same way as in the first exercises. Ask those participating to think of an image. It could be anything representational that pops into their mind: the sun, a cloud, a flower, a raindrop, a brick, a tornado, a camp fire, etc. Once they all have an image, give them time to think about what it might feel like to be the sun or a flower. Whatever feelings come, instruct them to fill the body with those feelings. This provides the impetus for movement. As they begin to explore the movement, they will naturally fall into a set rhythm. Once they have a established a rhythm, ask them to begin moving around the stage. If anyone loses their rhythm, chances are they've lost their concentration and should return to their resting position to rekindle their original impression of the image.

Steer them away from a tendency to fall into clichés. It is not important that they 'look' like a flower; it is far more useful as an actor to understand how it feels to be that flower, and to communicate that fact to an audience. Likewise, discourage them from 'playing' the mask at this point in the work. The neutral mask intentionally takes focus away from the face, forcing the actor to communicate with the body.

The next step involves removing the neutral mask to allow words to come organically from the character emerging from the movement. This step can be made more accessible with the use of animal imagery. Repeat the above exercise, only now ask each individual to think of an animal. Stick to familiar land mammals, birds and reptiles. Fish and water mammals pose a problem because they exist only in water.

Once they begin to move, they immediately take on the nature of their chosen animal, for example the kitten plays with yarn, the dog lifts his leg, the squirrel collects nuts, the snake slithers through the grass, etc. Being able to relate to the animal's reality makes it easier for most people to begin interacting with the other 'animals' on stage. Encourage them to find a reason to 'meet'. If a particular couple or threesome appears to have tapped a potentially dramatic relationship, coach them from the floor on to their feet. Ask the actors to 'hold' and have several observers go on stage and remove the masks. It is important here for the actor to drop the notion of animals and move on to applying the animal's qualities and energy to the development of a human character.

The actors should continue developing the relationship as they move. The circumstances for the relationship mixed with the animals' energies give the actors the reason to speak. Begin with sound that is released as an extension of the movement, and therefore rooted in the body. Gradually, move to words and watch an improvised scene unfold before your very eyes! Later, commedia dell'arte masks may be added to objectify and exaggerate the character's qualities.

THE PROCESS

Now the work becomes more focused. We have been building skills for a purpose: to introduce each individual to the 'craft' of mask and puppetry so that they may now use these skills to explore the 'art'. At the same time, they've learned to adapt those skills to suit the needs of an integrated setting. Further exploration will now unite the group by taking them on a journey that begins with rehearsals, continues through the building of masks, puppets, costumes, sets, etc. and culminates with the actual performance. The process cannot, and should not, be avoided. The process enables the ensemble to grow and mature. The foundation for trust in an integrated group requires a shared commitment covering time and experience. With trust comes confidence in oneself and in others. This must be in place in order for each individual to make the transition from rehearsal to performance.

The decision to rehearse, build and present theatrical performance using mask and puppetry begs one primary consideration. Masks and puppets must begin as an integral part of the concept for the performance. First, masks and puppets are not props; they are the characters of the play, and in some cases even become actors themselves, playing beside their human counterparts. Second, the relationship between mask and actor or puppet and puppeteer must be given the chance to develop. Any inconsistency here would guarantee a superficial performance (see Astell-Burt 1981: 46). This can be prevented if the group becomes comfortable working with masks and puppets (those built for the performance or cardboard mock-ups) from day one. Animation with masks and puppets demands sensitivity and practice. Introducing them as an afterthought would disrupt the harmony of the performance and demonstrates a lack of respect for the art form.

REHEARSALS

The following suggestions offer two approaches to building material for a collective performance. I recommend building material over a script for several reasons. In an integrated setting, adhering to a specific text and blocking it (that is setting the actors' stage movements and 'business') might prove too sophisticated a proposition for some groups. The material to be performed must remain flexible enough to accommodate the unpredictable behaviour of certain individuals in the group with developmental disabilities. If the words and accompanying movement originate from them, the concept of interacting as characters by allowing words and movement to serve the characters' intention in the action of the performance becomes a less foreign proposition. Also, building material for a performance calls for the active participation of the ensemble at all times. Using a script may persuade some to separate themselves from the ensemble and concentrate only on what they've been given. Therefore, allow the ideas for the performance to stem from group involvement (Astell-Burt 1981: 103).

Storytelling

Assorted masks and puppets, or cardboard mockups will be required.

I developed my own approach to storytelling while working with Das Puppenspiel Puppet Theatre on their adaptation of *Jumping Mouse*. I've since used it for gathering material for collective creations and street theatre performances. Divide the group into sub-groups of three to four individuals. Give each sub-group a structure from which to build their story. This structure is arrived at by plugging in each one of the variables below to complete the equation.

Method		Media		Situation		Conflict
Narrator, Brechtian, or Realism	+	Mask and/or Puppets	+	Who, What Where and When	+	Obstacle

Under the 'Method' heading I've listed three choices. Narrator implies that one character is to tell the story, while the others act it out. The Brechtian method allows for all the characters to switch between narrating and acting out the story. Lastly, Realism simply requires the characters to act out the story with no narration.

An example of this approach was used to create a street theatre performance I directed with an integrated cast. They chose: (Brechtian) + (Mask) + (Mouse, running away from home, to the circus, in the early morning) + (must help his new friend, a Lioness, escape the inhumane conditions and abuse she has suffered at the hands of the ringmaster). From this scenario, the group worked together to flesh out the story, adding other circus characters, improvising sound effects and music and using their bodies as the actual circus tent. The group saw to it that everyone had a part to play, and when they weren't directly involved in the storytelling, individuals would provide the soundscape or become part of the set. In this particular group, there was an individual with a developmental disability who often grew restless and would wander away from the rehearsal. The group eventually solved this problem by bringing the entire rehearsal to them, thereby refusing to allow the work to be interrupted and reminding the individual of their importance and responsibility to the group. Throughout the rehearsal period, the group used neutral and character mask exercises to harmonise the energy and movement of the animals with the masks.

Theme-based performance

This approach follows a more loosely structured formula. The effect resembles that of a collage: an assemblage of separate scenes that share a common theme. With such compositions, the continuity or throughline becomes the theme itself, and not the chronology of any one story. Theme pieces also lend themselves to an eclectic blend of performing arts, taking full advantage of the spectacle aspect of theatre.

I collaborated on a street theatre performance with an integrated cast, using a carnival theme. The size of the group (over twenty people) permitted us to give each person performance as well as production responsibilities. The following illustrates the breakdown of these responsibilities.

Performance areas
   Punch and Judy scene
   King and Queen of the carnival
   Commedia dell'arte scene
   Clowns
   Side show acts
   Maypole dance

Kazoo marching band
Production areas
  Finding and building:
    Masks and puppets
    Sets, props and costumes
    Musical instruments
  Painting
    Scenery
    Masks
    Puppets
  Make-up workshops

Under such circumstances, I've found that the success of the rehearsal process rests with the ability of the director or instructor 'to provide an atmosphere in which creation can take place' (Appel 1982: 7). This can be done any number of ways, from ensuring a clean and clutter-free rehearsal space to rotating activities to keep the work fresh and interest alive. During this part of the process, every effort must be made to encourage the individual to believe in their ability to contribute in a useful way to the project. The more familiarity breeds a sense of ensemble, the more the individual will feel comfortable with sharing their ideas and cultivating them in a creative way.

BUILDING MASKS AND PUPPETS

There is much to consider before sitting down to build a mask or puppet:

1 How many masks or puppets are needed? Could some characters be played with a mask instead of a puppet, or vice versa? How many actors and/or puppeteers are required to animate them all? Is it possible for them to play more than one role?
2 Who are the mask or puppet characters? Which of their personality traits should I emphasise? How do I want the audience to feel about each character?
3 How is the mask to be used? Must the actor speak or not? Must the mask change expression or shape?
4 What must the puppet do? Speak? Handle and use objects? Fly or swim? Eat? Come apart? Breathe fire?
5 Where is the performance to be performed? Indoors (with or without lighting) or outdoors? In an intimate setting or a larger venue?
6 What size should the masks or puppets be? Do they fit the scale of the set or story board? Do they fit the scale of the venue?
7 What is the required life span of the masks or puppets? Will they be used once or twice or over a period of weeks, months or years? Will they be transported from place to place frequently?

8 How much can be spent on materials? Is there a cheaper way to achieve the same desired effect? Can found household objects be cleverly used?

Masks

Suggested materials: cardboard, markers, exacto knives, scissors, fabric scraps, trimmings, carpenter's glue, contact cement, 12-inch balloons, pieces of foam core, various styrofoam shapes, cheesecloth, paper bags cut into strips, multi-coloured construction paper cut into strips, plaster of Paris strips, petroleum jelly, acrylic or tempera paints, small to medium paint brushes, elastic strings and bands.

Masquerade, half-masks

This type of mask was built for the maypole dance sequence in the carnival street theatre performance mentioned earlier. The outline for the mask is drawn with markers on a piece of thin cardboard. Use scissors or an exacto knife to cut out the face, eye holes and any other details drawn. Poke holes at either end of the mask. Thread the elastic string through holes, knot and staple into place. Apply glue to the front and back of the mask. Stretch fabric over mask and add trimming.

For a more three-dimensional look, sculpt foam core pieces in the shape of eyebrows, cheeks and noses. Attach the foam pieces to the face of the mask with contact cement. Measure out the elastic band and attach both ends to the back side of the mask with contact cement. Allow to dry before stretching cheesecloth over front and back of the mask. Using a brush, cover the entire mask with a mixture of carpenter's glue and water. Be sure to keep the desired shape of the mask. Allow to dry before painting with acrylic or tempera paints.

Character, full masks

Here, I would recommend building the mask on a mould. Ready-made plastic masks make suitable moulds and can be found at the larger theatrical supply or craft stores. You might also check Chinese souvenir shops. A simpler way would be to use an inflated balloon. Blow the balloon up to the approximate size of the individual's head and tie a knot at the end. With a marker, draw on the balloon where the eye, nose and mouth holes will be as well as the perimeter of the mask. Treat the inside of the marked area with petroleum jelly. Dip the paper bag strips in a mixture of carpenter's glue and water and arrange them within the marked area on the balloon. Remember not to cover the eye, nose and mouth holes. Allow to dry before adding the next layer.

Once the second layer has dried, you may want to build up facial

Figure 10.3   Half-masks

features. This can be done by sculpting and arranging pieces of styrofoam on the mask. Set the pieces in place with carpenter's glue and secure them by adding a layer of wet plaster of Paris strips over the entire mask. For a more colourful alternative, cover the mask with several layers of construction paper strips (solid or multi-coloured) dipped in the same glue and water mixture as before. Once dry, gently lift the mask off the balloon. You may find it easier to pop the balloon. Acrylic or tempera paints can be used on the plaster of Paris masks. Attach an elastic string or band as described above, substituting plaster of Paris strips for the cheesecloth.

You can expedite the process by using the individual's face as a mould. This method takes about an hour, during which the individual must sit or lie still and not move a muscle on their face. Some individuals may not wish to place themselves in what they perceive to be such a vulnerable or terrifying position. However, those who wish to try could donate their masks as moulds for the others to use. Have the individual sit or lie down in a comfortable position. Ask them to tie their hair back from their face and to remove any jewellery. They should either wear an old shirt or wrap an old towel around their neck and shoulders. Spread a thin layer of petroleum jelly over their entire face. Then, apply a single layer of wet plaster of paris strips directly on to their face. Do not cover the eyes, nostrils or mouth; if need be, these areas can be covered with a second layer once the mask is removed from the face. Allow to dry and harden before lifting the mask off the face. I've found this experience most

enjoyable and relaxing, particularly if the entire group is involved all at
once and there is music playing in the background. You may then choose
to add more layers, build up the facial features, add paint or simply leave
the mask as is.

Puppets

Suggested materials: *head*: styrofoam balls (4–6 inches in diameter), large
cardboard boxes, foam core sheets (1 inch thick), toilet paper and paper
towel tubes, various styrofoam shapes, carpenter's glue, straight pins,
paper bags and multi-coloured construction paper cut into strips, cheesecloth, yarn or burlap threads, trimming, acrylic or tempera paints, small,
medium and large brushes; *body, arms and legs*: an assortment of colourful
and contrasting medium to heavy weight fabrics, cotton muslin, stuffing,
wire coat hangers, wood dowelling, pliers.

Hand puppets

This type of puppet was used for the Punch and Judy scene in the carnival
street theatre performance mentioned earlier. The head and neck of the
puppet consist of a toilet roll tube and a styrofoam ball. Treat one end of
the tube with carpenter's glue, then insert it into the styrofoam ball. From
here, follow the same basic procedure as with the masks. Sculpt facial
features out of the styrofoam shapes and arrange them on the face of the
puppet. You may wish to trace the features on to the face first before
gluing them on and pinning them in place. Then, use the papier mâché
technique described above to add several layers of either the paper bag or
construction paper strips to the entire head and neck of the puppet. For
such small work, you will need to use smaller pieces of the paper. Allow
for drying time between layers. Once dry, the puppet's face, head and neck
may be painted. You may wish to attach other trimmings for the eyes,
mouth, nose or ears (especially if the hand puppet is an animal). Arrange
yarn or burlap threads and glue on to the head for hair.

While one individual or group builds the head, another could build the
body of the puppet. Building the body of a hand puppet takes no time at
all if you have access to either a sewing machine or a glue gun. A simple
smock-like pattern can be traced or cut out and pinned on to double-width
fabric (shoulders at the fold). Make sure the length of the smock will cover
both the hand that is animating the puppet and most of the forearm. Stitch
or glue (right sides together) two side seams, from the underside of the
arms down to the base of the smock. Little mitt-like hands can be traced,
cut out of cotton muslin, and sewn or glued together in the same manner.
Stitch or glue the open wrists of the mitts to the open armholes of the
smock (again, right sides together). Now, turn the whole thing right side

Figure 10.4   Hand puppets

out. Glue the open neck of the smock to the tube neck of the puppet. Pin,
stitch or glue on extra trim for collars, hats, vests, aprons, jewellery, etc.

Rod puppets

Follow the same procedure as used for hand puppets but with a few
adjustments. Primarily, this kind of puppet is animated with rods and not
with the hand and fingers. Therefore, you will want to make some sort of
adjustment to the head and neck area as well as to the body. Try gluing
and inserting a piece of coat hanger or thin dowelling into the top or back
of the puppet's head. Bend a hook into the coat hanger or add a wooden
knob to the dowelling to improve the grip. This kind of adjustment enables
the puppeteer to animate the puppet in front of them and on the floor. If
you wish to play the puppet overhead, behind a story board, use a paper
towel tube instead of a toilet paper tube for the puppet's neck. The longer
tube now becomes the rod for head animation.

The body of a rod puppet is usually more detailed than that of the hand
puppet. So, adapt the smock pattern to include arms, hands, legs and feet.
When tracing or cutting the pattern, keep the arms and legs wide and long.
Make the body out of cotton muslin. Stitch or glue right sides together,
leaving the neck open. Turn right side out and stuff the body with

lightweight, synthetic stuffing. I recommend stitching joints for wrists, elbows, shoulders, hips, knees and ankles as you stuff the body. Glue the body to the neck of the puppet. If your puppet has the paper towel tube for a rod, make a slit in the fabric, from lower to middle back, to slip the tube through. Scout the thrift stores, jumble or garage sales for baby and children's clothes to dress your puppet in. Later, you may wish to add two more rods at the wrists or at the elbows, especially if you are animating the puppet overhead.

Larger-than-life-sized rod puppets

These were used for the King and Queen in the carnival street theatre performance mentioned earlier. The heads were cut out of the sides of large cardboard boxes. A layer of thin foam core was glued to the front and back of the cardboard. The foam scraps were sculpted to form facial features. Cheesecloth was then stretched over the head and brushed with the glue and water mixture. Multi-coloured papier mâché substituted for the actual painting of the faces. Burlap threads served for the hair and beard; mylar scraps and fancy trim were combined to make the crowns.

The bodies of the King and Queen puppets were basically two crosses, composed of 2 inch × 1/2 inch slats (shoulders) with a hole drilled through the middle to accommodate long, 1-inch thick dowelling (body). Cardboard tubing had been inserted into the puppets' heads in order to secure them on top of the dowelling. The cotton muslin hands were pinned to two large, heavy pieces of fabric draped over the shoulders as regal robes. Rods were inserted into the hands to aid in animating the arms.

Adapting the process for an integrated setting involves making mask and puppetry accessible to everyone. A strong sense of ensemble, therefore, is necessary to achieve this goal. This support system must ideally meet the needs of every individual in the group. For some it is a sense of achievement. For others it is knowing that they've helped one another to achieve something. It could be as simple as animating a rod puppet with three puppeteers instead of one, or building a mask and constantly asking for input or suggestions. Time restraints and safety considerations may require that many of the materials be prepared in advance. For some individuals, mixing and matching the finished pieces may prove a more accessible introduction to mask and puppet-building.

PERFORMANCE

Who is the group performing for and why? Again, it comes down to communication. The added element of a private or public audience allows the group to take the process one step further. That is to say, the time has

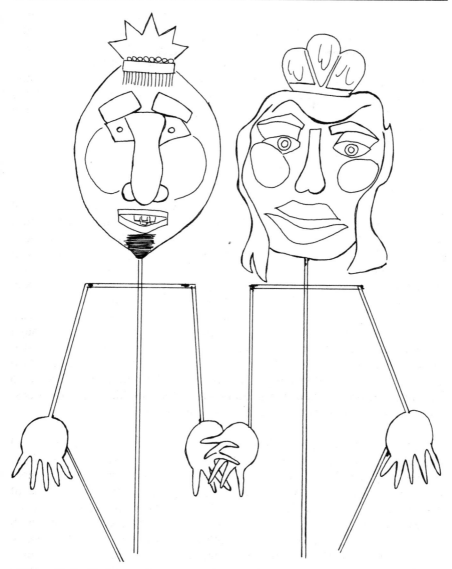

Figure 10.5 Rod puppets

come to share the story with someone new. By focusing on the process, and not the product, the group maintains a clear perspective on the work. Process brings us back to ensemble and the notion of working together to produce something. With an integrated cast, ensemble performance becomes a balancing act; it seeks to even out the scales by reducing any disparity in talent or ability.

In the carnival street theatre performance, Judy was played by a puppeteer with a visual disability. Her way of adapting to the experience was to set markers along the inside of the story board that she could feel with her left hand, while the right hand animated the puppet. This way, she knew exactly where to make her entrances and exits. The puppeteer who played Punch helped to make puppetry accessible to her by staying in constant physical contact with her and the puppet.

In this regard, it becomes apparent why we bother with mask and puppetry in an integrated setting. Some individuals require the added reinforcement of character that masks and puppets provide (Astell-Burt 1981: 109). Mask, puppetry and theatre combine to bridge, visually and orally, any communication gap between performer and audience.

The benefits from such a performance reach everyone involved. The experience yields an enormous sense of pride in the performers. It also promotes public awareness. Sharing the work with and for others may eventually succeed in conquering social stigmas surrounding disabilities in general, in favour of a healthier and more productive sense of community.

NOTES

1 I use the term 'integration' to describe 'the full, active and equal participation and acceptance of persons with disabilities into the society in which they live. A key to implementing this idea is to provide persons with disabilities the most "normal" environment possible in all areas of social life, which includes, in addition to education, employment, housing and medical care, the ability to participate in social, cultural and leisure activities', quoted in R. Richard (1992) 'A descriptive analysis of two approaches to the use of drama with persons with a disability', unpublished MA thesis, Concordia University, Montreal.
2 I use the term 'disability' or 'disabilities' to refer to 'a condition which makes the completion of a task or tasks more difficult. This condition may be sensory, intellectual or physical in nature', quoted in B. Warren (1991) 'Integration through the theatre arts: responses to theatrical performance integrating persons with a disability', unpublished paper.
3 I must acknowledge Bil Baird, renowned American puppet master, for this definition.
4 The concepts and exercises presented here stem from my own voice training. I have chosen to adapt and simplify them for the purposes of this chapter. They are discussed in greater detail in Linklater (1978)
5 This game was introduced to me by Dean Gilmour, a Toronto-based theatre artist and clown, to whom I am also indebted for my knowledge of neutral mask, clown and commedia dell'arte. I've adapted his Le Coq based mask exercises to suit the needs of this chapter.
6 I first did this exercise as a part of my actor voice training with David Smukler at York University. I have since adapted it for my work with mask and puppetry.
7 Enid Kaplan, an artist and a dear friend, shared this exercise with me as a technique for tapping into and trusting one's creative resources. I've chosen to take the exercise one step further, by including the actual building of puppets.
8 I use the term 'cotton drop' (known also in the theatre as a 'scrim' or 'cyclorama') to refer to any size, white or natural cotton fabric, stretched taut, on to which light and images are projected. In the case of shadow puppetry, the image

(puppet) is animated flush against the stretched cotton drop, with the light source (here, the flash light) defining the image from approximately 30 to 60 cm away (recommended for a 6 foot × 4 foot drop). The puppeteer(s) should position themselves outside the beam of light; otherwise they will destroy the illusion (with their own shadow) for the audience, viewing the image from the opposite side of the cotton drop.

9 This is actually 'muppeteering' technique, and the exercises were those taught to me by muppeteer Gordon Robertson.

10 A story board provides a proscenium style playing area for marionettes, hand and rod puppets. The puppeteer(s) are masked from the audience's view, animating the puppet(s) from behind the story board. The puppet(s) play to the audience from inside a picture frame 'stage' (proscenium). In the case of the marionette, the puppeteer(s) animate the puppet(s) from above the stage; with the hand and rod puppets, the puppeteer(s) animate them overhead. The colourfully striped booths used for Punch and Judy shows illustrate a classic example of a story board.

A 'makeshift' story board, therefore, can be any structure used to mask the puppeteer(s) from the audience, to focus attention on the puppet(s). It could be as simple as a table turned on its side, or a cardboard refrigerator box with a picture frame 'window' cut out. The cotton drop described in Note 8 may also serve as a makeshift story board.

11 See Note 5.

SUGGESTED READING

Appel, L. (1982) *Mask Characterisation: An Acting Process*, Southern Illinois University Press, Carbondale and Edwardsville.

Astell-Burt, C. (1981) *Puppetry for Mentally Handicapped People*, Souvenir Press, London.

Linklater, K. (1978) *Freeing the Natural Voice*, Drama Book Publishers, New York.

Name index

Amies, Bert 114, 130n11
Appel, L. 175
Aristotle 35
Astell-Burt, C. 166, 173, 182

Baird, Bil 182n3
Bartenieff, L. 80n6
Barton, B. 142
Beckerman, B. 129n
Browning, Robert 137
Burket-Smith, K. 26

Campbell, Joseph 133, 141
Chace, Marian 70
Copernicus, N. 137
Courtney, R. 130n7
Crickmay, C. 76

Dundes, A. 33n1

Eliade, M. 136, 137
Eliot, T.S. 137
Exley, H. 21n

Fox, Anne 154
Freud, Sigmund 35
Fulkerson, Mary 76, 80n2

Gettings, Fred 36
Gilmour, Dean 182n5
Gordon, D. 130n6
Gump, P.V. 33n3

Hillman, James 144
Hoffman, Malvina 56n
Homer 144

James, William 133

Johnstone, K. 130n9
Joyce, James 137
Jung, Carl 35, 136

Kaplan, Enid 182n7
Keen, Sam 143, 154

Laban, Rudolf 77, 148
Larsen, S.R. 138
Linklater, K. 182n4

McLuhan, Marshall 143
Messenger, J.C. 33n1
Moss, L. 4

Neihardt, J.G. 152
Neill, Cheryl 33n
Newhouse, Jane 72
North, M. 80n6

Opie, I. and Opie, P. 28, 33n2
O'Suillebahn, S. 33n4

Picasso, P. 48
Plato 35

Richard, R. 182n1
Robertson, Gordon 183n9

Shedlock, Marie 151
Sherborne, Veronica 81n18
Stanislavski, K. 119
Steinbeck, John 138
Sutton-Smith, B. 33n

Thomson, C. 77
Tufnell, M. 76
Warren, Bernie 77, 144, 182n
Wolkstein, Diane 136

Subject index

aggression, channelling 31

art, access to 4; artefacts 3; defining 3; demystification of 6; emotion and 35, 36–7, 53, 59; in healing 3; for health 5; as human exchange 54; professional artists 6; as recreation 12, 56; self-expression and 161, 162; social change and 3, 36; as therapy 4, 5; therapy 4

Arts for Health 4, 12

atmosphere, creation of 7, 41

body awareness 29, 65–9

cerebral palsy, dance and 59

collective unconscious 136

communication, drama and 112–13, 125, 126; mask and puppetry and 162; movement and 59; music and 93, 105, 106

concentration, developing 28

contract 10–14, 16, 50; between group and leader 123; conditions of 10; goals 10; problems of 10–14, 16; room 12–13

co-operation, promoting 27, 29

creation, act of 4, 6, 7

creative alertness 80n2

creative expression 7, 12

creative therapy, concept of 3; definition 8n1; employing 5–8; enjoyment of 11, 19; goals of 10; health and 4; interest in 3; patience, importance of 42–3; preparation and planning 10–14; problem of definitions 5; ritual and 32–3

creativity 37; music and 95; personal 14, 35, 111

dance/movement 58–71; balance 77; body awareness 65–9; cerebral palsy and 59; Change 70; clothing 60–1; control of body parts 60; creative alertness 80n2; Dance in/dance out 71; diagnostic tools 62, 64, 80n5; Electric Puppet 66–7; emotion and 59, 60, 63, 73; as 'emotion in motion' 66; equipment 60, 69; Follow My Dance I 63–5, 70; Follow My Dance II 72–3; Follow My Dance III 73–4; gesture 77; goals 60; group awareness 69–71; humour in 62; I Am Me 62–3; jump 77; Magic Aura 67; movement analysis 77–9; name games 62–3; Ninja 67–9; Parachute 69; practical activities 60–1; Reed in the Wind 69–70; repetition 80n7; Rob's Little Finger Game 61–2; sensory awareness, developing 76; spotlighting 63, 64, 71, 80n4; Stick in the Mud 67; travel 77; turn 77; warm-up 61–5; see also dancing; movement

dancing 71–6; environment 74, 81n21; Essences 74–6; feather dances 71–2; Follow My Dance II 72–3; music, photographs and painting 71; self-directed dance 74; sharing 76; see also dance/movement; movement

drama 111–29; actor, role of 130n12; auditory skills 118; blocking 123, 124; the censor 125–6; character 130n10; characters, creating 125–9; communication 112–13, 125, 126; contract between leader and group 123; definition 130n1; diagnostic tools 120, 121; director, role of 131n12; Dracula 115–16; dramatic actions

112, 130n5; dramatic process 113; equipment 116, 119; facilitator, role of 131n12; gaining confidence of group 114; guided fantasy 124; helpers 131n14; as human interaction 111; humour in 113–14; I'm Sorry I Must Be Leaving 127–8; imagination, awakening 117–25; improvisation 127; Keeper of the Keys 118; Liar's Tag 127; The Magic Box 119–20; Magic Clay 122; Magic Newspaper 120–1; Male or Female? 118–19; Mr/Ms Engine 114–15; name games 114–17; pattern 123; as personal activity 113; physical contact activities 119; Playing the crowd 126; practical activities 113–29; repetition 123–4; ritual and 111, 130n3; role 130n10; role-flexibility 125, 130n9; sex roles and stereotyping 119; spontaneity 111; spotlighting 117; storytelling and 111, 125; Tarzan 117; Tennis-Elbow-Foot Game 123–4; To Be Continued 126–7; the wall 125; Who Owned the Bag? 128–9
dreams 35

emotion, art and 35, 36–7, 53; dance and 59
environment 6; creating 8; dancing and 74, 81n21; guided fantasy and 124–5; importance of 11; interaction with, folklore and 27; room *see* room; space requirements 17; special settings 6; unsatisfactory 13; workplace 4; *see also* room
equipment, art materials *see* visual arts equipment; assessing need for 17; dance/movement 60, 69; drama 116, 119; mask and puppetry 167; pre-session check 18; sink 13

fantasy, visual arts in 54–5; *see also* guided fantasy
folklore 25–33; Anang of Nigeria 26; context and function 26–7; fairy tales 141; folktales 139–40, 141; games *see* games; history of 25–6; Inuit of North America 26, 30; Norse mythology 26; *see also* mythology; storytelling
folksongs 26, 94, 101

games, cumulative games 31–2;

development of spatial awareness 28; Do the Opposite 31; Irish wake games 30–2; leader joining in 31; London 26–7, 29–30; memory games 31–2; Muk 30; name games 18, 62–3, 114–17; Pig in the Sty 31; Stick in the Mud 28; Sun and Frost 28–9; traditional 27–30; warm-up 31
goals 10, 17, 20, 35; dance/movement 60
group, abilities of members 7, 11, 13, 15–16, 17; age of members 11, 13, 15; cohesion 29; composition of 10, 11, 15–16; co-operation 27, 29, 31; decision-making and 18; establishing trust 13, 47, 53–4; expectations and 12; gaining confidence of 114; generating security 13; goals 10; leader, contract with 123; mood 18; needs of members 7, 16, 17, 18–19; numbers in 15; response of 19; ritual and 33; sharing information with 18; trust exercises 47, 53–4; *see also* leader; sessions
guided fantasy 124; active participants 125; directive 124; environment and 124–5; leader and 124; non-directive 124, 125; passive participants 124–5; traditional narrative, using 32

home stories 142–4; beginnings 152–3; friends and enemies 155–6; heroes and villains 155–6; I am 153–4; My House 154; School days 155; sharing, techniques for 152–6
humour, in dance 62; in drama 113–14; effect of 8n2

individual, developing trust 17; health of 5; needs of 7; self-esteem 7, 35; self-expression 6, 43; self-help 4; self-image 37

language, common grammar 107; of the creative medium 8
leader 6–8, 13–14; and assistants 17, 20; contract *see* contract; flexibility of approach 18; games, joining in 31; goals 17, 20; group, contract with 123; guided fantasy and 124; material, knowledge of 26; objectives 50; patience, importance of 42–3; responsibilities of 16; role-flexibility 14; self-awareness 6–7; structuring

sessions 8; style of working 6, 14, 15; written records, importance of 20, 42; *see also* group; sessions

mask and puppetry, blind drawing 167; body warm up 164–9; breath support 163–4; Brechtian method 173–4; building 175–80; character masks 176–8; commedia dell'arte masks 172; communication and 162; creating 175–80; discovering character 163; equipment 167; full masks 176–8; function of 162; half-masks 176, 177; hand puppets 178–9; humming 164; Journey through the body 166; larger-than-life sized rod puppets 180; masquerade masks 176; materials for masks 176; materials for puppets 178; neutral mask 169–72; performance 180–2; performer and 163; process 172–3; putting on the mask 170; Realism 173–4; rehearsals 173–5; relating to inanimate objects 163; rod puppets 179–80, 181; Sartori masks 169; singing 164; sock puppets 168–9; storytelling 166, 173–4; theme-based performance 174–5; voice articulation 164; voice, warming up 163–4; Water babies 165–6; workshops 163–9
motor control, assisting 46; development of 27, 41
movement, and body awareness 29, 58; communication and 59; music and 107; and spatial awareness 28; *see also* dance/movement; dancing
music 84–110; articulated intervals 93–4, 100; ball of string 95; 'big-bang' 103; blocks of sound 99; body exercise 90–2; body as instrument 93; calling 103; centre, sense of 106; chords 99; communication and 93, 105, 106; court dances 98; depth of sound 94; duplet pulses 85; Eastern 94; the elements 102; events, improvising to cover 88; expression and 106; football chant 87, 97–8, 100; free sounds 94; gestures and 86–7, 1033; greeting the group 85–90; grounding 104; group formations 85; grunting 100; humming 90, 94, 164; imagination and 108; inner resources, finding 106; interlude in session 92–5; jazz 94; keening 101; lateral

dimension of sound 94; length of programme, agreeing 108; major and minor 99; melismatic intervals 94; memory, reflecting on session 104; microtonal intervals 94; minor third 101; mirrors 103; musical form 108; name chorus 104; noise 94; octave 100; opposites 102; organum 101; percussive and sustained songs 102; piano quintet 102; plainsong 99; practical activities 85–104; process of production 93; reflection on session 104; rhythm 94, 95–9; ritual and 108; rocking to 88–9; sense of form 107–8; session as journey or story 108; social-competence and 105; society, sense of belonging to 93; songs *see* songs; sound images 103; sound-play 95–104; sounds structured and free and silent 98; space, time and form, playing with 106; star points 96; star radials 96; stepping-stones 97; stereophonic sound 103; structured rhythms 93–4; subdivision 98–9; support music 96, 100; swanee whistle 94; swaying to 87; tactile objects 102; tennis 95; textures 94, 102–4; thumb fifths 101; tile-dance chorus 96; triplet pulses 85; tune 94, 99–101; unstructured rhythms 94; use of in session 41; vertical dimension of sound 94; visual arts, use of in 41, 51–4; vowels 103; within the interval 101; *see also* songs
mythology 134–5, 136–7; archetypes 136; concretised symbols and 136–7; goal of 136; as picture language 136; psychological insights 136; ritual and 136; symbolic images 136, 137; teaching stories 140; universal images 136; *see also* folklore; storytelling

name games 18, 62–3, 114–17
naming songs 85–6, 104

puppetry *see* mask and puppetry

ritual 25–33; artificially imposed 33; creative therapy and 32–3; drama and 111, 130n3; in music therapy 108; mythology and 136; predictability of 33
role-flexibility 14, 113, 125, 126, 130n9

role-theorists 111–12
roles, context of 112; function of 112; interactions 112; stereotyping 119
room 12–13, 17–18, 19; requirements 13; security of 13; unsatisfactory 13; *see also* environment

self-esteem 7, 35
self-expression 6, 43; theatre and 161, 162
self-help 4
self-image 37
sessions, continuity and scheduling of 13; ending 19; equipment required 17; evaluating 19–20; goals 17, 20, 35; as journey or story 108; planning 13–14, 17–18; planning next 20; preliminary questions 15–18; pre-session planning 16–17; questions during 18–19; questions following 19–20; running 18–19; structuring 8, 17, 18; warm-up 18, 31, 61–5; *see also* group; leader; room
society 3–4; culture and 25, 36; development of, arts and 3; folklore 25; health of 3, 5, 36; industrialised 3, 5, 25; sense of belonging, music and 93, 107; traditional 25
songs, action songs 88–9; Body blues 91; body exercise 90–2; breath 92; familiar, repetition of 88; folksong 26, 94, 101; football chant 87, 97–8, 100; grunting 100; humming 90, 94, 164; as journey 107; keening 101; melisma 101; naming songs 85–6, 104; Oh What a Beautiful Morning 87–8; ornamented folksongs 101; percussive and sustained songs 102; plainsong 99; Rockets 91–2; rocking to 88–9; sentence repetition 92; silent song 90; swaying to 87; Tarzan song 91; tile-dance chorus 96; Toe song 90–1; *see also* music
spatial awareness, development of 28
spotlighting, in dance/movement 63, 64, 71, 80n4; in drama 117
storytellers 136
storytelling 133–59; audience participation 137; beginning of story 134–8; bound flow 151; characters, creating 125; choosing stories 138–44; conflict in stories 145–6; creating highs and lows 146; credibility 147;

drama and 111; fairy tales 141; the finale 146; finding stories 139–40; flow 150–1; folklore 135; folktales 139–40, 141; force 150; free flow 151; general characteristics of stories 145–8; gesture 151–2; group 126–7; home stories *see* home stories; I knew her when 158–9; learning and sharing stories 144–59; legends 135, 140–1; Liar, liar, pants on fire 157–8; masks and puppetry and 166, 173–4; metaphor 133; myths and mythology *see* mythology; as oral tradition 137–8; pacing 146; physicalising the story 148–52; shape of stories 145; space 149–50; spiritual concerns 135; stories in pictures 147–8; Super Man, Wonder Woman 158; symbolic images 136; tall tale 157; teaching stories 138–42; technology and 138; time 148–9; traditional narratives 32; truth 133–4, 143; universal images 136; *see also* folklore; home stories; mythology

theatre 161; collaborative nature of 161–2; ensemble 161–2; as microcosm of life 161
trust continuity and 13; developing 17
trust exercises group 47, 53–4; partner 52–3

unconscious 35, 133; collective 136

visual arts 35–56; art history books, use of 43; collage 50–1; equipment *see* visual arts equipment; group 'trust' exercises 47, 53–4; honest expression, encouragement of 44; initial experience 45–6; as inner discovery 41; kits, use of 45; materials *see* visual arts equipment; mixed media work 50–5; music and drawing game 54; music, use of 41, 51–4; negative space 38, 42; painting 48–50; partner 'trust' exercise 52–3; patience, importance of 42–3; positive space 38; practical activities 45–55; storage and transport of works 41–2; suggested fantasy 54–5; written records, importance of 42
visual arts equipment, acrylic paint 39; brushes 40, 49; chalk 48; charcoal 38, 46; conte 38, 47; erasers 38, 42, 46,

47; graphite pencils 37–8, 46; inks 40; introduction of 40–1; kits 45; liquid soap bottles 41; oil paints 39; oil pastels 47–8; paint 39, 48–9; paper, size of 41; paper, supplies of 42; pastels 38–9, 47–8, 50; pencils 37–8,

46, 50; selection of 37; velcro 41; watercolours 39, 48–9

workplace 4
written records, importance of 20, 42